The Small Wood Shop

The Small Wood Shop

The Best Of Fine WoodWorking

The Taunton Press

Cover photo by Vincent Laurence

Taunton

BOOKS & VIDEOS

for fellow enthusiasts

First printing: September 1993
Printed in the United States of America

A FINE WOODWORKING Book

FINE WOODWORKING® is a trademark of The Taunton Press, Inc.,
registered in the U.S. Patent and Trademark Office.

The Taunton Press, Inc.
63 South Main Street
Box 5506
Newtown, Connecticut 06470-5506

Library of Congress Cataloging-in-Publication Data

The small woodshop.
   p.   cm. — (The Best of fine woodworking)
   "A Fine woodworking book" — T.p. verso.
   Includes index.
   ISBN 1-56158-061-9
   1. Woodwork — Amateurs' manuals.   2. Workshops — Equipment
and supplies — Amateurs' manuals.   3. Woodworking tools — Amateurs'
manuals.   I. Series.
   TT185.S587   1993
   684'.08 — dc20   93-2346
                                                          CIP

Contents

Introduction

For most woodworkers, there's just never enough room in the workshop. No matter how big and commodious the work space seems to be at first, tools and projects fill it up too quickly. In that way, regardless of the square footage, we all have small shops. Learning how to work well and efficiently in a limited space fast becomes an important part of a woodworker's repertoire.

A lot goes into making the most of a work space. How it is designed and arranged, what tools fill it up and how they are used are only a part of the equation. In these 32 articles collected from the pages of *Fine Woodworking* magazine, woodworkers share their solutions to the unique problems of the small wood shop. There is a wealth of practical information from three pros' recommendations about outfitting a first shop to how to get the most out of fundamental machine tools and bring old ones back to life. Some of the more important tips go beyond the basic operations of taking tools to wood. Issues of safety, electrical wiring, proper disposal of solvents and insurance are also covered.

No matter how small your shop, there's plenty of room for this valuable information.

—*William Sampson, executive editor*

The "Best of *Fine Woodworking*" series spans issues 46 through 100 of *Fine Woodworking* magazine, originally published between mid-1984 and 1993. There is no duplication between these books and the popular *"Fine Woodworking* on..." series. A footnote with each article gives the date of first publication; product availability, suppliers' addresses and prices may have changed since then.

Rolling Chop-Saw Stand Saves Space

Folding wings support long stock

by Charles Jacoby

Anatomy of a mobile chop-saw stand

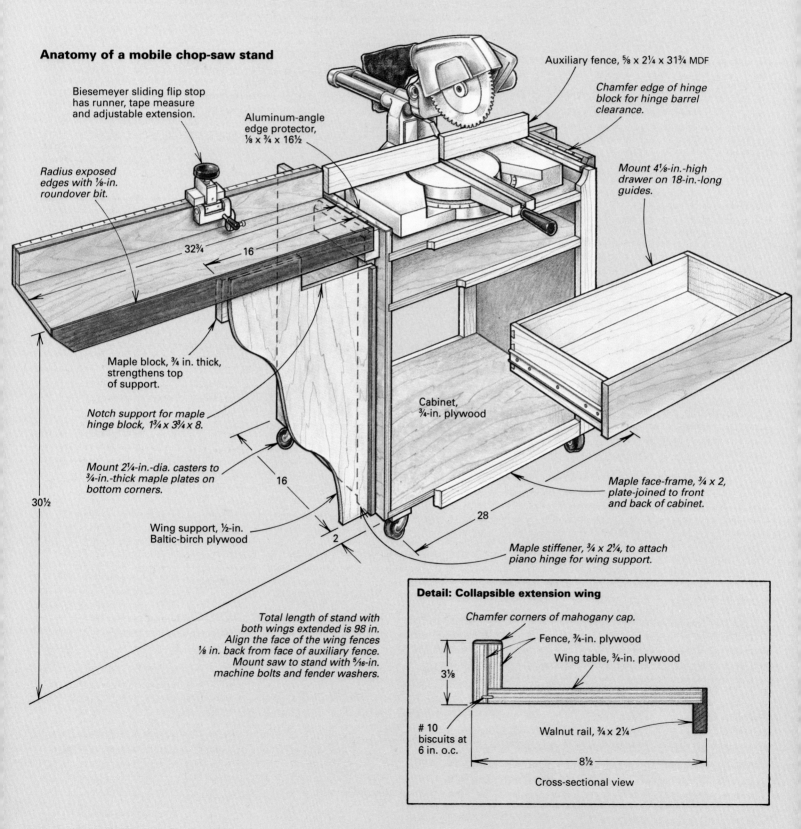

Biesemeyer sliding flip stop has runner, tape measure and adjustable extension.

Aluminum-angle edge protector, ⅛ x ¾ x 16½

Auxiliary fence, ⅝ x 2¼ x 31¾ MDF

Chamfer edge of hinge block for hinge barrel clearance.

Mount 4⅛-in.-high drawer on 18-in.-long guides.

Radius exposed edges with ⅛-in. roundover bit.

32¾

16

Maple block, ¾ in. thick, strengthens top of support.

Notch support for maple hinge block, 1¾ x 3¾ x 8.

Cabinet, ¾-in. plywood

Mount 2¼-in.-dia. casters to ¾-in.-thick maple plates on bottom corners.

16

Maple face-frame, ¾ x 2, plate-joined to front and back of cabinet.

30½

Wing support, ½-in. Baltic-birch plywood

2

28

Maple stiffener, ¾ x 2¼, to attach piano hinge for wing support.

Total length of stand with both wings extended is 98 in. Align the face of the wing fences ⅛ in. back from face of auxiliary fence. Mount saw to stand with ⁵⁄₁₆-in. machine bolts and fender washers.

Detail: Collapsible extension wing

Chamfer corners of mahogany cap.

Fence, ¾-in. plywood

Wing table, ¾-in. plywood

3⅛

10 biscuits at 6 in. o.c.

Walnut rail, ¾ x 2¼

8½

Cross-sectional view

My shop is pretty crowded, so when I acquire a new tool, I have to create efficient ways to store and use the tool. Such was the case after I bought a new sliding compound-miter saw. The saw needed a permanent, but mobile, home where I could do accurate cutoff and miter work. I first tried using the saw on planks and horses. This worked fine for single cuts, but I really needed a fence with a stop for cutting multiples. And the extensions that came with the saw limited its cutting to short pieces. Also, I still had to break things down to put the saw away.

About this time, my wife, Rosemary, gave me a benchtop oscillating-spindle sander. Again I wondered where I would store the tool. Building a stand to house both tools was the answer—make that a movable stand with folding extension wings. I designed the stand with crosscutting and mitering in mind but with a place to store the sander. I also left room for a top drawer to hold my shaper cutters and accessories. When I'm not using the saw, I drop the wings and roll the stand into a corner (see the photo). And even with the wings folded down, I can still do short chop-saw work by clamping a stop block to the saw's auxiliary fence.

Cabinet construction—For the stand's carcase, I made a ¾-in. birch-plywood box. To make storing the sander easy, I left the stand's lower compartment open (back and front). I dadoed the box's top, middle and bottom ¼ in. into the sides. Then, using #10 biscuits and glue, I plate-joined maple face frames to the front and back of the carcase to make the box rigid. Because my miter saw has its own base with four feet, I recessed the top of the cabinet so that the saw's work surface would be at the same height as the wings (see the drawing). I also fastened four 2½-in.-dia. casters (two of them locking) to hardwood plates that I glued to the bottom of the cabinet. The added height of the casters puts the top of the stand at a comfortable working level. To protect the top edges of the plywood sides, I mounted strips of ¾x¾ aluminum angle.

Collapsible wings—What makes the stand accurate and maneuverable are the folding pair of wings attached to the side of the cabinet. Each wing basically consists of a table, a support and a fence. The tables are ¾-in. plywood and the supports are made from ½-in.-thick Baltic-birch plywood for strength. To stiffen the wing tables, I made front rails using walnut I had on hand. The wave-like curves of the supports aren't necessary, but I wanted to use my new spindle-sander. To strengthen the top of the supports, I glued and screwed on a maple block to the back side of each. Finally, I made the fence for each wing from two pieces of ¾-in. plywood, staggered and glued together to form a rabbet (see the drawing detail). I glued and biscuited the fences' rabbets to the wing tables, and then I capped the top of the fences with mahogany. I chamfered the caps' edges, so there would be enough clearance for the runner block of an adjustable stop.

A flip stop for the fence—By securing a flip stop to the left fence, I'm able to measure precise lengths. The stop I use is made by Biesemeyer Manufacturing Corp. (216 S. Alma School Road, Suite #3, Mesa, Ariz., 85210; 800-782-1831). I purposely made my fence higher than what the flip stop requires to permit a full 2x4 to go under the stop. Because of the extra height, I had to make a metal stop extension to get it low enough for thin boards.

Aligning the wings and mounting the saw—The collapsible wings are strong; I can crosscut 14-ft.-long 2x8s in half on a fully extended stand. To achieve this kind of load, I had to first add blocks and stiffeners to reinforce the cabinet where the wing-table and wing-support hinges attach. I secured 1¾-in.-thick support blocks

Getting sent to the corner doesn't always mean you've been bad. After a well-executed cutting performance, Jacoby's cutoff-saw stand (with a sander stowaway) gets its wings lowered and is rolled to a tidy corner in the shop. The stand, with its wings extended, makes a level assistant when mitering the ends of long stock or crosscutting exact-length workpieces.

to the top of the cabinet sides. Then I fastened ¾-in.-thick strips of maple to the plywood sides. For the hinges, I fastened two Corbin ball-bearing (large door) hinges to the wing tables and mounted a pair of 2-in. by 24-in. piano hinges to the wing supports.

Before I screwed the hinges to the cabinet, I lined up the tables and fences as follows: First, I propped each wing assembly in place with buckets and blocks. Next, I set my saw down at the rear of the cabinet top and laid a 6-ft.-long straightedge across the front of the fences. After I had shimmed each wing so its fence was properly aligned (an extra pair of hands are a big help), I flipped the straightedge 90° to set the height of the wing tables. Once the wings were in position, I carefully clamped the hinges in place, so I could make pilot holes. Finally, I screwed the table hinges to the support blocks and the piano hinges to the stiffener strips.

I offset the saw's auxiliary fence about ⅛ in. ahead of the wing fences so that they won't influence the alignment of long boards held snugly to the saw's fence. I fastened the saw to the cabinet top using ⁵⁄₁₆-in. machine bolts with large fender washers under the plywood. With the wings extended, I originally figured I'd have to clamp the supports to the front rails. But the wing tables are heavy and rest on the supports unaided.

Finishing touches—To complete the stand, I made a simple drawer for the upper cabinet opening. Before installing the drawer on a pair of 18-in.-long slides, I notched the top of the drawer back to clear the ends of the saw-mounting bolts. Finally, I sealed the drawer, cabinet and wings with clear Watco oil. Once my mobile stand was finished, I put the saw right to work, cutting everything from baseboard to pull-out dish racks for the kitchen. □

Charles Jacoby is a retired men's clothing store owner who enjoys making furniture for his family in Helena, Mont.

Photos: author; drawing: David Dann

An Easy-to-Build Workbench

Bolted butt joints for rigid construction

by Richard Starr

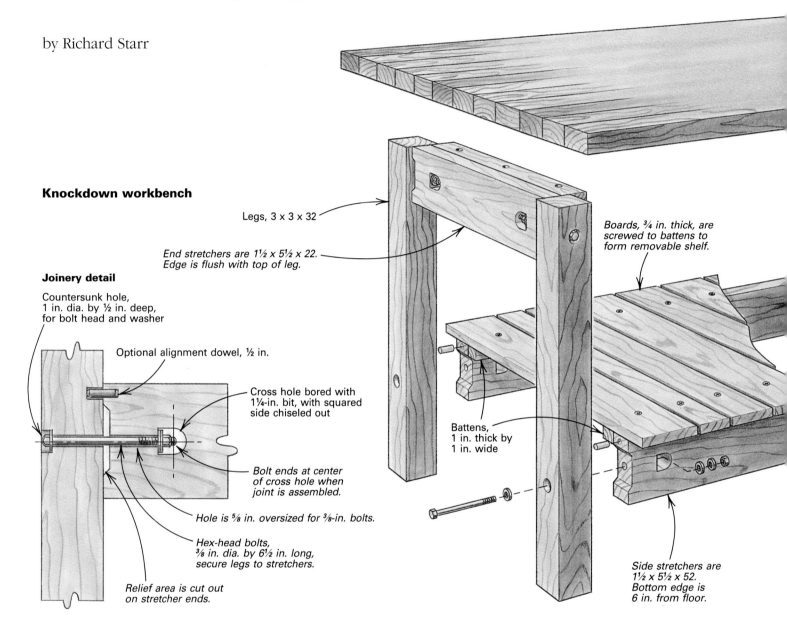

Knockdown workbench

Legs, 3 x 3 x 32

End stretchers are 1½ x 5½ x 22. Edge is flush with top of leg.

Joinery detail

Countersunk hole, 1 in. dia. by ½ in. deep, for bolt head and washer

Optional alignment dowel, ½ in.

Cross hole bored with 1¼-in. bit, with squared side chiseled out

Bolt ends at center of cross hole when joint is assembled.

Hole is ⅝ in. oversized for ⅜-in. bolts.

Hex-head bolts, ⅜ in. dia. by 6½ in. long, secure legs to stretchers.

Relief area is cut out on stretcher ends.

Boards, ¾ in. thick, are screwed to battens to form removable shelf.

Battens, 1 in. thick by 1 in. wide

Side stretchers are 1½ x 5½ x 52. Bottom edge is 6 in. from floor.

As a school woodshop teacher, I must often solve problems on the spur of the moment. That's how the design for my easy-to-build workbench came to me. A couple of kids wanted to build a bench as a gift for a neighboring preschool. The bench had to be quick and easy to construct, yet professional looking and, above all, absolutely rigid. When all the elements for a simple, bolt-together frame came together in my mind, I hit my palm to my brow. It seemed so obvious. I wondered why I hadn't thought of it before.

Designing the workbench

The workbench mainly consists of four legs and four stretchers held together with eight identical joints. The joints are easy to cut yet forgiving because they are fastened with common hex-head bolts available at any hardware store. The joint, equally effective in hardwood or cheap construction-grade lumber, is also perfect for many types of knockdown furniture. It's even solid enough for permanent installations, such as a built-in work counter.

The first step in building the frame is to decide the dimensions

of the top. This decision should be based on the bench's intended use (a carving bench should have a narrower top than a cabinet-maker's assembly bench) and on the shop space you have available. The bench I built has a 42-in.-wide by 72-in.-long top, good for general woodworking tasks. From these dimensions, I calculated the size of the frame and the length of the stretchers. You can determine the length of each pair of stretchers by subtracting twice the thickness of a leg plus the amount the top will overhang at each end from the length and width of the benchtop. When deciding on the amount of overhang, keep in mind that it's a good idea to leave plenty of room on all sides, for mounting vises and for clamping things to the top. For example, I chose a 7-in. over-hang and used 3-in.-thick by 3-in.-wide legs, so my end stretchers were 22 in. long and the side stretchers were 52 in. long. I made my stretchers from 2x6 stock.

I used soft maple for my bench's legs, but you can use glued-up hardwood or construction-grade 4x4s. Cut the legs to a length that equals the height of the bench less the thickness of the top. I find that bench height is largely a matter of personal taste. I'm a six-

Drawing: Mario Ferro

Solid-maple top, 1½ x 42 x 72

Battens, 1 x 2 x 22, are glued to stretchers. Lag bolts attach top.

ends than that or you risk the force of the bolt splitting out the endgrain and ruining the stretcher.

Bore out the cross holes with a 1¼-in.-dia. bit, which will leave a hole large enough to allow a box wrench to fit around the nut during assembly. Next, the portion of the hole facing the end of the stretcher is squared up for the nut. I used a try square to mark out the pocket, as shown in the drawing. Then I chopped out the waste with a chisel. If you like, you can whittle or sand the edges of the opening to give them an attractive chamfer.

To locate the bolt holes in the ends of the stretchers, I made a thin-plywood (you could use cardboard) template cut to the same dimensions as the cross section of a stretcher, in this case about 1½ in. by 5½ in. The template is used to mark the center for each ⅝-in.-dia. bolt hole, and then these holes are drilled through until they intersect with the cross holes. A spade bit in a portable electric drill works fine in endgrain, although I prefer to use a modified auger bit in a hand brace. To modify the bit, I just filed the spurs off, and it chewed right through endgrain. I tried to drill accurately by checking that the bit was parallel to the face and edge of the stretcher, and stopping and rechecking frequently. Because the hole is much larger than the bolt, dead accuracy isn't necessary; as I've said, this joint is very forgiving.

If you plan to disassemble and assemble the bench often, you might want to add an alignment dowel on the end of each stretcher. This short, ½-in.-dia. dowel keeps the stretcher aligned during assembly and mates to a slightly oversized hole in the leg.

Next, mark and cut out the relief area on each stretcher end, leaving two 1-in.-long contact areas. A ¼-in.-deep relief is all you need, but if you'd like to add a decorative touch, you can cut a fancy shape; just avoid cutting too near the cross hole or you'll risk splitting the joint when you tighten the bolt. I cut out the relief area on a bandsaw, but you could use a sabersaw or chop out the waste by hand with a chisel.

Use the same template described above to mark the positions of the bolt holes on the legs. Each pair of legs is laid out differently, so be sure to mark carefully. If you choose to countersink the bolt heads, drill the countersunk holes first. A 1-in.-dia. hole matches the diameter of washers normally used with ⅜-in. bolts. Drill the bolt holes oversized—⅝-in. holes for the ⅜-in. bolts—as you did on the stretcher ends earlier.

Assemble the bench frame by first bolting together the legs and end stretchers, and then joining them with the side stretchers. The joints will seem loose and sloppy when first assembled; simply position and tighten them using two washers under each nut. You might need to retighten the joints after they've settled for a few days.

Fitting the benchtop

For my benchtop, I glued up some 1½-in.-thick maple I had lying around. An easier (although more expensive) alternative is to buy a length of ready-made butcher-block countertop, available from many building-supply stores, home centers and lumber dealers.

Bolt the top to the frame through a batten glued to the inside faces of the end stretchers (see the drawing). Bore three ⅝-in. holes in each batten, and then fasten the top with ⅜-in. lag bolts and washers. While the battens keep the top flat, the oversized holes allow the solid-wood top to move with changes in humidity. If you want to add a shelf under your workbench, screw battens to the underside of some ¾-in.-thick shelf boards; then drop the shelf in place, as shown. □

footer, and I like a 34-in.-high bench whenever I'm sawing or planing wood; for small assembly work, though, I'd want the benchtop an inch or two higher. The workbenches in my school shop are 30 in. high, which is right for most adolescents, although younger woodworkers might do best with a 26-in.-high bench.

Making the stretcher joints

The function of a stretcher is to prevent the frame from racking and the bench from rocking, so it's imperative that each stretcher connection be rock solid. A joint held together with a single bolt focuses pressure at the center of the joint, which doesn't adequately prevent the joint from racking. Two bolts are better because they pull the stretcher against the leg closer to the edges, thus keeping the joint square. But you need to buy twice as much hardware, plus it takes twice as long to knock down or assemble the bench. After trying several variations of the bolted stretcher joint, I finally came up with the version shown in the drawing. A single bolt is used for each joint, and an arched relief area is cut out on each end of the stretcher. As the joint is tightened, pressure is focused at the outer edges (like a two-bolt joint), effectively locking the stretcher square to the leg and preventing racking.

To begin making the joints, crosscut the stretchers square and to length, and drill cross holes to provide the space for the nut and washers that are fitted to the end of each bolt. The center of each cross hole is located where the bolt end will be when the joint is assembled. For my bench, I used 3-in.-sq. legs and 6½-in.-long bolts with the heads countersunk ½ in. deep. This places the center of my cross holes at 3½ in. from the end of each stretcher. You should avoid locating the cross holes any closer to the stretcher

Richard Starr is a teacher and author. Building this workbench is the topic of the first show in his television series, Woodworking for Everyone, *on PBS this fall.*

All these tools fit inside the pine chest on the left. Saws hang inside the lid; planes sit on the bottom; a drawknife, spokeshaves and chisels hang on the chest's ends; long marking and measuring tools hang on the front and back; everything else fits inside eight drawers or in two removable boxes. Konovaloff built the walnut chest on the right to refine some of the storage systems.

A Cabinetmaker's Tool Chest

A home for hand tools

by Tony Konovaloff

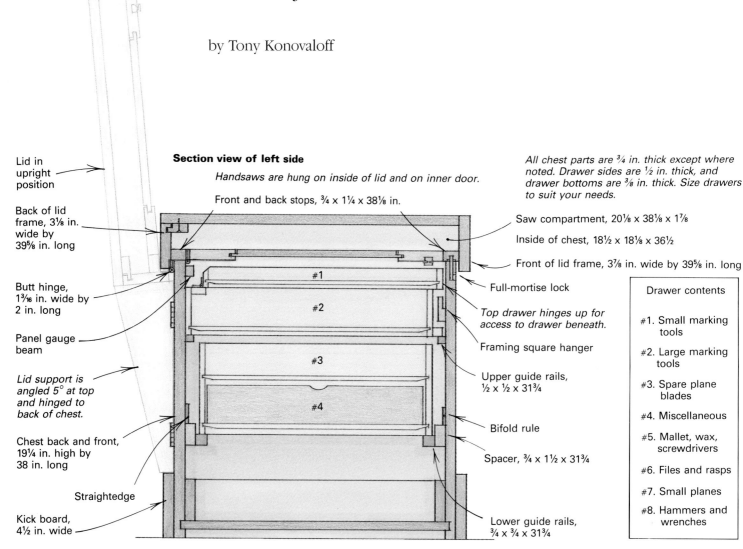

Section view of left side

Handsaws are hung on inside of lid and on inner door.

Front and back stops, ¾ x 1¼ x 38⅛ in.

Lid in upright position

Back of lid frame, 3⅛ in. wide by 39⅝ in. long

Butt hinge, 1³⁄₁₆ in. wide by 2 in. long

Panel gauge beam

Lid support is angled 5° at top and hinged to back of chest.

Chest back and front, 19¼ in. high by 38 in. long

Straightedge

Kick board, 4½ in. wide

#1
#2
#3
#4

All chest parts are ¾ in. thick except where noted. Drawer sides are ½ in. thick, and drawer bottoms are ⅜ in. thick. Size drawers to suit your needs.

Saw compartment, 20⅛ x 38⅛ x 1⅞

Inside of chest, 18½ x 18⅛ x 36½

Front of lid frame, 3⅞ in. wide by 39⅝ in. long

Full-mortise lock

Top drawer hinges up for access to drawer beneath.

Framing square hanger

Upper guide rails, ½ x ½ x 31¾

Bifold rule

Spacer, ¾ x 1½ x 31¾

Lower guide rails, ¾ x ¾ x 31¾

Drawer contents
#1. Small marking tools
#2. Large marking tools
#3. Spare plane blades
#4. Miscellaneous
#5. Mallet, wax, screwdrivers
#6. Files and rasps
#7. Small planes
#8. Hammers and wrenches

From *Fine Woodworking* (September 1991) 90:62-65

If you work wood, you need a place to store your tools. So for many of us, a tote box, a tool cabinet or a chest is one of the first woodworking projects we undertake. My pine tool chest, shown on the left in the photo on the facing page, was one of my earliest projects, and it served me well for years. Each tool has a home—on the bottom of the chest, in one of eight drawers, in removable boxes or on a rack inside the chest or its lid. As I collected new tools and learned new storage tricks, I altered the chest's storage layout by moving drawer guides and tool racks. The inside of the chest is now pockmarked with screw holes, as evidence of these alterations. So after too many alterations on my pine chest, I decided to build a new chest of walnut.

Since the size of my first tool chest is as practical as it is big, I made the new one, which is shown in the drawing on the bottom of these two pages, the same size. I wanted the chest to be portable, although it takes two people and a forklift to carry it. I was so familiar with my first chest that I could find anything with my eyes closed. So, I reasoned, why not just refine that same storage system in the new chest?

I went through the same steps to plan my new chest as I did when I built the first one—listing, grouping and measuring all my tools (as well as some I hoped to buy)—but in the end, I only altered my original design slightly. I decreased the tolerances between drawers and boxes, I made some drawers shallower, and I added a couple of drawers. And, for appearance sake, I made the kick board wider so it would be in balance visually with the sides of the lid. I'll tell you how the new chest was built and more about its design, but remember that the compartments inside (see the drawings) are for my tools. So use the drawings as a guide to customize a chest for your own tool collection.

Planning a place for each tool

A snug home for the tools not only saves space, but also prevents them from banging around when I move the chest or shuffle through its contents. I arranged my planes and other large tools on a "floor plan" of the bottom to arrive at the chest's overall length and width. The chest's depth was determined by the 16-in.-long tongue of my framing square, which I decided to hang between the drawers and the front. And I designed a compartment within the lid for storing my handsaws.

Once I knew the chest's overall size, I turned my attention to the storage racks, drawers and removable boxes inside. Since I had already decided to store my planes on the bottom, I needed to devise a way to get them out without having to remove everything else first. The solution was to have a bank of drawers at each end of the chest with an open well between them. I can lift the planes out through the central well, or I can slide all the drawers to one end of the chest and lift the planes out through the open space at the other end. I filled the space in the well with two removable boxes. One box holds my screwdrivers and my drilling tools (bits, a brace and a geared drill). All my sharpening equipment fits in the other box. The minimum size of the well was determined by how much space I needed to remove my largest plane, a Stanley #7 jointer. Once I knew the minimum size of the well, I divided the remaining space between the two banks of drawers and racks for hanging tools on the back and on the sides, as shown.

Like the framing square, long or awkward tools hang on racks between the drawers and the chest's sides and ends. I also hang the tools I use often, like a folding rule and chisels, because this way they're always visible and accessible. My drawknife and spokeshaves hang on one end; chisels hang on the other end; a square, straightedge, folding rule and panel gauge beam hang on the front and back sides. I then sized the depth of the drawers according to their contents. I put a mallet and commonly used screwdrivers in one top drawer, and measuring and marking tools in the other. Each of the other six drawers contains a different tool group, with the least-used tools in the lower drawers.

The chest holds too many tools to list. I'm amazed that everything fits inside when I see all the tools spread out on the floor in front of the chest, as shown on the facing page. In that photo, the empty walnut chest is almost complete, except for the drawer guides and tool racks. Although I could have glued the guides and racks into carefully spaced grooves, I chose instead to screw them to the chest sides so I can alter their arrangement easily.

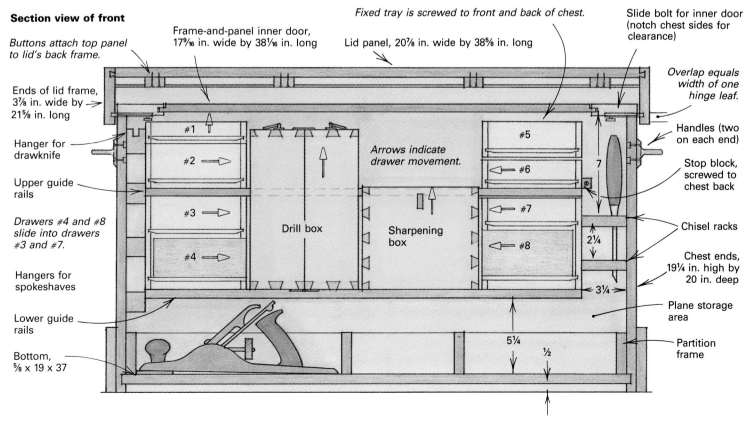

Section view of front

Buttons attach top panel to lid's back frame.

Frame-and-panel inner door, 17⁹⁄₁₆ in. wide by 38¹⁄₁₆ in. long

Fixed tray is screwed to front and back of chest.

Lid panel, 20⅞ in. wide by 38⅝ in. long

Slide bolt for inner door (notch chest sides for clearance)

Ends of lid frame, 3⅞ in. wide by 21⅝ in. long

Overlap equals width of one hinge leaf.

Hanger for drawknife

Upper guide rails

Drawers #4 and #8 slide into drawers #3 and #7.

Hangers for spokeshaves

Lower guide rails

Bottom, ⅝ x 19 x 37

#1
#2
#3
#4

Arrows indicate drawer movement.

Drill box

Sharpening box

#5
#6
#7
#8

7

Handles (two on each end)

Stop block, screwed to chest back

Chisel racks

Chest ends, 19¼ in. high by 20 in. deep

Plane storage area

Partition frame

2¼

3¼

5¼

½

Photos: Gary Weisenburger; drawings: Kathleen Rushton.

Sliding dovetails on the ends of the lid are hand-cut with a dovetail plane (left). The scoring blade on the plane's side prevents tearout when cutting across the grain.

Konovaloff hangs the lid by screwing hinges to the chest's back. Then he turns the lid upside down, props up the chest to align hinges and mortises, and screws the hinges to the lid (below).

Making the chest

I made the chest and most of its drawers, boxes and racks from walnut. My first chest is a testament to the durability of pine, but hardwood can take more abuse and still look good. However, I used alder for the bottom panel because its lighter color improves visibility inside the chest. Before starting the project, I bought 80 bd. ft. of 4/4 lumber: 50 bd. ft. for the chest, kick board and lid, and 30 bd. ft. for the storage compartments inside. I also used a lot of scrap.

I began by gluing up all the large panels for the sides, ends, top and bottom, and then I thickness-planed them after the glue dried. I work exclusively with hand tools, and so I scrub-planed the panels nearly to thickness (see the sidebar on the facing page for more on this) and then surfaced them flat with a jointer plane. Next, I cut each panel to size (given in the drawings) and plowed a groove in the sides and ends ½ in. from their lower edge, for the bottom panel. The sides and ends are joined with dovetails, and I cut the tails first because I find that it's easier to make the pins fit the tails. As unorthodox as it may sound, I used a file and fine-tooth rasp, rather than a chisel, to trim the pins.

I made the kick board next. Although it strengthens the bottom of the chest, the kick board is really just a protective base molding. On my first chest, I made the kick board the same width as the sides of the lid, but the kick board looked too narrow. So on the walnut chest, I made the kick board ½ in. wider, and it looks more balanced. To ensure that the dovetailed kick board fit the chest tightly, I cut the pins on the end pieces first, glued them to the chest, screwed them in place from inside, and then held the front and back pieces up to mark for the tails. After cutting and fitting the tails, I glued and screwed the front and back pieces in place.

Making the lid

The lid is basically a shallow box that overhangs the outside of the chest. Long wood cleats, glued inside the front and back of the lid frame, act as stops and rest on the top edges of the chest when the lid is closed. An inner frame-and-panel door is hinged to the back stop and held closed with slide bolts that engage the sides of the lid frame. The space between the underside of the lid and the inner door is 1⅞ in.—enough for saws to be hung on both surfaces.

The construction of the lid is somewhat unconventional unless you think of it as a traditional dovetailed drawer turned upside down. In traditional drawermaking, the back is made narrower than the sides so that the bottom can slide over the back and into grooves in the sides. In the case of my chest's lid, the top-to-side-frame joints aren't just tongues in grooves, they're sliding dovetails. The top panel is butted and glued to the frame in front and secured to the back with cabinetmaker's buttons, like those used to hold solid tabletops to aprons. This construction anchors the panel at the front while allowing it to expand or contract at the back.

I cut the sliding dovetails on the ends of the top panel and the mating grooves in the sides of the lid frame before joining the frame parts. The sliding dovetails, which are half as thick as the top panel, are not centered on the panel's ends. I located the tails close to the panel's inner surface so there would be as much wood as possible above the mating grooves in the side frames. I cut the tails with my Ulmia dovetail plane, as shown in the top photo. (I bought my Ulmia plane from Woodcraft Supply, 210 Wood County Industrial Park, Parkersburg, W.V. 02102-1686.) After planing the side frame's grooves, I cut the angled sides by tilting a side rabbet plane to match the dovetails' angle. It may seem imprecise to do this by eye, but it's easy with practice.

When the panel slid freely in the grooves, I cut the dovetails that join the lid-frame corners. I laid out the corner dovetails so that the sliding-dovetail groove would fall between two pins at the frame's front and in the middle of a wide pin at the frame's back. I cut the pins on the side pieces first, and then slid them onto the top panel's dovetails to mark the tails on the front and back frame pieces. When assembling the lid, I was careful not to get glue in the dovetail grooves, lest the panel not be able to expand and contract.

Hanging the lid

After planing and scraping the lid smooth and gluing the stops inside, I hung the lid on the chest. The brass butt hinges that mount the lid to the chest are screwed to the back of the chest and to the inside edge of the lid's back frame (see the bottom photo). I used five 1³⁄₁₆-in.-wide by 2-in.-long hinges, which fit perfectly on the ½-in.-wide overlap below the stop on the back of the lid frame. The hinges ¹⁄₁₆-in. overhang on the back of the lid frame allows the lid to open slightly past 90° and rest on two fold-out supports hinged to the chest's back (see drawings on pp. 12-13). The lid tilts just enough so I can unlatch the inner door without it falling open.

I first chiseled hinge mortises in the lid's back frame and temporarily mounted the hinges so I could set the lid in place and mark the hinge locations on the chest. Then, after chiseling the hinge mortises in the back of the chest, I removed the hinges from the lid and screwed them on the chest, since the hinge screws in the chest aren't accessible with the lid in place. To screw the hinges to the lid, I put it upside down on my bench, laid the chest on its back, and propped up the chest with a piece of wood to align the hinges in their mortises on the lid (shown in the bottom photo).

The chest was complete except for installing the lock. I chiseled the front of the chest for a full-mortise lock and screwed its strike plate on the lid's front stop. I didn't use a spring-loaded lock, as is suggested in early-cabinetmaking texts, because I was afraid I might leave my keys inside the chest. If I were to close it with a spring-loaded lock, the chest would lock automatically. Need I say more?

Installing the storage compartments

I built the storage compartments from the bottom up. First, I divided the bottom of the chest for individual planes by dadoing partitions to a 3-in.-high frame that fits around the inside perimeter of the chest. Next, I screwed the tool racks to the sides and ends of the chest and then installed the drawer guides around them. The L-shaped guides keep the drawers and removable boxes at various distances from the hanging tools. As shown in the drawings, the framing square and 24-in.-long straightedge sit in their own racks or directly on the drawer guides. After installing the drawers, I added the two top trays; one is hinged to the drawer beneath it, and the other is screwed to the front and back of the chest.

I finished the chest's outside with three coats of a mixture of 4 oz. of beeswax melted in 1 gal. of boiled linseed oil. I applied a coat on the inside too, leaving the chest open to dry. Then I fastened bronze handles on the ends with 1/4-20 stove bolts. □

Tony Konovaloff formerly made furniture in Tahoe Paradise, Cal. He is presently a woodworking student at the College of the Redwoods.

Thicknessing boards with a scrub plane

If you've ever considered working wood only by hand, you probably shuddered at the idea of thickness-planing rough boards. But I flatten and thickness a board quickly with a scrub plane and smooth the board with a jointer plane.

A scrub plane, which has a flat sole and a convex cutting edge, leaves a rough, fluted surface, and removes stock quickly. I not only use mine in the shop, but also to preview lumber I want to buy. You can even scrub-plane tabletops or panels that are too wide for your thickness planer. A wood scrub plane sells for about $50; but you can use a plane you already own and just regrind an extra blade. (A new blade is about $12 at hardware stores.)

Turning a jack plane into a scrub plane: The difference between my jack plane and its scrub plane alter ego is how the blades are ground: A jack plane's blade is straight and a scrub plane's blade has a 3/32-in.-high convex curve (see the top photo). You don't need more curve than that because it's hard enough to plane a 1/16-in.-thick shaving. To make the curved edge, I first beveled each corner 3/32 in., and then I ground the curve from the outside corners of the bevels to the middle of the cutting edge. I worked slowly with a hand-crank grinding wheel and quenched the edge often so I didn't anneal the tempered blade. While grinding, I maintained a 27° bevel, and I sharpened the cutting edge by honing a secondary bevel on it.

Since a scrub plane removes thick shavings, I opened the throat by setting the plane's frog as far back as possible. However, when scrub-planing figured wood, I move the frog forward a bit. To set the depth of cut, I align the edge of the cap iron with the corners of a convex blade, as shown in the top photo, and put the blade in the plane. I start by exposing about 1/32 in. of the blade and adjust depth to suit the wood's hardness and figure.

Using a scrub plane: I use my scrub plane to cut with the grain, shown in the bottom photo, diagonally to the grain or, with care and a sharp blade, directly across the grain.

To flatten and thickness-plane a warped or twisted board, I first scrub equal amounts of wood off the high spots on one side, and ensure that it is flat by sighting across winding sticks and planing the board until the sticks are parallel. I then finish that surface with a jointer plane. Lastly, I scribe a line on all four edges to mark the desired thickness of the board, and then I scrub the other side to the line and joint it flat. When removing lots of wood like this, I plane with the grain and diagonally to it.

When planing a large panel, the blade can get hot, so I'm careful not to lay the plane where the blade could burn me or the workpiece. To keep the blade cooler and to avoid dulling it, I don't drag the plane blade back over the wood before taking another cut. I also scrub-plane dried squeeze-out from glued-up panels before I thickness-plane and smooth them. I use the leading edge of the plane body, not the blade.   —T.K.

A scrub-plane blade can be made by grinding a convex edge on a 2-in.-wide jack-plane blade (left). In use, the cap iron's edge should align with the blade's corners.

To thickness-plane a panel, the author scrub-planes diagonally to the grain. Then he scrubs with the grain (below) and smooths the panel with a jointer plane.

Making a Chisel Cabinet

A simple case for an elemental tool

by Carl Dorsch

The slanting sides of this chisel cabinet emphasize the subtle concave curve of the door. Although Dorsch used magnetic strips to secure his chisels, the cabinet could easily be customized for other types of collectibles.

Wood chisels are some of my favorite tools. I have a rather extensive collection that includes two sets of bevel-edge chisels: one set of five for general work and one set of seven for fine paring. Rounding out this collection are a couple of firmer chisels and three mortise chisels that I made. I had built a large, double-door cabinet for my handplane collection, and there was enough space on the doors to hang the chisels. But I knew I would despise the rattling when opening and closing the cabinet doors; besides, I wanted to store the chisels in their own case to reflect my appreciation for them.

The small, single-door wall cabinet shown here is perfect for the chisels. Although a bit extravagant, the cabinet fulfills my storage needs and was fun and easy to make. Cabinet construction is straightforward. The two sides are doweled into the bottom and top, as shown in figure 1 on the facing page, and angle toward the front at 15°; the cross-grain quartersawn oak sides further emphasize the concave door. The chisel handles rest on narrow shelves and magnetic strips hold them in place. You could substitute deeper shelves and other fasteners to display your favorite collectibles. Tablesawn cove moldings trim the top and bottom.

Building the cabinet—My chisel cabinet was inspired by James Krenov. After seeing a curved-panel cabinet he had made, I knew just what to do with a warped panel left over from another project. I had glued up the book-matched, ⅜-in.-thick oak panel, but never used it because it bowed about ½ in. across its width. While nature did a good job creating the curved panel that became the door on my chisel cabinet, a more controlled approach would be to cooper the door by gluing up beveled staves (see *FWW* #56, pp. 36-39) and then shaping the panel with a round-bottom plane. This way, the door can be made to predetermined specifications to suit your requirements. For this project, though, I would still make the door first and then build the cabinet carcase to fit.

Since the door was already done, I began by cutting identical pieces of ¾x4¾x17 oak for the top and bottom so that my cabinet would be ¼ in. wider than the overlaid door. This leaves ⅛ in. showing on either side of the door. The ends of the top and bottom are mitered at 15°, as shown in figure 1. Crosscut two ⅝-in.-thick cabinet sides to 35 in. long and then rip them to 4½ in. wide with the blade tilted to 15° to match the angle of the top and bottom. With the blade still at 15°, rip ¼-in. wide by ¼-in. deep rabbets on the back inside edges of the sides to accept the cabinet

(continued on p. 18)

Fig. 1: Chisel cabinet

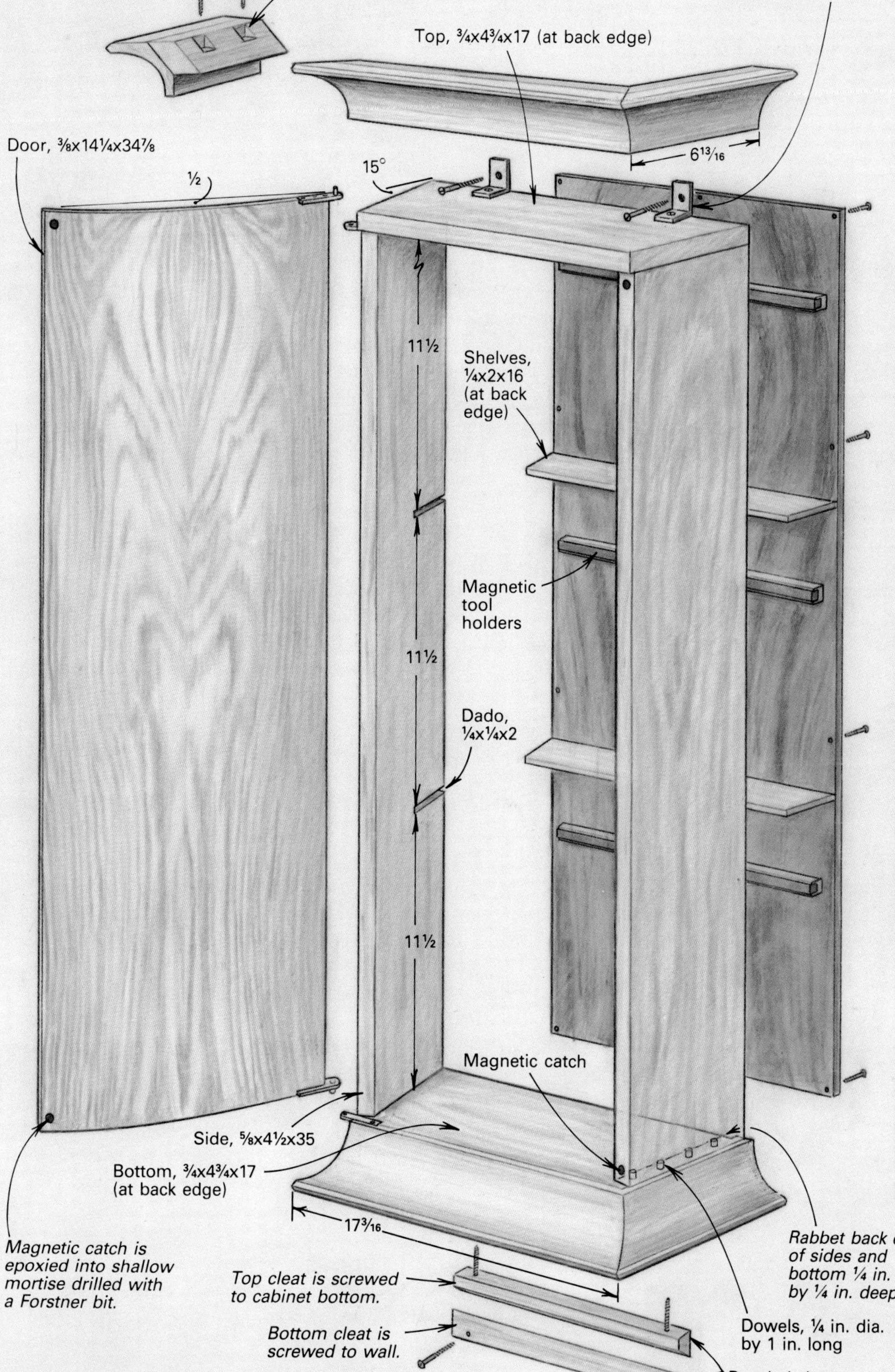
Drill a slotted hole to allow cross-grain movement of top and bottom.
Screw L-bracket to cabinet top and wall.
Top, ¾x4¾x17 (at back edge)
6¹³⁄₁₆
Door, ⅜x14¼x34⅞
½
15°
11½
11½
11½
Shelves, ¼x2x16 (at back edge)
Magnetic tool holders
Dado, ¼x¼x2
Magnetic catch
Side, ⅝x4½x35
Bottom, ¾x4¾x17 (at back edge)
17³⁄₁₆
Magnetic catch is epoxied into shallow mortise drilled with a Forstner bit.
Top cleat is screwed to cabinet bottom.
Bottom cleat is screwed to wall.
Rabbet back edge of sides and bottom ¼ in. wide by ¼ in. deep.
Dowels, ¼ in. dia. by 1 in. long
Beveled cleats

Fig. 2: Making the cove molding

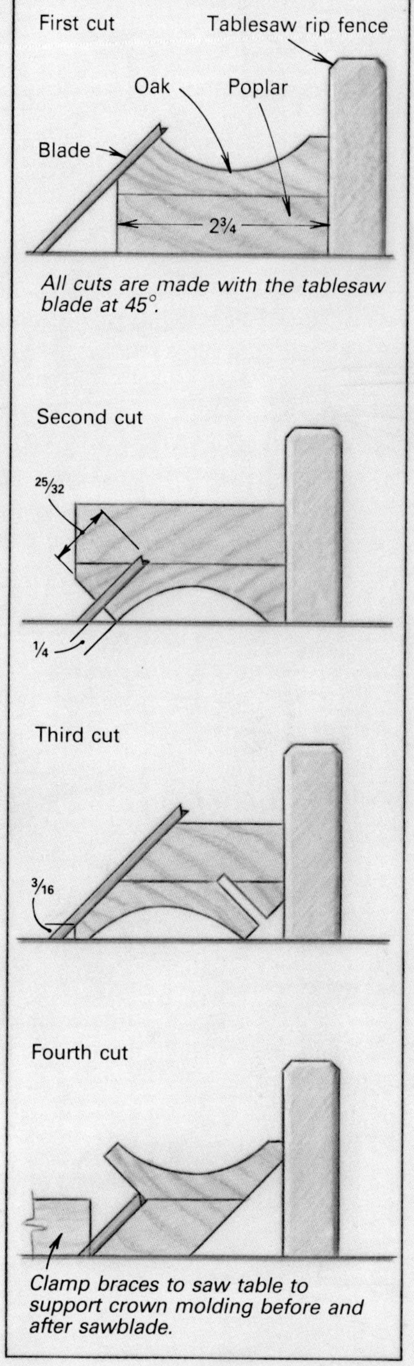
First cut
Tablesaw rip fence
Oak
Poplar
Blade
2¾
All cuts are made with the tablesaw blade at 45°.
Second cut
²⁵⁄₃₂
¼
Third cut
³⁄₁₆
Fourth cut
Clamp braces to saw table to support crown molding before and after sawblade.

Detail: Section view of cabinet bottom

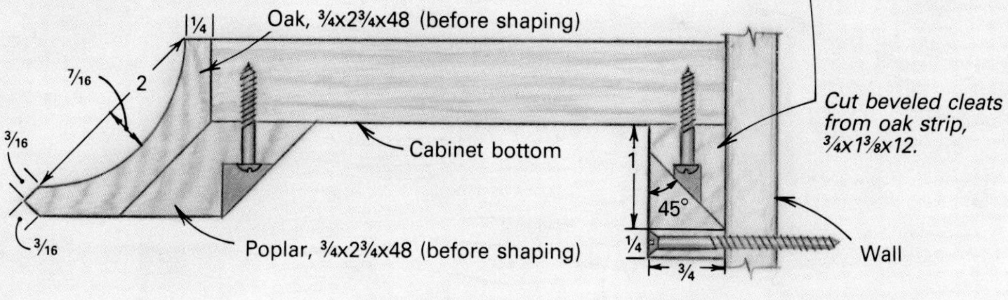
¼
Oak, ¾x2¾x48 (before shaping)
⁷⁄₁₆
2
³⁄₁₆
Cabinet bottom
Cut beveled cleats from oak strip, ¾x1⅜x12.
1
45°
³⁄₁₆
Poplar, ¾x2¾x48 (before shaping)
¼
¾
Wall

Detail: Magnetic tool holders

Three layers of flexible magnetic strips, ¹⁄₁₆ in. thick by ½ in. wide, are glued into ½-in.-wide by ⁵⁄₃₂-in.-deep dado.

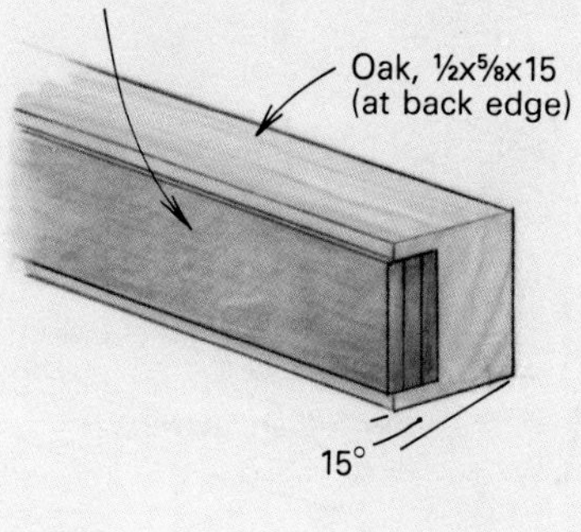
Oak, ½x⅝x15 (at back edge)
15°

back. With the blade at 90°, cut matching rabbets in the top and bottom pieces. The cove molding will hide the ends of these rabbets.

If you want shelves in your display cabinet as I did, you should crosscut their ends 15° to match the angle of the sides. Then dado the cabinet sides to receive the shelves. I used a marking knife to trace the outline of each shelf end onto the sides and then I pared the dadoes with a chisel. You could also rout the dadoes using a straightedge clamped across the sides as a guide.

To locate and drill the holes for the dowels that join the sides to the top and bottom, I made the maple doweling jig shown in the photo below. When using the jig, keep the cleats that are nailed to the edges of the guide block on the outside and rear surfaces of each piece, as shown below. Securing the jig to the workpiece with 4d finishing nails keeps it from shifting during drilling and the nail holes are hidden when the carcase is assembled. Drill the dowel holes $\frac{9}{16}$ in. deep to prevent the 1-in.-long dowels from bottoming. The $\frac{1}{2}$-in.-thick doweling jig also makes a good depth stop when inserting the dowels into their holes. (For more on this, see *FWW* #70, pp. 69-73.)

Before glue-up, I dry-assembled the carcase to ensure everything fit and the carcase was square. When you are satisfied with the fit, disassemble the carcase, put glue in the dowel holes in the cabinet sides and insert the dowels. Then put glue in the holes in the top and bottom pieces, and assemble and clamp them to the sides. Measure across the diagonals and clamp as needed to square up the carcase; don't overtighten the clamps or you will bow the sides. When the glue has dried, measure and cut the back to fit into its rabbets. I used $\frac{1}{8}$-in.-thick hardboard, veneered on the inside face with goncalo alves, for its striking appearance, and on the other side with mahogany, to balance construction and prevent bowing. I test-fit the shelves and back, but didn't permanently install them. I'll do this after I apply the finish later in the construction process.

Making and installing the cove moldings—Rather than rout the edges of the top and bottom, I made and attached cove molding from a separate piece of straight-grained quartersawn oak. This eliminated shaping endgrain and also conserved wood by reducing the thickness needed for the top and bottom. Although the molding can be made from $1\frac{1}{2}$-in.-thick stock, I didn't have any this size and so I laminated $\frac{3}{4}$-in.-thick poplar to the back of $\frac{3}{4}$-in.-thick oak. It is easier and safer to make all the molding from two 4-ft.-long pieces of stock and then crosscut and miter the individual short pieces to length.

This jig guides the bit for drilling dowel holes, and serves as a depth gauge when setting the dowels. Be sure to position the cleats against the outside and back edges of the workpiece.

I coved the molding by clamping a fence diagonally across the tablesaw and running the molding stock over the blade at an angle, taking very small cuts and raising the blade slightly after each cut, as discussed in *FWW* #87, p. 51. I then beveled and rabbeted the back edge of the molding following the sequence of tablesaw cuts shown in figure 2 on the previous page. When making the fourth cut, be sure to clamp braces to the tablesaw, as shown, to support the molding. If your cabinet sides are angled 15°, then the moldings should be mitered at $37\frac{1}{2}$°. If not, you can figure the angle for each miter by measuring the included angle between the front and side and dividing this angle by two. Subtract the result from 90° to get the correct miter-gauge angle, and cut the miters on the tablesaw.

Glue and screw the front pieces of molding to the top and bottom of the cabinet and then fit each side piece individually. If the miters do not fit as cut on the tablesaw, pare the side molding miters with a sharp chisel to match the front moldings. After the front corner miters fit, trim the back ends to length by crosscutting at 15°. Attach the side moldings with a dab of glue and a screw at the front and with a screw that fits into a slotted, countersunk hole at the back, to allow for seasonal wood movement.

Hanging the door—Fitting the door to the cabinet is the most critical part of construction because there is little room for error. Install the moving half of the knife hinges in notches cut in the door, and then test-fit the door to the cabinet. Because my door was slightly bowed along its length, I had to spokeshave the cabinet sides' edges to accommodate the bow, as well as slightly trim their 15° bevel to the door's curve. When the door fits, use it to mark the top and bottom for the locations of the pin half of the hinges. Pare the hinge mortises with a chisel, but stop short of the mark for the hinge end. Test-fit the door again, this time by holding the pin half of the hinge on the door while sliding the hinge into its mortise. Do this for both the top and bottom. Center the door on the cabinet by adjusting the length of the hinge mortises. The door is held closed by two round magnets that are epoxied into holes drilled into the edge of the unhinged cabinet side. Strikes for the magnets are epoxied into shallow mortises drilled into the inside face of the door with a Forstner bit.

Now, remove the door and the hardware before finishing the cabinet. I applied a light coat of Minwax Golden Oak and rubbed on a mixture of tung oil and polyurethane. I added extra polyurethane to the mixture that was applied to the shelves and bottom for more protection where the handles of the chisels will rest. When the finish is completely dry, slide the shelves into their dadoes from the rear, fasten the back panel into its rabbet with 10 #6 by $\frac{3}{4}$-in.-long screws and reinstall the door.

The magnetic strips that hold the chisels are screwed to the cabinet back from the rear. Although magnetic tool holders are commercially available, I think they look too bulky and their magnetism is so great that they make tool removal awkward. So I made my own holders, as shown in the detail in figure 1 on the previous page. For each holder, I used cyanoacrylate to glue three flexible magnetic strips together and then into a dado in a $\frac{1}{2}$x$\frac{5}{8}$x15 piece of oak. Flexible magnetic strips are available from most craft-supply stores and many mail-order tool companies. The three strips provide just enough magnetic attraction to keep the chisels in position, yet allow them to be removed easily.

I hung the cabinet on beveled cleats at the bottom and two small L-brackets at the top, as shown in figure 1. Cove molding around the top and bottom hides these attachment fixtures when the cabinet is hung on the wall. □

Carl Dorsch is an amateur woodworker in Pittsburgh, Pa.

Photos: Charley Robinson; drawings: Lee Hov

For practice cutting dovetails, this cabinet with drawers is a great project. Through dovetails join the carcase while tapered, sliding dovetails secure the shelves and vertical dividers. The banks of graduated drawers include lots of through and half-blind dovetails.

Making a Case for Dovetails

A wall-hung tool cabinet that will hone your joinery skills

by Carl Dorsch

When I needed a tool cabinet, I saw it as a great opportunity to practice cutting dovetails. The cabinet I designed features through dovetails, half-blind dovetails and tapered, sliding dovetails. All of these joints can be cut either by hand or by machine; I cut mine by hand except for the tapered, sliding dovetails, which I cut with a router (see the sidebar on the following page).

Because my cabinet shown in the drawing on p. 21 and in the photo above has doors, it protects the tools from dust and curious visitors, yet it leaves them readily available. The upper portion of the cabinet displays my antique planes. The shelves are spaced to hold the handplanes upright, and the cabinet is deep enough so that two planes fit side by side. The bottom of the cabinet contains several drawer banks for storing accessories and other tools.

Building the carcase

The carcase sides are joined to the top and bottom with through dovetails. (For machine techniques on cutting through dovetails, see Mark Duginske's article in *FWW* #96, p. 66.) I cut the dovetails with the tails on the sides and the pins on the top and bottom so that the mechanical lock of the joint resists the weight of cabinet and its contents. I used stopped, tapered, sliding dovetails for the shelves and drawer dividers because I prefer them functionally and aesthetically. The taper makes this strong joint easy to assemble, as discussed in the sidebar below, and stopping the dovetail leaves a cleaner appearance than exposed joinery. After cutting the tapered, sliding dovetails, but before assembling the carcase, I trimmed the back of the shelves to provide space for the flush back. The back of the top section of the cabinet must be rabbeted to accommodate the inset cabinet back and the hanging cleat.

Drawer construction

The drawers have through dovetails at the back and half-blind dovetails up front. Instead of installing the bottom in grooves in the sides and in the front, they're screwed to the assembled drawers and extend past the sides to create slides that ride in dadoes routed in the carcase sides and dividers, as shown in the drawing on the facing page. The bottom drawer in each bank slides on the shelf beneath it. I leave the bottoms slightly wide until the drawer bodies are attached, and then I plane each one to fit its dado.

Making and fitting the doors

The doors are typical frame-and-panel construction and overlap where they meet at the cabinet's center. To accommodate the overlap and to keep the gap between the doors centered, I made the center stile of the left door ¼ in. wider than the center stile of the right door. Both of these stiles are rabbeted to make the lap joint.

Because the knife hinges that I used to mount the doors have no provision for adjusting the doors' fit, they must be accurately mortised in place. I've found that by mounting the hinges to the doors first and leaving the hinge mortises in the carcase slightly short, I can chisel out the mortises to sneak up on a perfect fit.

The cabinet can be set on a bench or hung on the wall. I hung mine on the wall using beveled cleats, one on the rear of the cabinet and one on the wall. When using this hanging system, the wall cleat should be fastened with two screws into each stud. ☐

Carl Dorsch is a woodworker in Pittsburgh, Pa.

Tapered, sliding dovetails with a router

Sliding dovetails provide extremely strong carcase joints. But the wider the stock, the more difficult it is to slide home a straight dovetail because glue tends to bind and grab the tight-fitting pieces. By tapering one side of both pin and socket, the joint remains loose, as the two pieces are assembled, until the pin is fully seated in the socket.

The trick is to get a matching taper on the pin and the socket for a perfect fit. To ensure an identical taper, I use the same ¹⁄₁₆-in.-thick shim for routing first the socket and then the pin, as shown in the drawing below. I cut the tapers on the upper edges of the dovetails; the straight bottom edges of the dovetails then serve as references to ensure that the shelves are flat, square and evenly spaced.   —C.D.

Routing tapered, sliding dovetail sockets

When routing tapered, sliding dovetails, the socket stock (cabinet sides) and pin stock (shelves) must be the same width, or the tapers will not match. Trim shelves to accommodate cabinet backs after routing the mating sockets and pins.

Routing a tapered dovetail socket requires three passes. For ¾-in.-thick pin stock, make the first pass with a ⅜-in.-dia. straight bit to hog out most of the waste. For the second pass, use a ½-in.-dia. dovetail bit, and cut a typical straight dovetail socket. The final pass with the same dovetail bit, but with the guide fence shimmed at a slight angle, routs the socket's tapered top edge.

First and second pass: Clamp guide fences A and B to the cabinet component to align the cutter with the dovetail layout line and use this setup for both passes; one with straight bit, one with dovetail bit.

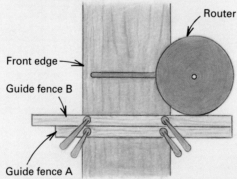

Router

Front edge

Guide fence B

Guide fence A

Third pass: Leave guide fence A clamped in place, and insert a spacer and a shim between fence A and B. The spacer determines the width of the socket (use a ⅛-in.-thick spacer for ¾-in.-thick pin stock). The ¹⁄₁₆-in. shim creates the taper angle.

Spacer must be flush with front edge of workpiece.

Guide fence B
Guide fence A

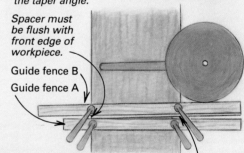

Tape shim flush with back edge of workpiece.

Routing tapered, sliding dovetail pins

The pins are cut in two passes using the same dovetail bit as for the sockets but in a table-mounted router. The tapered pin side is cut in all stock before resetting the fence to rout the straight pin side. Be sure to rout a tapered side on some scrap stock to test fence setup for routing the straight side.

First pass: Adjust fence so that the dovetail bit protrudes ³⁄₃₂ in. Tape a ¹⁄₁₆-in.-thick shim flush with rear edge of workpiece and high enough to clear router bit.

Front edge of workpiece   Auxiliary fence   Router table fence

³⁄₃₂

Shim

Second pass: Set the fence to dovetail the pin's straight side. Make a test cut on the scrap stock and readjust as needed for a snug fit in the socket.

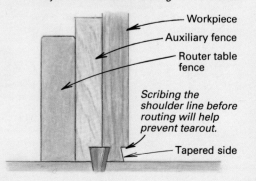

Workpiece

Auxiliary fence

Router table fence

Scribing the shoulder line before routing will help prevent tearout.

Tapered side

A dovetailed tool cabinet

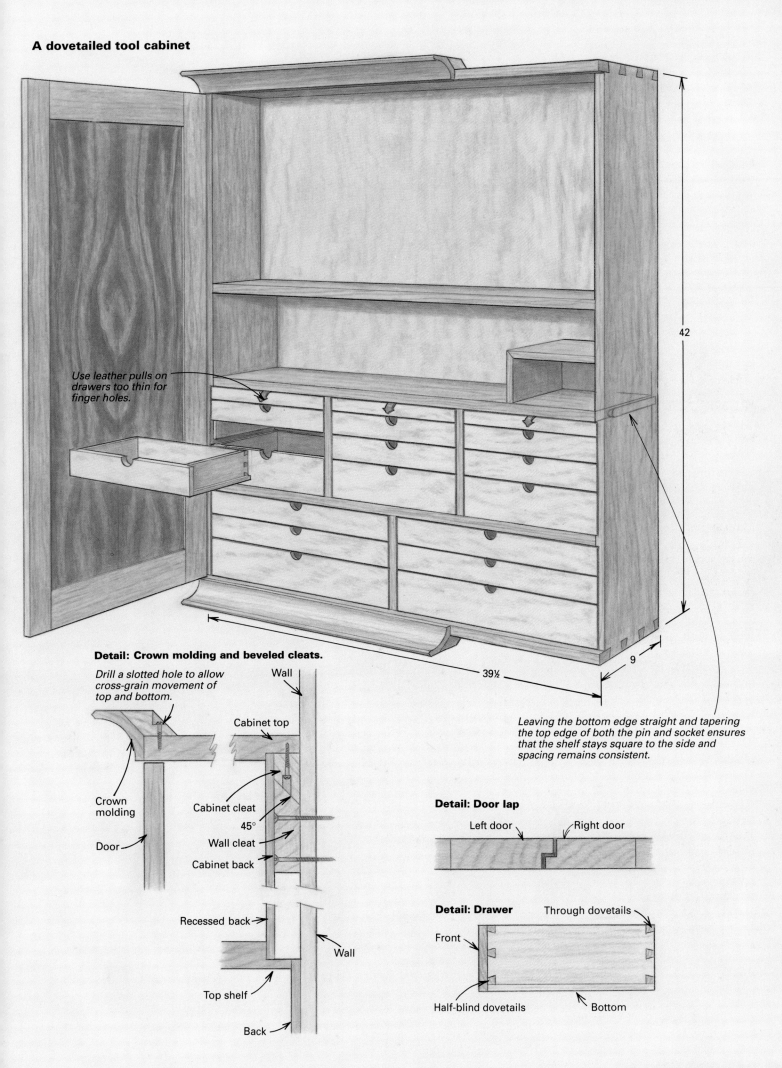

Use leather pulls on drawers too thin for finger holes.

42

9

39½

Leaving the bottom edge straight and tapering the top edge of both the pin and socket ensures that the shelf stays square to the side and spacing remains consistent.

Detail: Crown molding and beveled cleats.

Drill a slotted hole to allow cross-grain movement of top and bottom.

Wall

Cabinet top

Crown molding

Door

Cabinet cleat

45°

Wall cleat

Cabinet back

Recessed back

Top shelf

Wall

Back

Detail: Door lap

Left door   Right door

Detail: Drawer

Through dovetails

Front

Half-blind dovetails

Bottom

With its surface at 20 in. Chuck Davis' assembly table puts the work at a comfortable height and also allows him to put a foot up to rest and stretch his back.

Cabinetmaker's Assembly Table

Torsion-box construction and a wooden brake make this mobile work surface strong and stable

by Charles Davis

There's never enough bench space in a shop. At one time or another, almost every horizontal surface in a shop will get pressed into service as an ersatz assembly table. Through the years, I've had to improvise to come up with assembly space: at times using my workbench, a solid-core door placed over two sawhorses, my tablesaw and extension tables and (all too often) the shop floor. All the projects assembled on these makeshift assembly tables were completed, but there were always compromises and inconveniences.

My workbench is too narrow for many projects, solid-core doors aren't as stable as I would like and I hated to tie up the tablesaw from glue-up until I removed the clamps—usually the next morning. Clamping around the casting on the bottom of the tablesaw is a pain, too, and extension tables just aren't meant to take the weight or the pounding that assemblies often entail.

I wanted a table that was large enough to stack standard sheet goods on and flat enough to screw face frames together on. I wanted it stationary most of the time (and able to be locked in place) but capable of being moved around the shop when needed elsewhere. I also wanted the table to support relatively large loads (I figured up to 3,000 lbs. or so), such as for stacking sheet goods at the infeed side of the tablesaw. Through a process of trial and error, I found that a surface height of 20 in. provided comfortable access to my work and allowed me to set one foot comfortably onto the table, which makes it easier to reach the middle of the table and also relaxes my back. I mulled over the design for several months; then, during a lull between jobs, I did some serious design work and began construction. The result (with a few modifications) is shown in the photo at left and in the drawing on p. 24).

A torsion box for a flat, strong surface

Torsion-box construction was really the only solution to my design dilemma. A torsion box consists of a core grid with a skin on both sides. The resulting box is stronger (especially in resisting bending or twisting forces), more stable and far lighter than a block of solid wood of equivalent size. I decided on ¾-in. birch plywood for the torsion box's core members and for the two full sheets that would sandwich the core. I wanted a flat surface on which to build the table, so I put a sheet of Kortron (an acrylic-faced pine particleboard) on—you guessed it—the floor to smooth out any slight irregularities in the concrete. Kortron is more rigid than plywood, so it's ideal for this application. Also, my floor is very nearly flat to begin with, but if yours is not, you may need to shim beneath the Kortron to eliminate any tendency for the sheet to rock.

I cut the box's sides, ends and all core members and then marked the long core members where the short pieces would butt against them. I stapled together the perimeter of the box first and then proceeded from one side of the box to the other. Because I didn't have a giant, industrial milling machine handy to surface the core and perimeter, I didn't glue the core members to each other. The core members must be able to move slightly to come flush with the box's top and bottom when the whole is assembled. I stapled across each joint line to provide sufficient hold till the box was glued up and made sure all the staples were set below the surface of the core members.

After checking corner to corner for square, I marked the box's perimeter where the core members were stapled to it. I then applied glue to the top edge of all core members and, with my wife's help, carefully laid the box's top in place. Working quickly, I snapped chalklines to define the core's grid on the top, using the marks I'd made around the perimeter for guidance. I nailed off the perimeter first, placing a nail every 6 in. and did the same in the interior of the grid. I was careful to avoid intersections of the core members because I didn't want to hit staples or split the core members' ends.

Shopmade cam brakes hold the table immobile. A little wax on the fulcrum screw keeps the cam working smoothly.

I wanted even pressure over the entire surface until the glue set, so I placed six sheets of Kortron on top of my now half-finished tabletop. I calculated this would provide approximately 140 lbs. per square inch of "clamping" pressure on the glue joints. By now it was late afternoon, so I left the "clamps" on overnight. The next morning, I removed the sheets of Kortron, flipped the assembly over and attached the box's bottom in the same way.

To provide a means of attaching the leg assembly, I glued and screwed pairs of leg-attachment plates to the bottom of the torsion box, one over the other, at the four corners. I positioned the outside edges of the plates directly beneath two core spacers. Besides transferring the load more directly (than if the leg were positioned over a void), this placement provides plenty of stability to the table as a whole and keeps the brake-cam lever under the table and out of the way. Although I used two pieces of plywood for the leg-attachment plates, in retrospect, using one good piece of Douglas-fir 2x4 would have been adequate and would have saved me some time and effort.

Designing the legs and brake system

I'd already determined the overall height for the table, so I had a rough idea of the size of the leg assembly. I also knew about how much weight I wanted the table to be able to support. I had since revised my original goal of having the table support 3000 lbs., figuring instead on a maximum of 19 sheets of ¾-in. stock, which would stack level with the height of my Unisaw's tabletop. At just over 98 lbs. a sheet, 19 sheets of Kortron weigh almost 1900 lbs., and the table itself would weigh over 300 lbs. complete. Even with my reduced-load requirement, I needed a set of casters with a load rating of more than 500 lbs. each! After an extensive (but ultimately futile) search for rubber casters with brakes that could accommodate this load, I realized I'd have to compromise a bit. I decided I could do without the mobility when the table was fully loaded. I settled on some 4-in. casters, load-rated at 200 lbs., which had been kicking around in a dark corner of my shop ever since I'd salvaged them from a defunct dolly. They had no brakes, so I redesigned the leg assembly to incorporate a shopmade, cam-operated brake, separate from the swivel casters (see the drawing on the following page and the photo above).

The legs on my table consist of a core of 4x4 Douglas-fir, two L-shaped leg braces, the caster mounting plate and two filler plates that help support the caster mounting plate (see the drawing on p. 24). The cores, braces and filler pieces are glued and nailed together with 1½-in. finish nails, and the caster mounting plates are glued and screwed to the leg braces. I bored a ½-in. hole in each of

Fig. 1: Cabinetmaker's assembly table

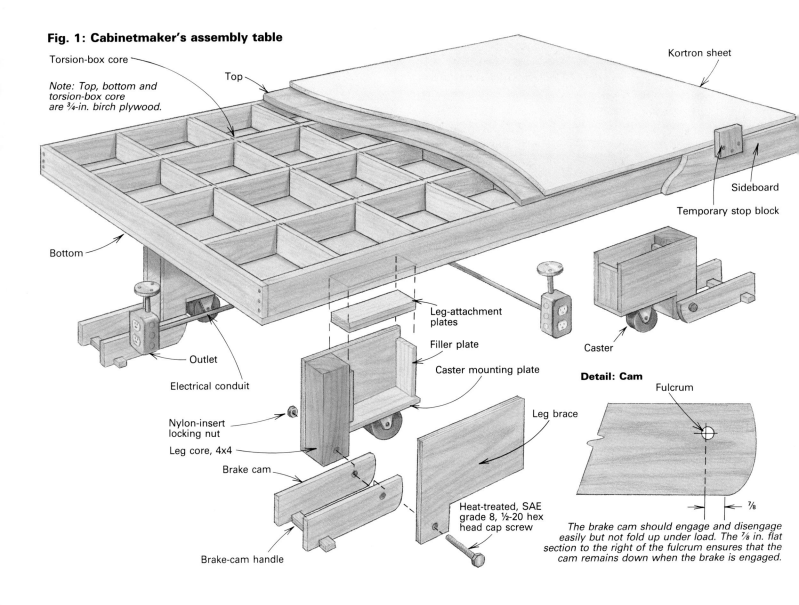

Torsion-box core

Note: Top, bottom and
torsion-box core
are ¾-in. birch plywood.

Top

Kortron sheet

Sideboard

Temporary stop block

Bottom

Leg-attachment
plates

Filler plate

Caster mounting plate

Caster

Outlet

Electrical conduit

Nylon-insert
locking nut

Leg core, 4x4

Brake cam

Leg brace

Heat-treated, SAE
grade 8, ½-20 hex
head cap screw

Brake-cam handle

Detail: Cam

Fulcrum

⅞

*The brake cam should engage and disengage
easily but not fold up under load. The ⅞ in. flat
section to the right of the fulcrum ensures that the
cam remains down when the brake is engaged.*

Would you believe, a saw pony?

by Pat Paterson

A sawhorse is a sawhorse is a sawhorse. Right? Well, not exactly. Occasionally, I need a low-assembly table when I'm working on a set of cabinets, but I don't want to monopolize a lot of space in my shop on a permanent basis. So I simply throw some 2x4 ribs and a sheet of plywood over four of these low sawhorses. Problem solved.

These little horses have come in handy on more occasions than I can count. I've used them, stacked two high (they nest perfectly), as supports for an auxiliary bench of normal height. They're great step stools for working on crown molding, installing a ceiling light fixture or for poking around in some long-forgotten wood you stashed in the rafters. Someone 6-ft.-tall standing on one of these horses will have 4 in. of clearance to an 8-ft. ceiling. They also provide a comfortable seat for lunch, for a cup of coffee or for looking at plans. When you're not using the horses, stack them four high, out of the way; they take up almost no space.

If you build one set of sawhorses, you'll never stop building them. Because they're so versatile, people want them as soon as they see them. A gardener friend wanted only one horse. She put all her hand tools inside and placed her seedlings on the open lid while she worked her garden. The bottom of the legs were wide enough to keep the sawhorse from sinking into the soft soil. My brother uses one for stepping into and out of his truck camper. Others have used the horses as picnic tables at the beach and as extra chairs at a backyard barbecue.

Back in prehistory—before the existence of chop boxes, or power miter saws—I used a manual miter box. My backsaw had very little set, and the saw occasionally bound in the kerf. I'd clamp the miter box to the top of one of these horses, and it never tipped, even during one of those binding thrusts. The stability of the horses will also keep them upright in the back of a pickup no matter how sudden the stop.

One of the best things about these horses is that you can build them for next to nothing. I use 2x4 cutoffs and any plywood scraps that are big enough. I cut pieces to size as I get them, and I set them aside. When I have some slack time, I put together a set of sawhorses. Old horses can be reconditioned quite easily, too, by replacing the lid, which takes all of the abuse. If you're starting from scratch, you can make five horses from a standard sheet of plywood (lids excepted).

I gave two horses from the first set I made to a friend. He immediately bemoaned the fact that the narrow opening made access to bulkier tools, like the router, jigsaw and hammer drill, a bit difficult. He was happy to use them nonetheless but only until he got around to building something better. That day never arrived, though. So he's still using the same two horses—23 years later. □

Pat Paterson is a retired steam engineer. He works wood as a hobby in Victoria, B.C.

From *Fine Woodworking* (July 1992) 95:38-41

the leg assemblies for the brake-cam fulcrum, and glued and nailed the leg assemblies to the attachment plates on the table's bottom.

I used heat-treated, SAE grade 8, 1/2-20 hex head cap screws as fulcrums for the brake cam (a screw with a smaller diameter may not have been strong enough under full load, and a lower-grade steel probably would have bent). To secure the screws, I used aviation-style, nylon-insert locking nuts. These nuts permit me to keep the brake cam in the upright "off" position by just snugging the nuts against the leg braces, yet they don't interfere with the cam's operation.

Getting the brake to work properly required a good deal of trial and error. Setting the brake cam has to cause the caster to rise off the ground, but only slightly; the greater the distance, the more stress on the cam and the more difficult the brake will be to operate. I settled on a design whereby the wheel rises $\frac{1}{8}$ in. off the ground when the brake is engaged. Ensuring the stability of the leg assembly under load required that I design the cam with a flat section on both sides of the fulcrum. Arriving at an optimal length for the flat at the end of the cam ($\frac{7}{8}$ in.) and an optimal curve for the cam end, required some experimentation and several trips to the bandsaw. The drawing detail on the facing page shows the final shape I arrived at.

A couple of oversights rectified

I used my table for a couple of weeks, very contentedly, but soon discovered, as often happens, that I'd overlooked a thing or two in my design. I noticed that I was always just beyond the reach of an electrical outlet. I remedied this situation by adding four outlets below the torsion box, one at the midpoint of each side and one at each end. I used metal handy-outlet boxes because both boxes and cover plates have round corners to prevent snags or cuts. I installed Leviton #5014 special-service duplex outlets into these boxes. These outlets were considerably more expensive ($2.99) than standard-service outlets ($0.39), but they're designed to stand up better to rough conditions, such as those found in a woodworking shop. I connected a 14-gauge, Type SJ electrical-cable supply line with a nylon grounding plug to one of the boxes at the end of the table.

All 115-volt outlets in my shop are protected with Ground Fault Circuit Interrupter (GFCI) breakers. If yours aren't, you may wish to install one instead of a duplex outlet in the handy box where you have attached the supply line, and feed the power through it to the other three boxes. Select a receptacle-type GFCI device with a rating of at least 15 amperes at the receptacle and 20 amperes feed-through to the other three outlets. My shop outlets are protected with the Leviton #6599. (For more on GFCI breakers, see pp. 45-49.)

Working on my new assembly table was infinitely better than working on any of the previous surfaces I'd used, but I did notice that some of my face-frame joints were slightly offset. The only thing I could attribute this to, since I was using the table as reference, was a slight deflection in the tabletop. I'd screwed a sheet of $\frac{1}{4}$-in. hardboard to the top of the birch plywood after I'd finished the table (intending it to be a replaceable, smooth work surface), but, evidently, it wasn't stiff enough. I replaced it with a $\frac{3}{4}$-in. sheet of Kortron, and that solved the problem. I'd also noticed—especially with the Kortron—that whenever I really bore down on a face frame, it would tend to slip. I fixed this by installing side and edge boards all around (to get the sides out beyond the 49x97 sheet of Kortron) and using temporary stop blocks whenever I'm assembling cabinets.

Since completing the assembly table, over 100 sets of cabinets have moved across it on their way through my shop. The table's low height has saved my back (as has being able to use the table at the tablesaw's infeed side); the flat, stiff reference surface has saved me untold hours of sanding; and the convenience of electrical outlets—where I need them, when I need them—has eliminated many snake-like tangles and saved me plenty of time as well. □

Chuck Davis is a cabinetmaker and licensed contractor in Watsonville, Calif.

A combination mini-sawhorse and toolbox, these saw ponies are extremely versatile. Their rugged construction and low stature make them very stable.

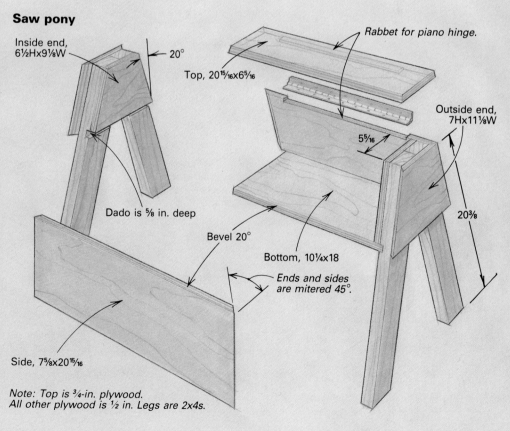

Saw pony

Inside end, 6½Hx9⅛W

20°

Rabbet for piano hinge.

Top, 20¹⁵/₁₆x6⁵/₁₆

Outside end, 7Hx11⅛W

5⁵/₁₆

Dado is ⅝ in. deep

Bevel 20°

Bottom, 10¼x18

Ends and sides are mitered 45°.

20⅜

Side, 7⅝x20¹⁵/₁₆

Note: Top is ¾-in. plywood. All other plywood is ½ in. Legs are 2x4s.

Making a Machinist-Style Tool Chest

Weekend project helps clear workshop clutter

by Ronald Young

Fig. 1: A machinist-style tool box

Using the simplified construction techniques illustrated here, you can build this tool chest in a weekend.

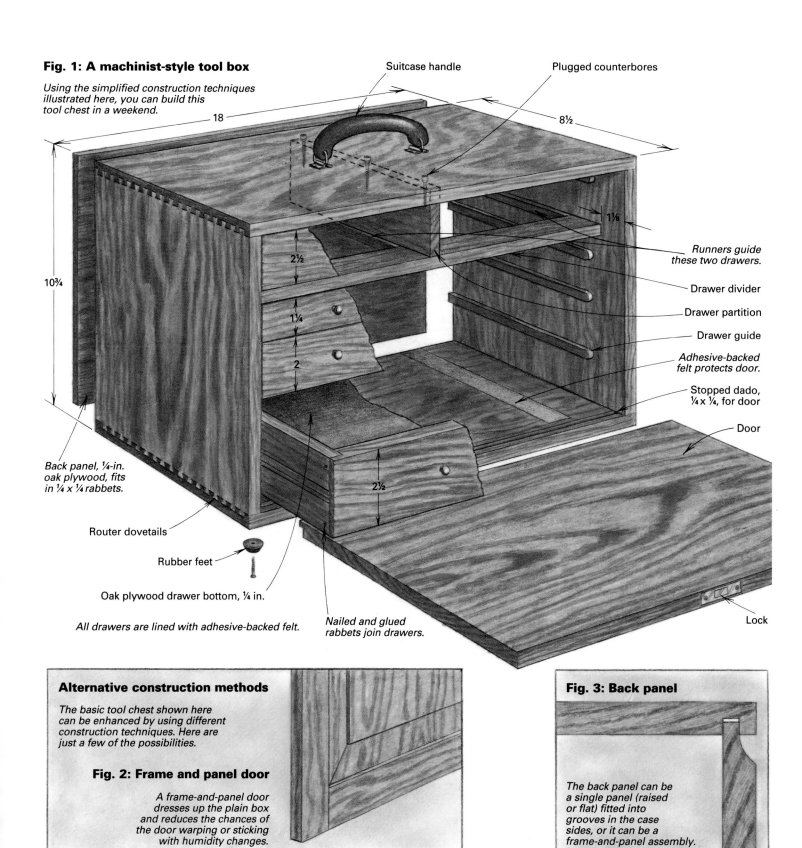

Suitcase handle

Plugged counterbores

18

8½

1⅛

2½

Runners guide these two drawers.

Drawer divider

Drawer partition

Drawer guide

Adhesive-backed felt protects door.

Stopped dado, ¼ x ¼, for door

Door

1¼

2

10¾

Back panel, ¼-in. oak plywood, fits in ¼ x ¼ rabbets.

Router dovetails

Rubber feet

Oak plywood drawer bottom, ¼ in.

All drawers are lined with adhesive-backed felt.

2½

Nailed and glued rabbets join drawers.

Lock

Alternative construction methods

The basic tool chest shown here can be enhanced by using different construction techniques. Here are just a few of the possibilities.

Fig. 2: Frame and panel door

A frame-and-panel door dresses up the plain box and reduces the chances of the door warping or sticking with humidity changes.

Fig. 3: Back panel

The back panel can be a single panel (raised or flat) fitted into grooves in the case sides, or it can be a frame-and-panel assembly.

From *Fine Woodworking* (March 1993) 99:52-53

F ashioned after the old-style machinists' boxes, this small tool chest provides convenient, portable storage for your finest tools, instruments, rules and other small items. The original machinists' chests were traditionally made of walnut or fumed oak. I made mine of oak and stained it to match the rich brown tone the old-timers achieved through the chemical reaction that occurs when oak is exposed to ammonia fumes. The stack of graduated drawers helps prevent small objects from being inextricably buried at the bottom of the box. A separate door can be locked covering the drawers for security during storage. The door also keeps the drawers from falling out when you're carrying the box from job to job. When you're using the box, the door slides neatly into the chest under the bottom drawer, as shown in the photo at right.

My 18-in.-wide by 10¾-in.-high tool chest suits my space and storage requirements, but you should modify these dimensions and the drawer configuration to suit your particular needs. I used ⁹⁄₁₆-in.-thick oak for most of the chest. The drawer backs and sides are ⁵⁄₁₆-in.-thick poplar, and the back panel and drawer bottoms are ¼-in.-thick oak-veneer plywood. All the hardware for my chest came from Constantine's (2050 Eastchester Road, Bronx, N.Y. 10461; 212-792-1600). I suggest buying your hardware before you begin construction, so you can be sure you've dimensioned the chest appropriately.

The main body of the chest is a dovetailed box, which I constructed using a commercial dovetail jig and ¼-in.-dia. dovetail bit (see *FWW* #99, p. 58). You could tablesaw finger joints instead (see *FWW* #84, pp. 74-75), or you could use this project as a great opportunity to practice handcutting dovetails.

Constructing the carcase

After selecting the stock for the carcase, lay out and cut the pieces to size, as shown in figure 1 at left, selecting the best wood for the top and sides. You will assemble and disassemble the parts several times while cutting the dovetails and constructing the chest, so be sure to mark the pieces on the inside faces to prevent layout mistakes.

After cutting the joints, dry-assemble the four sides, and check for square fit. Disassemble and cut the back-panel rabbets in the top, bottom and sides. Because I ripped the rabbets on my tablesaw, I had to fill the gaps that resulted in the dovetail joints with small blocks of wood during final assembly. Using a plunge router, I cut a stopped dado along the front edge of the case bottom for the door. Although I chiseled out the mortises in the carcase sides for the drawer divider, it would have been as easy to cut them with the plunge router. Next you should cut out the drawer

A machinist-style tool chest is a perennial favorite for storage of treasured tools because the stack of felt-lined drawers provides easy access and a safe haven.

partition, and then lay out and attach the drawer guides and runners with glue and small brads to the drawer partition and the carcase sides, as shown in figure 1. The drawer divider is cut to size, tenoned and screwed to the drawer partition.

A final dry-assembly lets me check the sides, divider and runners for square before I bore and counterbore holes for the drawer partition to the carcase top. If everything is square, I cut and fit the plywood back. I then disassemble and reassemble the chest with glue, screws and clamps (checking for square as I go) and allow the assembly to dry overnight.

Making the drawers

Drawer construction is straightforward with simple butt and rabbet joints, as shown in figure 1. Be sure, however, to cut the drawer-slide grooves slightly oversized to allow for smooth movement. I did mine with a dado head on my tablesaw before assembling the drawers. A little paste wax or paraffin on the drawer runners contributes to smooth operation.

Finally, cut and fit the door, mortise the lock and attach a suitcase handle to the top. A large chest might be better off with a handle on each side. To finish the chest, I rubbed on two coats of Watco Danish oil and then sprayed two coats of Deft spray polyurethane on the exposed surfaces. And to protect my finest tools, I lined the drawers with adhesive-backed felt.

Because of the simple construction shown in figure 1, I was able to build this chest in a couple of days. If you would prefer less of a plain-vanilla chest, you might want to consider using some alternate construction methods, as shown from left to right in the bottom drawings. These techniques will probably take you a little longer and call for a little more material. ☐

Ron Young is a woodworker in Decatur, Ala.

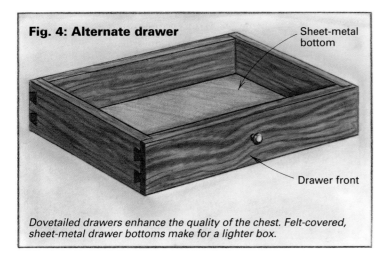

Fig. 4: Alternate drawer

Sheet-metal bottom

Drawer front

Dovetailed drawers enhance the quality of the chest. Felt-covered, sheet-metal drawer bottoms make for a lighter box.

Building a mahogany breakfront like the one in the photo at left is a big job for most small shops. But Doug Schroeder, left, along with Jon Schmalenberger and one other helper, invested nearly 3,000 hours to build four of them in Schroeder's shop. The slender dovetail pins and impeccably detailed fronts for the 40 drawers (above) were accomplished with the aid of some low-tech production methods.

Handling Large Commissions
Overcoming the limitations of a small shop

by Douglas Schroeder

Sometimes the small-shop operator shies away from that big job because it seems to be too much of a good thing. But with careful attention to details and a prudent awareness of the pitfalls, you can turn that major commission into the boost that will raise your work to a whole new level.

In January, 1986, I was one of four staff conservators at the Society for the Preservation of New England Antiquities (SPNEA). Three days a week I worked on some of the finest 17th- and 18th-century furniture at the SPNEA Furniture Conservation Center near Boston, Mass. The rest of the week I struggled with my own start-up business designing and building custom furniture and kitchen cabinets and doing odd repair jobs. One day, the head conservator, Robert Mussey, asked me if I would be interested in building some bookcases in my shop for one of SPNEA's private clients. Because I had a sizable opening in my schedule, I looked into the job.

The bookcases turned out to be four matching mahogany break-fronts, one of which is shown in the photos above. Each of the four breakfronts is 9 ft. wide, 8 ft. 8 in. tall and 20 in. deep. They were designed by one of the nation's premier architects, Robert A. M. Stern of New York, N.Y., specifically for one room of a 20,000-sq.-ft. Stern-designed home being built in eastern Massachusetts.

I was familiar with Robert Stern and the quality of his work primarily through his PBS television series, *Pride of Place: Building the American Dream.* But the opportunity to build furniture of uncompromised quality was on a collision course with my inadequate shop space and meager tooling. Ever the optimist, my fears of economic ruin, starvation, debtor's prison or worse were scattered before the hurricane-force winds of "the job of a lifetime." With Robert Mussey's offer of an open-ended leave of absence, I bid on the project and got it.

The job of a lifetime or a lifetime job?—From the day I started this project to the last, sweaty, 13-hour day nearly 18 months later, the horizon always seemed mountainous. I am still amazed at what my two helpers and I accomplished.

We milled, joined and sanded 2,600 bd. ft. of lumber to make:
- 24 separate dovetailed cases,
- 32 frame-and-panel backs, half mahogany and half poplar,
- 16 upper-case doors with 15 lights each,
- 320 separate pieces of upper-case door muntin and mullion stock,
- 40 drawers, dovetailed front and back with solid wood bottoms,
- 72 shelves with beaded edges,
- 144 mahogany horizontal shelf supports,
- 64 mahogany vertical shelf standards with bird's-mouth notches.

On top of that, there were:
- 1,384 ft. of moldings to set up, run and sand twice,
- 240 panes of glass to be installed and glazed,
- 192 mortises for hinges and locks,
- 64 brass key escutcheons to be individually fit,
- 6 coats of oil-varnish finish wiped on and wiped off.

We put in a total of 2,746 hours. The total labor charge was $63,600 and the total materials charge was $10,400.

The sheer volume of work was often very demoralizing. There were sustaining moments along the way whenever one particular phase of the project was completed, but the day when the four completed breakfronts could be set up in my shop as they would stand in the house always seemed a long way off. However, the wait for that moment was worth it, and if given the opportunity, I would do it all again. Here then are some thoughts on the process, the problems and the solutions encountered along the way.

The estimate–Before I could be considered for the job, I met with architect Edward R. Mudd who was supervising the construction of both the house and its interior furnishings. The purpose of the meeting was twofold: For me to become familiar with the specifications of the job and the expectations of the clients; and for the architects to evaluate my qualifications for meeting those expectations.

The scale drawings indicated that the clients not only wanted the breakfronts in the style of the late-18th-century Georgian period, but they also wanted them built using period construction techniques and tools. This discussion necessitated my first sales pitch. Building these cabinets was going to be time-consuming enough *with* the aid of power tools; using only hand tools would make the price of the job astronomical. Besides, I believe that 18th-century craftsmen would not have hesitated to use power tools had they been available. In support of this assertion, I gave a brief demonstration to show how much more quickly a jointer and thickness planer could dimension rough stock as opposed to a handplane. Then, to assuage any doubts about my devotion to traditional woodworking practices, I also demonstrated how cleanly and efficiently a handplane and cabinet scraper could prepare surfaces for a final finish, relative to a thickness planer, belt sander or pad sander. The economic implications of a totally handmade piece versus a combination of modern horsepower and hand-tool finesse were obvious. In addition, I explained that many period construction techniques (especially cross-grain construction) fail the test of seasonal temperature and humidity changes. As a staff conservator with SPNEA, the experience of literally taking apart (when necessary), repairing and conserving some of New England's finest period furniture taught me traditional construction from the inside out, including its failings.

At the end of this meeting, it was clear that the historical period, dimensions, proportions and styling of the breakfronts were already established. But there were myriad other details that still needed to be worked out, such as molding profiles, drawer and door decoration (crossbanding and cock bead, for example) and choice of hardware, as well as the engineering of the actual construction of the breakfronts. With these considerations in mind, I was invited to submit an estimate for approval.

Because of the unknowns, I prepared a "range" estimate, from a very plain, stripped-down model to the top-of-the-line model with all the extras. After a lot of figuring and head-scratching, I finally arrived at a range of $12,000 to $15,000 as the cost in labor and materials to build *one* breakfront. Normally I would add a margin of profit to the estimated cost to arrive at my final estimate, but I didn't do that. I assumed that by building four identical breakfronts simultaneously, I would gain a rate of efficiency over the entire project roughly equal to what I wanted for a profit margin. Yes, very sound reasoning if one is building hundreds of wooden widgets; somewhat sound reasoning even if one is building only four wooden widgets; but very poor reasoning when one is building four huge, highly detailed, structurally complex and labor-intensive period reproductions. The extensive amount of handwork required to produce these four breakfronts more than negated the advantage I'd expected to gain through the principles of building multiples. It's important to remember that the first time you build any piece of furniture, you're making a prototype; production doesn't begin until after the prototype is built and the construction and processes are evaluated. On top of that, the logistical nightmare of having four large pieces in my shop for 18 months and having to move, stack, work under, around, between and through them was something I didn't foresee. The amount of time spent just moving parts around was enormous. To my credit, I did have the sense to avoid some potential problems. I let the architects take care of hiring professional movers to transport these behemoths from my shop to their new home. And I also charged separately and on a time-and-materials basis for installation.

It was quite apparent that I needed to enlarge my 800-sq.-ft. shop so I would have room to set up the cabinets as they took shape. I also needed to buy a good thickness planer, drill press and jointer. I figured I'd need some extra carbide sawblades and an extra set of knives for both the jointer and the planer to avoid downtime while items were out for sharpening. Of course, I didn't figure the cost of the shop expansion or the major tools directly into the estimate since their service to me would obviously extend far beyond the duration of this one job. However, one advantage of a large job is the excuse and opportunity to add tools to your shop. Because this was a big investment for me, I wrote into my estimate a system for receiving partial payments based on regular inspection periods, along with a sizable down payment upon acceptance of my estimate. In hindsight, it would have been prudent to add in a factor to cover the time involved in setting up and taking down the breakfronts for the purpose of these inspections.

My high-end estimate got me the job, covered wages and expenses and provided a steady income for 18 months. However, there was no real profit because I really didn't take the dark side of building multiples seriously enough. Small mistakes become large mistakes; large mistakes go off the scale.

Help!–Upon receiving word that I'd been awarded the job, I immediately began expanding my shop by building an 11-ft. by 20-ft. addition, a space roughly equal to the size of the room for which the cabinets were designed. Because my shop is contained in one section of a large barn, I was able to add the extra square footage within the already-covered space in the barn. So I now had the job and the space. But this was more of a job than

Above: The author worked out all the details, including molding profiles, on a full-scale drawing for approval by the architect and clients to ensure there would be no surprises at the end of the job.

Below: The waist assembly frame, shown sitting atop the lower cabinets, is glued up with the endgrain continuous across its ends. To allow for the frame's expansion and contraction, the upper-case retainer molding is attached at the back with screws through slots.

Photo: Paul Bertorelli

I could handle alone, either physically or emotionally; I needed help, and very good help at that.

I was extremely fortunate to find the two people I hired. As a graduate of the North Bennett Street School in Boston, Mass., Jon Schmalenberger was well trained in period furniture construction. The combination of this training and the first-hand, practical experience gained by running his own business made him the ideal candidate for this job. He agreed to temporarily put aside his own shop activities and commit himself fully to 10 months of very intense work. Jon needed virtually no supervision, and he single-handedly did all the milling, gluing up, dimensioning and carcase dovetailing for the breakfronts.

My other assistant, Kirsten Mong, worked for a luthier and had built her own guitar. Although her furniture-making experience was limited, the work she had done showed great skill and attention to detail. Most of the jobs requiring patience and stamina fell to Kirsten throughout the five months she worked on the breakfronts. She planed, scraped, sanded and resanded miles of mahogany and yellow poplar, and she fine-tuned the surfaces and joints, a step necessary to create a beautiful piece of furniture.

Plan of attack—Good communication with the architect and the client was vitally important. To ensure the customers would be satisfied, I began a full-scale drawing on drafting vellum pinned to a wall, shown in the top photo at left. With this medium for creating and exchanging ideas, together with ¼-scale working drawings, models of some components and various types of displays, all the details were worked out in advance and approved by all parties. This process, although very time-consuming, was invaluable in avoiding ugly surprises at the end of the project.

Figure 1 on the facing page shows how the pieces were constructed. Each breakfront consists of six separate dovetailed carcases and a separate base, waist and cornice section. This makes it possible to disassemble these huge pieces for moving them through doorways, around corners and up flights of stairs. Each base section is equipped with eight, heavy-duty leveling guides so it can be put in position and leveled. After leveling the base, the three lower cases are set in place. They fit inside the base molding and are joined with screws inserted from inside the two drawer cases.

As you can see in the bottom photo at left, the ends of the mahogany frame of the waist assembly are edge-glued to the front and back members so the endgrain shows, giving the appearance of a solid top. Because the waist molding and the upper-case retainer molding run cross-grain to the frame along the case's sides (including where the sides of the center cabinet section protrude forward), the molding couldn't be glued down without restricting the frame's expansion and contraction: an accident waiting to happen. Instead, the front 3 in. are glued and screwed to the frame while the rear ends of the moldings are held snugly with screws in slots, as shown in the bottom photo. The moldings along the front edge of the frame can be glued and screwed to the frame because the grain orientation of all the pieces is the same. The completed waist assembly then just drops onto the lower-case assembly, and the upper cases are set on top of the waist and screwed together side to side.

The cornice is actually made up of two architectural elements: the 3-in.-high frieze and the cornice or pediment. The frieze board is glued up from mahogany and poplar and assembled to make a mitered frame that fits perfectly on the upper cases. Then, moldings are glued and screwed to the poplar portion of the frame to create the massive cornice. Like the base and waist assemblies, the completed cornice simply drops into place. Perhaps I use the word simply a little too freely. Getting the cornice into place requires considerable muscle power, two stepladders and two fools perched on those parts of the stepladders that warn: *not a step*. The cornice is held in position by locater blocks glued to the top of the upper case and secured with screws through a cleat glued to each end of the cornice.

Construction details—The first step in building any piece of furniture should be careful wood selection. Figure and grain are as important as any other design element, and they often make the difference between a good piece and a great piece. With four matching pieces in the same room, judicious wood selection takes on an entirely new dimension. As an image of the four breakfronts formed in my mind, I began to know where I wanted a highly

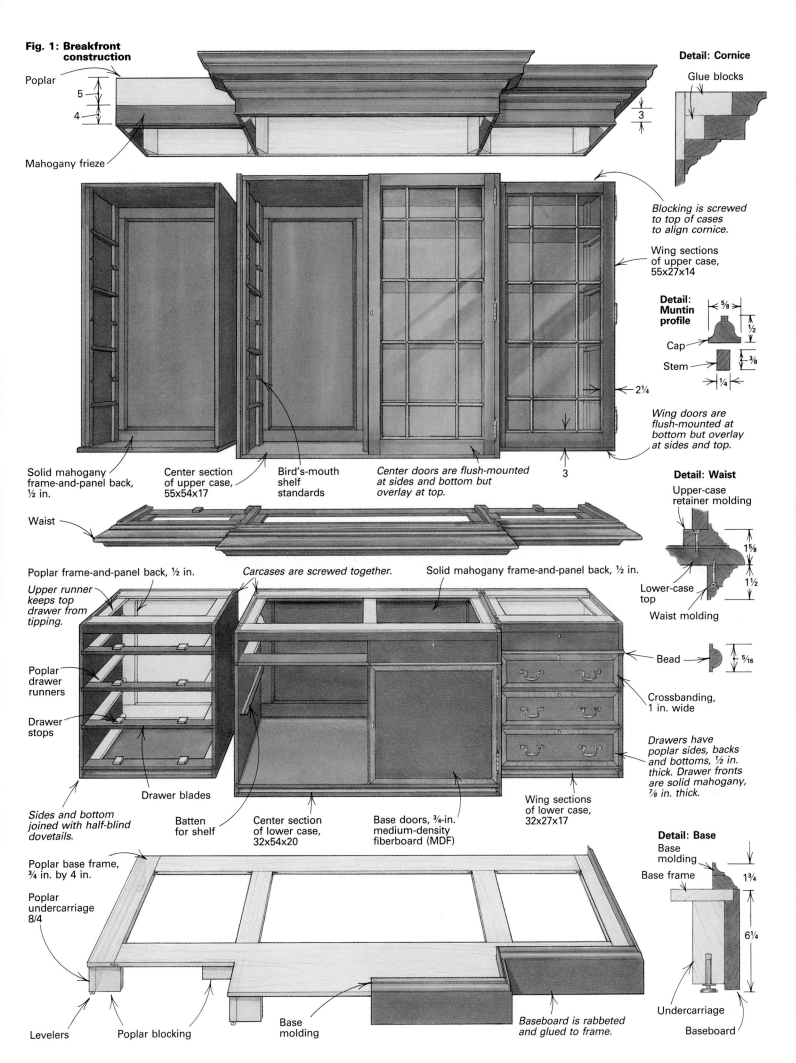

Fig. 1: Breakfront construction

Poplar

5
4

Mahogany frieze

Detail: Cornice

Glue blocks

3

Blocking is screwed to top of cases to align cornice.

Wing sections of upper case, 55x27x14

Solid mahogany frame-and-panel back, ½ in.

Center section of upper case, 55x54x17

Bird's-mouth shelf standards

Center doors are flush-mounted at sides and bottom but overlay at top.

3

Wing doors are flush-mounted at bottom but overlay at sides and top.

Detail: Muntin profile

⅝

½

Cap

Stem

⅜

¼

2¼

Detail: Waist

Upper-case retainer molding

1⅝

1½

Lower-case top

Waist molding

Waist

Poplar frame-and-panel back, ½ in.

Carcases are screwed together.

Solid mahogany frame-and-panel back, ½ in.

Upper runner keeps top drawer from tipping.

Poplar drawer runners

Drawer stops

Bead

5/16

Crossbanding, 1 in. wide

Drawers have poplar sides, backs and bottoms, ½ in. thick. Drawer fronts are solid mahogany, ⅞ in. thick.

Sides and bottom joined with half-blind dovetails.

Drawer blades

Batten for shelf

Center section of lower case, 32x54x20

Base doors, ¾-in. medium-density fiberboard (MDF)

Wing sections of lower case, 32x27x17

Detail: Base

Base molding

Base frame

1¾

6¼

Poplar base frame, ¾ in. by 4 in.

Poplar undercarriage 8/4

Levelers

Poplar blocking

Base molding

Baseboard is rabbeted and glued to frame.

Undercarriage

Baseboard

Drawings: Kathleen Creston

figured board to provide a focal point, where I wanted a pale, straight-grain board to provide a static field and how the eye should travel across the whole piece. The challenge was previewing the nearly 2,000 bd. ft. of rough-cut Honduras mahogany I had in my shop and barn. After a few frustrating attempts with a handplane, I realized that one lifetime would not be enough; I needed an alternate method. In an especially illuminated moment, I ran down to the local hardware store and bought a small Skil portable power-planer for $29.99. With it I was able to preview mahogany planks, 16 ft. long by 30 in. wide, in a matter of minutes.

After all the boards were marked for their intended use, they were crosscut, ripped, milled and, where necessary, glued up to make the parts for the four breakfronts. Figure 2 below shows how we avoided one of the most typical problems of period furniture: case sides that have split because the drawer runners were glued and/or nailed cross-grain to the wide panels. On our cabinets, the drawer runners are fitted, but not glued, into ⅛-in.-deep dadoes in the case sides. The front end of each runner is tenoned and glued into a ¼-in.- by 1-in.-deep mortise in the back edge of the drawer blade (horizontal dividers between drawers). The back end of the drawer runner is screwed to the case through a slotted hole to allow for expansion or contraction of the case side. An S-curve bandsawn on the runner reduces the width of the piece so I can use

Clamping the cock bead with masking tape, while gluing it to the doors and drawer fronts, eliminates the need for clamps and cauls.

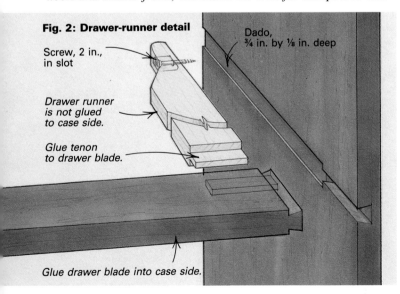

Fig. 2: Drawer-runner detail

Screw, 2 in.,
in slot

Dado,
¾ in. by ⅛ in. deep

Drawer runner
is not glued
to case side.

Glue tenon
to drawer blade.

Glue drawer blade into case side.

a 2-in. screw rather than a 4-in. screw to secure it to the case side.

Perhaps the greatest challenge in creative jigging was producing dovetails for 40 drawers in four different sizes using slender, fine pins typical of the 18th century. Fortunately, Robert Mussey had told me about a shopmade dovetailing jig devised by Mario Genevesse, a master cabinetmaker in Natick, Mass. The jig lets you quickly rout out the sockets for either half-blind or through dovetails, thereby creating the pins. Even though the tails are then sawn and chiseled out as in normal hand-cut dovetails, a great deal of time is saved in laying out and executing the pins. For details on making this jig, see my article in *FWW* #68, p. 56.

Of the 40 drawers, 24 have cock bead and crossbanding. The other 16 are the top-most drawers, and they're left unadorned to make up the lower-case frieze. We didn't come up with any shortcuts for applying the crossbanding to the drawer fronts. A shallow rabbet was machined in the solid-mahogany drawer fronts and the veneer was mitered and glued in place, strip by strip, using cam clamps and cauls. However, we found that clamping with masking tape, a trick I'd used in small-scale repair work, worked beautifully for applying the cock bead (see photo at left). Once I learned how to maneuver the tape to vary the pressure, I had no trouble gluing in the bead, quickly and evenly. Not having to wrestle with clamps and cauls was well worth the cost of a few rolls of masking tape.

The lower-case doors provided another arena for creative woodworking. We chose to use mahogany-veneered medium-density fiberboard (MDF) for the door panels because it's considerably more stable than plywood or hardwood. However, because the edges are weak and they can't hold hinge screws, it was necessary to edge the doors in solid mahogany. Knowing how time-consuming it had been to cross-band the solid drawer fronts, we looked for a way to save time. We planed and ripped the solid edge stock to size and then glued the crossbanding to it. It wasn't necessary for the veneer to fit perfectly. Therefore, we cut it so we could hold it in about ¹⁄₁₆ in. from each side of the edge stock. As we machined the veneered edging stock, first for the tongue to mate with the groove in the edges of the MDF door blanks, and then for the cock bead rabbet, these cuts simultaneously trimmed the crossbanding. Then, all we had to do was miter the crossbanded edging stock and glue it to the door panels.

When it came time to think about building the 16 upper-case doors, I immediately realized that I needed an alternative to the labor-intensive, traditional, hand-coped muntin detail. The obvious alternative of using cope-and-pattern shaper cutters didn't seem like the solution, considering the fine and fragile muntin profile I wanted and the limited machinery I had. So necessity once more reared her motherly head. A cutaway section of muntin stock looks like a mushroom with a long stem. It's easy to imagine it as a two-part affair: The stem or rabbeted part that actually divides the panes of glass is one part, while the top or molded cap becomes the second part. We used this two-part construction to our advantage.

After the door stiles and rails were mortised and tenoned and the rabbet was cut for the glass, the ogee detail was run on these parts and mitered at the corners, as shown in the top photo on the facing page. The mortises for the muntin stems and the V-miters for the muntin caps were laid out and cut into the ogee molding on the door frame. I then assembled the door frame with the horizontal and vertical stems half-lapped and glued to each other at their junctures and tenoned and glued into the door frame. The half-lap joints of the stems were installed so the horizontals (mullions) ran through on the outside face. To complete the doors, the muntins and mullions needed the double ogee molding detail, or cap as I call it. I ran the vertical cap pieces (muntins) full length so they overlapped and strengthened the stem's lap joints. I carefully fit the ends of the muntin caps into the V-miters on the door rails and then marked the locations where the V-miters intersected the mullion caps. Then, I removed the muntins, sawed the V-miters into them and glued them back in place. All of the horizontal cap pieces were then cut slightly long and individually mitered and glued to the stem frame, as shown in the bottom photo at right. I mitered all the ends with my Lion Miter-Trimmer, which is available from Pootatuck Corp., Box 24, Windsor, Vt. 05089; (802) 674-5984, and a number of mail-order houses. All the V-mitering was done on my tablesaw with a miter gauge and a simple system of stops, often running as many as four parts at once. Making muntins using this two-part process may sound difficult, but it is easier, quicker and stronger than traditional methods if you mark accurately and take care in making your setups. Mac Campbell describes a similar method in *FWW* #72, p. 48.

Lessons learned—As I mentioned earlier, there was no real profit margin in this job. The additional $27,000 in work that I've done for the same clients has helped considerably to soothe the sting; and perhaps the lessons that I've learned have compensated for the lack of profit. But, of course, this logic is only valid if I don't make the same mistakes twice. Aside from being overly optimistic about the economic advantages of building four identical pieces, unforeseen details probably caused me the most trouble.

One of the details that hurt me the most, glazing the upper-case doors (a period detail), was the only work I planned to subcontract. I based my estimate on the very rough estimate I got from a local glazier. When the doors were built and finished, I took four of them down to the glazier for a trial run. The completed work would have looked bad in the top floor of a 10-story building viewed from the back seat of a speeding taxi cab in a heavy fog. The hours it took to clean the brown-putty fingerprints and gobs of silicone from both sides of 60 panes of glass (not to mention from my million-dollar oil-varnish finish) convinced me to glaze the remaining 12 doors myself. Even without the cleanup time, the original estimate came up short and cost us some money.

When I submitted my estimate, there were still many unknowns about the job. One was the cost of the shaper cutters I'd need to cut the molding profiles that I was working out with the architect. Unfortunately, I didn't delve deeply enough into this aspect before submitting my estimate, and so I was surprised to find that I was unable to use *any* off-the-shelf cutters. I had to have them all custom-made, which added a few hundred dollars to the cost of the job. Making assumptions like this during the estimating stage, especially on large projects, is asking for trouble.

Finish-sanding was another area I underestimated. I had more than ¼ mile of moldings and who knows how many acres of case surface area to sand, dampen and sand again. I just didn't allow enough time.

Although making multiples didn't work out the way I hoped it would, in any large job there are repetitive machining operations that you can treat as "production" runs. Here are some ideas that can help your repetitive operations go smoothly. Pay attention to accuracy; the smallest error can multiply to create a cumulative error factor that can put you out of business. Double-check your setups often as you work; it's much easier than redoing a whole run because something moved after the first pass. Make up plenty of extra stock before you start the operation; anything can go wrong from a slip on the saw to a flaw in the wood, and besides, you'll need spare parts to test succeeding setups. Finally, don't skimp when making jigs and fixtures; if you make them accurately and to last, you'll probably use them again.

Photos below: Paul Bertorelli

The photo above shows the detailing and joinery for the upper door frames. The muntins and mullions are assembled in two parts (see photo below). The "stems" are crosslapped and mortised into the door frame, and the molded "caps" are glued to the stems after being notched where they intersect.

Documentation and photography—Part of growing and prospering as a woodworker is learning the importance of documenting your work. Throughout the course of this project, I kept a comprehensive file of literally every bit of information that passed through my hands: all my scale drawings, sketches, molding profiles (some of which were taken from tracings I had previously made from period pieces), lists of sources and copies of written communications with the architect and client. It was a pain to keep up with it all, but this information will always be useful in future work.

It's also very helpful to have photographic documentation of the job through each phase of its construction. Take these photos yourself from time to time as work progresses to record joinery details and unusual jigs or setups. Sometimes a finished piece warrants professional photography, and sometimes it doesn't; quite often you can get by on your own. Inexpensive cameras, tripods and lighting equipment will do, but there's really no substitute for photo background paper, which is sold at most photo-supply stores in rolls of various widths. A bright, unbroken background dramatically sets off a piece of furniture, and a great photograph will help make that big job continue to pay off in the future by testifying to the quality of your work and the seriousness of your endeavors. □

Douglas Schroeder builds custom furniture and reproductions and does restoration work in Hudson, Mass.

Production Basics for a Small Shop

A *reversal of fortune with a revision of procedures*

by Jim Tolpin

One of the luckiest days in my woodworking career was the day I realized I was going broke. I can now joke about "back then" since my situation is much better today, 20 years later. But in my first 10 years as a cabinetmaker, working out of a one-car garage, I barely provided for myself, let alone the family of four I now support. I could often be found constructing highly refined pieces of casework that required hours of hand-joinery and tedious detailing. I bathed in each client's approval of my work at the time of delivery, but little did I know that much of their joy was in obtaining such work for such a price. Fortunately, I learned that it wasn't the woodworking itself that forestalled my financial success, but rather the way in which I was working the wood.

I decided to unplug myself from the shop to figure out what I was doing wrong. It didn't take long before I had three answers. First, I didn't have the faintest idea of how to build consistent production cabinets; second, my methods and tools were primitive and counterproductive; third, I was a poor businessman. To continue woodworking as a livelihood, I'd have to learn how to build pieces of high-quality cabinetry as efficiently as possible. So to fix my career and resolve my earlier woes, I chose to revise the shop first and then the process, before looking at the business affairs (which is another story). In this article, I'll examine some specific processes in my revised system, along with their applications to my woodworking. To explain the system's benefits, I'll show how I group operations, and then I'll take you through the ordering and layout processes for solid-stock components of a typical cabinet project. Finally, I'll describe my methods for joining face frames (see the sidebar on p. 36). But first, let me give a few examples of how I reorganized my shop.

Work flow and block production—To better use the space in my 22-ft. by 24-ft. garage shop, I replaced some machines and upgraded others. My major purchases were a more powerful tablesaw, an 8-in. jointer and a lighter planer. I also installed a dust collector and an air compressor, and I revamped fence systems for the tablesaw and radial-arm saw and added shop-built extension tables to both. Then I concentrated on the floor plan. Proper placement of major stationary tools and work surfaces reduces operator fatigue, allows smoother material flow through the shop and increases production. For example, I clustered tools into symbiotic groups (like the jointer/tablesaw/router-table arrangement in the bottom photo on the facing page) to enable quicker operation changes. To maximize open floor space, I built knockdown work surfaces, shown in the top photo on the facing page, and a support grid for my portable thickness planer. When not in use, the thickness planer is suspended from the ceiling joists, and the platform stands hang on the wall. With the physical plant in shape, I turned my attention to the production process.

I realized that to make the shop really work for me, the tasks involved in building a set of cabinets had to be sequenced carefully. Again, the flow of materials through the shop is critical. Products of one operation must not prevent access to the machinery and space requirements of the next; components must be grouped so that a particular tool setup is created only once; and functions must be organized so all materials reach the same production phase at the same time. I first analyzed the material flow and grouped processes to see how they could be sequenced, from layout and cut lists, to the fabrication stage, to the installation of the product on-site. Over the past 10 years, through much thought, many trials and errors, and with advice from tool and hardware manufacturers, I've developed what I call a block production method (shown in the flowchart on the facing page) to make the most of my time and modest floor space.

The premise of block production is that all the tasks involved in the manufacture of cabinets can be grouped into exclusive "blocks." The materials intended to undergo a certain block operation are carefully ordered so that all steps occur at the proper time. I keep a large copy of the flowchart hanging on the wall of my shop to remind me where to turn at the end of each production block. In addition to the vast time savings that have resulted from implementing this method, there have been other benefits as well. First, it's possible to accurately generate data on the amount of labor required in any given process (valuable information when estimating the costs of proposed projects); second, breathing spaces are built into the work pace so that between blocks, you can catch up and clean up (for most independent cabinetmakers, this really makes a difference in work quality); third, it's possible to do more than one project at a time without confusion, and a small job automatically nets a higher profit margin as it rides through the tool setups of a larger one.

From cut lists to ordering—Once I had created a well-oiled procedure for cabinetmaking, I was ready to plan out some work. When figuring materials for a cabinet project, I've found that one of the most necessary shop drawings is an elevation of each module to be built. I do this on a 5-in. by 8-in. index card, which provides space for a drawing and a list of pieces with their dimensions. I keep all these elevation cards handy in a file-card box, and from them, I develop two master cut lists: one for solid stock and one for sheet goods. The amount and sizes of materials that need to be ordered are compiled from these cut lists.

In my early cabinetmaking days, preparing and assembling solid stock were more than two production blocks; they were almost my entire operation. The involved procedures of milling, dimensioning and joining solid stock filled my shop with fragrant aromas, but

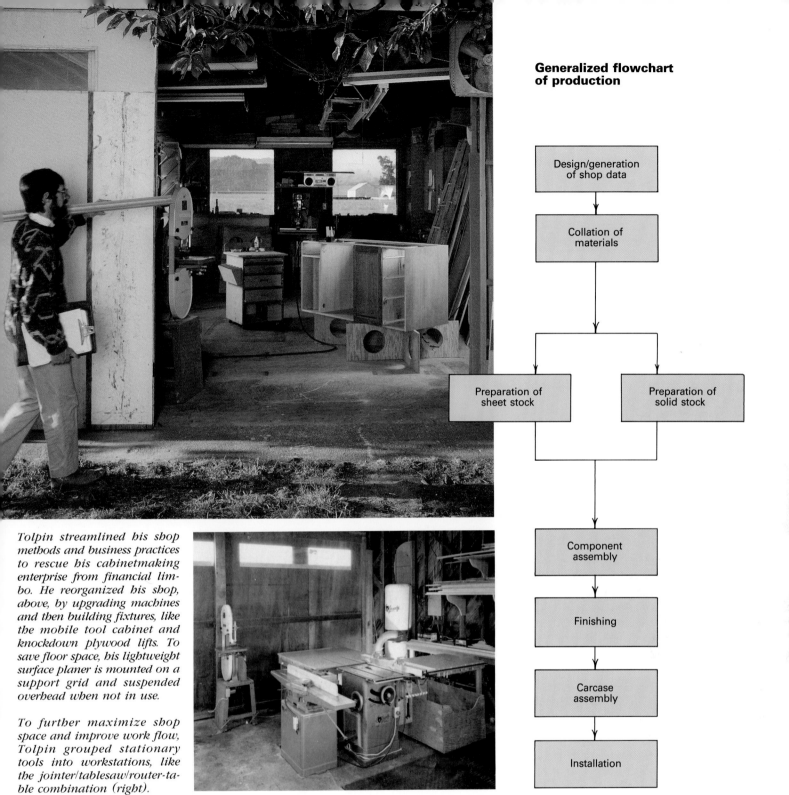

Generalized flowchart of production

```
Design/generation
of shop data
        │
        ▼
Collation of
materials
        │
   ┌────┴────┐
   ▼         ▼
Preparation of   Preparation of
sheet stock      solid stock
   │         │
   └────┬────┘
        ▼
Component
assembly
        │
        ▼
Finishing
        │
        ▼
Carcase
assembly
        │
        ▼
Installation
```

Tolpin streamlined his shop methods and business practices to rescue his cabinetmaking enterprise from financial limbo. He reorganized his shop, above, by upgrading machines and then building fixtures, like the mobile tool cabinet and knockdown plywood lifts. To save floor space, his lightweight surface planer is mounted on a support grid and suspended overhead when not in use.

To further maximize shop space and improve work flow, Tolpin grouped stationary tools into workstations, like the jointer/tablesaw/router-table combination (right).

they did little to fill my pockets. Now I make much of the casework from sheet stock, but solid stock remains the material of choice for select components, like doors, drawer faces and face frames. The processes I use in solid-stock preparation can also be applied to simple wood-furniture projects. First, when figuring how many board feet of solid stock you'll need, add about 15% to account for defects and waste. Then, when you order the wood, ask your supplier(s) to plane it to ⅛ in. thicker than the finished dimension you need and to leave the edges unjointed, which is referred to in the trade as S2S (surfaced two sides). Final-planing the material yourself is the only way to ensure that it will be smooth and uniform. I surface 1-in.-thick stock down to ¹³⁄₁₆ in., which lets me shape more definition into the molded edges of doors and drawer faces than would be possible with ¾-in. stock. Another advantage is that edgebanding for ¾-in.-thick sheet goods can be ripped from

the stock in one operation. After you've ordered materials, you can start planning how you'll lay out and cut the components.

Laying out solid stock—I anticipate the layout stage for solid stock with some trepidation; so I quickly set aside as much material as possible—before my brain overheats. I begin by sorting through the pile, and separating the widest pieces of stock. After spreading these out, I refer to my solid-stock cut list. Since the pieces in this list are in widths, it's simple to assign the widest components to the widest stock, which soon commits a significant amount of board footage. The layout task then becomes more manageable. While taking care to avoid defects in the wood, I chalk the layout lines directly on the stock, and allow at least 1 in. of waste at the board ends. Since many of the wider components are drawer faces, I lay out adjoining drawers end to end on the same board to ensure a continuous flow of grain patterns from one cabinet to the next. Boards to be glued up into panels should also be cut from the wide stock.

Door-rail and stile stock is selected from the straightest wood left in the pile. If there are paired doors, I try to lay out adjoining stiles side by side, and then rip the stock into two pieces. This allows the grain to match perfectly from door to door, and any wood movement will be similar. Whenever possible, I group components of similar length on the stock so I can rough-crosscut the boards into lengths that are easy to handle. When all the parts are laid out, I'm ready to rip them to width and crosscut them to length in preparation for the component-assembly block.

In creating my block production method, I discovered some dif-

ferences between the avocation and the occupation of custom woodworking. Today, the revised system I use to process materials enables me to pursue my favorite work as a legitimate business. I hope these methods will be useful to others too, because even though our endeavors as independent cabinetmakers won't be found on the charts that list growth industries, there's no doubt in my mind that we're doing important work. □

Jim Tolpin owns a custom cabinetmaking shop in Ferndale, Cal. He is the author of Working at Woodworking, *the new book from which this article was adapted. The book is available from The Taunton Press, 63 S. Main St., PO Box 5506, Newtown, Conn. 06470-5506.*

Joining cabinet face frames

If a project calls for face frames, I've found that I don't need to join the parts with dowels, mortises and tenons, or even biscuits because my cabinet's plywood carcases keep the face units in place. To improve efficiency and maintain frame quality, I adapted the standard industry techniques of screwing face-frame components together through angled holes in their back sides for use in my one-man production shop. The resulting joints are strong, stay flush and don't require clamps while the glue dries. To drill the angled pockets, I use a Ritter bit (available from Woodworker's Supply of New Mexico, 5604 Alameda Place N.E., Albuquerque, N.M. 87113; 800-645-9292), which is a long countersink bit designed to drill at a low angle. The joint is glued and fastened with square-drive face-frame screws (also carried by Woodworker's Supply of New Mexico), which have pan heads that won't split out endgrain.

In addition to the bit, you'll need a jig to hold the pieces in position for drilling. You can either buy the jig or make your own; the left photo below shows my shop-made jig in place on the drill press. The support for the stock to be drilled is 22½° from vertical, and has lines drawn on its surface 90° to the base of the jig. These lines indicate proper alignment of the stock.

To prepare for countersinking, chuck the bit into the drill press, and set the speed at 1,000 RPM. Place the jig on the drill-press table in its approximate position, and lightly clamp it down. Run a series of test holes in scrap the same thickness as the frame until the exit hole is centered in the end of the stock and the countersink is deep enough to bury a screw head. When you're satisfied, set the stop for the quill travel, and tighten the jig's clamps.

Now, arrange the precut face-frame parts into the configuration shown on the elevation drawing for that cabinet. Mark

the back surface of each end that butts one another, and drill the holes where indicated. Pieces 1¼ in. to 2¼ in. wide receive two holes, while narrower stock receives only one. Wider stock can receive a hole every ¾ in. to ⅞ in. While drilling, hold the stock tightly to the sloping jig and perpendicular to the drill-press table, using the reference lines on the jig. After drilling all the holes required to join the frame, turn the components over face down. It's tricky to lay out from the perspective of inside the cabinet, but you will soon get used to it. Once the parts are properly oriented, mark the position of the interior joints. Measure carefully, unless the components themselves can be used as spacers.

You should fasten the innermost joints of the frame first. Secure the pieces to receive the screws along the edge of your work surface, using two C-clamps at the joint, as shown in the photo on the right. Firmly butt the component to be fastened against the clamped piece at its marks, and drill pilot holes for the screws. Back off the free piece, clear out the chips and apply glue to its end. Then reposition the piece, and drive the screws home. Release the clamps, lift up the joined components and remove any excess glue with a damp rag. When the whole frame is together, check diagonal measurements to ensure that it's square (if needed, clamp a temporary brace across it), and set the assembly aside to dry.

Be sure to let the structure sit overnight to reach full glue strength. Then, to clean up the frames, block-plane the surfaces and edges of the joints, and sand the wood to 220-grit. The assembled units are ready for the next production block, where I apply the finish and install hinge plates. The completed face frames are then mounted to the cabinet carcases in another stage, before final installation.   —J.T.

The angled pockets for the face-frame assembly screws *are drilled with a special shallow-angle countersink bit and with the frame member held 22½° from vertical on a shopmade jig.*

When joining the face-frame parts, *Tolpin double-clamps one of the solid-stock workpieces securely to his bench to counter its strong tendency to slide out of flush as the screws are driven home.*

Shop Insurance
Taking the splinters out of buying the right coverage

by Gary B. Savelli

I f you're a self-employed woodworker, you should consider liability, business and personal property insurance as important as your shop equipment. Even if you're an amateur woodworker, it's wise to check your homeowner's insurance policy to make sure that your home and shop equipment are adequately covered and that having a shop in your house doesn't jeopardize your home coverage. This is especially true for hobbyist woodworkers who earn money on the side by selling products made in the shop, because a homeowner's policy might not cover commercial operations.

Insurance can be expensive, but it could determine whether your business survives should you incur losses through lawsuits,

fire or theft (to name a few potential catastrophes). Although I feel a woodworker should be adequately insured across the board (no pun intended), you have to balance the total amount you spend on insurance against the risks you are facing. For instance, if you specialize in restoration work and installing architectural elements, your equipment and tools may be minimal, so fire insurance might not be terribly important to you. Instead, you might prefer to spend your money to insure your health and income in case a fall off a scaffold leaves you unable to work. On the other hand, if you located your cabinet business in a bad neighborhood to take advantage of low rents, you might concentrate on insuring your tools against fire and theft.

Liability insurance—I advise my woodworking clients that business liability coverage is essential. This insurance covers you if a judge finds you liable for losses or damage incurred by another person (or corporation). The settlements and the legal expenses here can be so large that were you *not* insured, you might be forced into bankruptcy. I recommend Comprehensive General Liability insurance. This broad liability policy covers court settlements, the cost of legal defense and medical expenses that arise from the operation of your shop. If your business is in your home, you still need a separate CGL policy—homeowner's insurance will not cover losses from running a business. The CGL policy does not deal with lawsuits brought by employees, however. These are generally covered by worker's compensation.

As a product-liability insurance, CGL also pays claims resulting from property damage or injury that your product causes. It does not cover loss to property in your care. For instance, suppose you're in the process of delivering a cabinet and accidentally drop it on my car. The car damage amounts to $200; the cabinet damage is $450. Your insurance may pay for car damage, but the cabinet is not covered. If the cabinet tipped over and hurt someone, the insurance would pay the court costs and any settlement against you to the full extent of the policy.

CGL costs vary widely, depending on the state and the situation, so it's impossible for me to give specific costs, but here's a typical case based on rates in California. The premiums are usually determined with a formula based on your gross annual receipts, employees'

"As a manufacturer, a woodworker might be liable for injuries caused by a product, even if the customer abused it."

annual payroll and, sometimes, the square footage of your shop. If you have a sole-proprietor shop with no employees and a gross income of $40,000, you would pay between $500 and $800 for $300,000 of liability coverage. A two-worker shop with 3,000 sq. ft. and gross annual receipts of $100,000 would pay between $2,000 and $3,000 for $300,000 of liability coverage. One caution: The policy is auditable, meaning that your agent will base the initial premium on payroll and income figures you supply. Then, at the end of the year he'll require audited figures, which will be used to calculate the actual cost of the policy. Should the audited figures vary from your original estimates, your insurance company will either bill you extra or pay you a refund. When shopping for a CGL policy, be wary of very low rates—the agent may have deliberately low-

"If you have antique hand tools, their value should be listed on your homeowner's insurance."

ered the figures to offer you a deceptively lower initial premium, but will make up the difference at the end of the year. Also, many agents offer low prices because their policies are not true CGL policies, but actually owners, landlords and tenants policies that cover only your premises, not products or business operations outside your shop.

If you cannot find a CGL policy, the next best policy is one that contains "manufacturers and contractors" and "products and completed operations" coverage. A policy that contains these coverages protects the same major elements of a CGL policy.

In addition to your CGL policy, you may want to cover your business personal property, such as machines, inventory, raw materials and office equipment. Two basic types of policies apply. The least expensive is Named Perils Coverage, which covers losses from fire, windstorms, water, smoke, vandalism and other specified problems. The other, more expensive, coverage is called All Risk, which covers theft, as well as damage from fire, windstorm, water, smoke and vandalism. These policies can cost anywhere from a couple of hundred dollars to more than a thousand dollars, depending on the company and the state where you live. Some companies also combine business personal property and liability coverages into a single package often called Multi-Peril Package, Artisan Package or Manufacturers and Contractors Package.

Worker's compensation—This insurance, which covers employees for occupational diseases and injuries, is mandatory in most states. In addition to covering injuries while on the job, this insurance will pay employees' salaries while they are recovering from a disease or injury. The policy also includes employer's liability insurance, which generally protects an employer found liable for the employee's injury. Usually the premiums are set by the state and will not vary from company to company.

A type of worker's compensation you should look for is a "participating" policy. This kind of policy pays back a dividend (though usually small) if your insurance company remains profitable. The dividends are not guaranteed, but at least it's good to know you may be able to recoup some of the insurance costs. Many states also

have a state compensation fund, making compensation coverage available to those who cannot afford or qualify to purchase from a private company.

Homeowner's insurance—This insurance generally excludes most damages involved with operating a business in your home. For instance, if a professional woodworker working at home has a fire in his basement shop, homeowner's insurance would cover only the losses to the home, not the business losses. Similarly, a homeowner's insurance policy won't cover court costs stemming from a product-liability suit.

Hobbyist woodworkers (those who don't sell their product) generally are covered by their homeowner's policy, but you should check with your agent to be sure. Generally, a fire that originates in a hobbyist's shop is covered under homeowner's insurance because insurance companies recognize that virtually every house has a shop or work area of some kind.

Homeowner's insurance usually deals with the cost of replacing your personal property in one of two ways. One type of policy will reimburse you for the cost of your tools and machinery (or any other household item) minus the depreciation. The other type pays you the current replacement cost. This type is slightly more expensive, but is worth it because you'll have to replace an item at current costs. If you have many machines and hand tools, they should be listed on your insurance policy. This could result in higher premiums, depending on the limits set in your policy. Your agent may require copies of the receipts from the tool purchases to determine their value. If you have antique hand tools, their value should be listed on your homeowner's insurance. Once again, your agent may want them appraised.

Whether you are a hobbyist or a professional, read your policy. I can't overemphasize this. You should find out what you are insured for *before* a catastrophe happens. Your policy may not exactly qualify as light reading, so if you have any questions, contact your agent. You should shop for insurance in the same aggressive manner you would shop for a tablesaw—prices and policies will vary significantly. A good way to shop for insurance is to join your local woodworker's trade association. Ask members what company they use, then go with a proven specialist. Also, the American Craft Council makes group medical insurance and an all-risk property policy available to its members. For more information, write: American Craft Council, 40 W. 53rd St., New York, N.Y. 10019.

Finally, if you're dealing with an independent agent, ask what company the agent is offering and if the company has an "A" rating by the A.M. Best Co.'s rating method, which gauges the financial health of insurance and other companies. And again, trying to save money by not buying insurance is false economy, especially if you're an incorporated business and the premiums are tax deductible. □

Gary Savelli is vice president of Basic West Insurance Co. located in San Francisco, Calif.

Limiting your liability

by Peter A. Lee

Woodworkers selling their products risk the same kinds of product liability and personal injury suits as do industrial giants. The cash amounts involved may be more modest, but any woodworker can be held legally liable if an employee or customer is injured in the shop or if an employee injures someone or damages their property. As a manufacturer, a woodworker might be liable for injuries caused by a product, even if the customer abused it.

Liability laws are complex and vary from state to state, so in a short article, I can give only general advice on limiting liability. There are prudent, common sense steps you can take to reduce risks, and you can organize your business in ways that will reduce your personal financial liability if you are sued.

Suits arising from shop accidents may be the most serious risk faced by a woodworking business. You have an ethical and legal obligation to the public and your employees to run a safe shop.

Housekeeping is important. Keep your shop clean and in a good state of repair. Safety hazards, like piles of dust and scrapwood, should be corrected immediately.

Equip all your machines with necessary safety devices, such as guards for blades, cutters, belts and other moving parts, even though it sometimes seems easier to work without them. Post clearly visible safety procedures around the shop and near machines. Provide and require all employees to wear eye, hearing and breathing protection. Other safety gear such as push sticks, featherboards and hold-downs should be available in abundance so there's never an excuse for not having them handy. Be sure each employee is properly trained to handle the assigned jobs and machines, and if you can, keep written records of how and when the training was conducted. By practicing rigorous safety procedures, you reduce the likelihood of an accident; if one does occur, you have documented your concern for safety and reduced your chances of being found negligent.

Keeping the public at large out of the shop is also important. Posting a prominent warning sign at your shop entrance is not enough. Locate your office in the front of the shop to discourage walk-throughs. At a job site, stand sawhorses to block traffic through dangerous areas.

Fellow woodworkers may want to trade their labor for shop time and the use of your machinery. This can be especially risky. A newcomer might not be familiar with the safe operation of your machines or tools, putting themselves or others at risk. Don't enter into such an arrangement unless you're sure they can safely operate your machinery. Have them sign a "release in indemnity" agreement—if the person is injured, you are not liable. These agreements, however, don't afford protection in all states, so check with your attorney.

The major product liability risks come from poorly thought-out designs that in normal use can injure a person; defectively made items that could break easily or operate improperly, injuring someone; or items sold without warnings advising the customer of hazards relating to their use or misuse.

You must ensure that someone using your product won't be easily injured by it (the same holds true for your premises). Furniture should be proportioned so it won't tip unexpectedly and so it's strong enough to stand up to the use it's reasonably expected to see. Take extra steps to ensure safety, like fastening a tall cabinet securely to the wall, instead of just letting it stand on its own. Take the trouble to gently round sharp edges on furniture. If you're making toys, make sure there are no small parts that a child could break off and swallow and that the finish you're using is non-toxic. Establish your concern for safety by documenting any specific actions you take to ensure product safety.

In instances where safety is still a concern, provide the customer with a written explanation—a tag, label, letter or card—explaining any precautions that might be appropriate. None of these precautions can be overemphasized when designing children's furniture or toys. For more information on this, write the Consumer Product Safety Commission, whose address is given at the end of this article.

You must insure yourself within economically realistic bounds—without going broke. Your insurance should be comprehensive enough to cover your business premises and products (see main article). If you have employees, you must carry state-mandated insurance, such as worker's compensation. Contact your state labor board to find out any additional obligations.

In spite of all your precautions, you could find yourself the loser in a business-related civil suit. Therefore, in addition to insurance coverage, one of the simplest and most economical methods to protect your personal assets is incorporation. The beauty of the corporate structure is that, as long as you are operating under the legal formalities of the corporation and holding yourself out to the public as a corporation, only corporate property and assets (bank accounts) can be used to settle a claim. In rare cases, the so-called corporate veil can be pierced and personal assets reached, but the corporation still affords effective protection. If you wish to incorporate, you should seek the advice of your attorney and public accountant.

In most states, you can also protect your assets by holding personal property jointly with a spouse. Spousal-protection laws (and homestead acts) allow that judgements (including those judgements initiated by trade creditors) against one spouse cannot reach assets that are held jointly by both spouses—a spouse who is an innocent bystander should not have to act as the insurer for the other spouse's business misfortunes. One can debate the complexities in considering this tactic for asset protection, but in most cases the benefits outweigh the detriments.

Many corporations, woodworking businesses included, involve partners. While there are benefits to partnership, an "innocent" partner may still be liable if the other partner injures someone in the course of business. If that partner has no assets, the injured party can satisfy his claims against the assets of the solvent partner, even though the solvent partner may not have had any direct part in causing the damage to the injured party. Once again, a corporation would afford some protection in this case.

Discussion of insurance and liability may sound like a doomsday approach to craft, but it simply amounts to good business, and this ultimately benefits you and your customers.   □

Peter A. Lee is an attorney and woodworker in Honolulu, Hawaii.

Further reading

Additional material for this article came from:
The Law (In Plain English) For Craftspeople by Leonard D. DuBoff. Madrona Publishers, Inc., P.O. Box 22667, Seattle, WA 98122; $7.95 plus postage.
DuBoff has written two other books useful for the small craft business:
The Law (In Plain English) For Small Businesses ($8.95 plus postage) and *Business Forms and Contracts (In Plain English) For Craftspeople* ($14.95 plus postage).
For information on federal regulations for toys and children's articles, write:
U.S. Consumer Product Safety Commission, Washington, DC 20207.

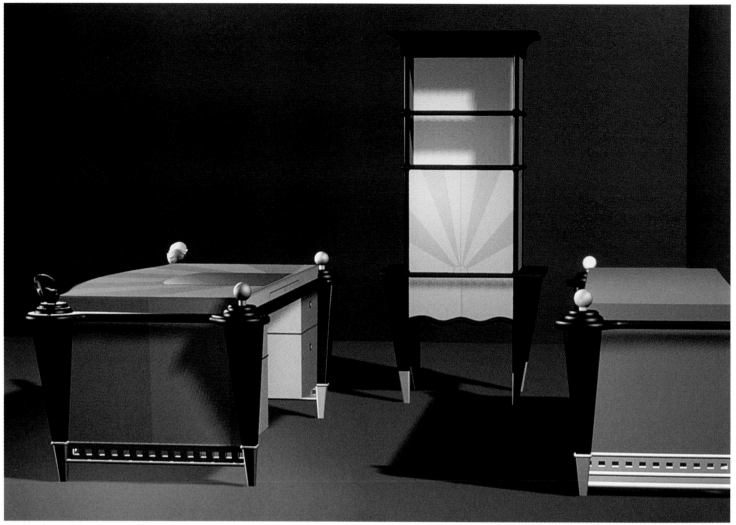

As real as it appears, this photo of Po Ku's "Hawksmoor" desk and computer cabinet was created and printed on a powerful computer system called Alias. Ku initially made drawings of the desk using CAD software on a personal computer. Then the data was fed into the Alias system, which animated the three-dimensional image, rendering realistic wood grain, metallic and painted surfaces, and shadows.

Computers in the Shop
From microchips to wood chips

by Sandor Nagyszalanczy

If you bought a personal computer years ago with dreams of using it to educate your children or balance the family budget, chances are that microchip-minded marvel has seen more action propelling heroes through game mazes. But if you're a woodworker, it's probably time to consider reclaiming your computer from the kids and putting it to work in the woodshop. Today woodworkers can use computer devices and programs to perform design and construction tasks undreamed of a very few years ago.

Many full-time woodworkers have been using computers in their businesses for years, doing bookkeeping, preparing job estimates and client correspondence, yet affordable computer technology has also become available to the amateur woodworker.

While advanced computer-aided design (CAD) systems are replacing drafting tables in professional shops, personal computers and inexpensive drawing and drafting programs are helping hobbyists design more complicated projects. And affordable computer-aided manufacturing (CAM) devices, like computer-numerically controlled (CNC) routers, have started to appear in small, one-man businesses—for custom work as well as for production.

Even though this article isn't a comprehensive survey of computer software or hardware, it will give you some idea about how woodworkers are putting modern computer technology to work in their shops and businesses. Perhaps you'll want to take a trip to your local computer store—on your way back from the lumberyard.   —*S.N.*

A computer's image of furniture

Even if you're really good at visualizing a piece of furniture in your mind's eye, you must have had occasions when you wished for a more concrete representation before actually making a model or building the piece. Drawings are helpful, but imagine having a realistic photograph of a piece of furniture that doesn't yet exist. That is exactly what you're being shown in the photo on the facing page. That photograph of Canadian furniture designer Po Ku's "Hawksmoor" desk and computer cabinet was generated by a sophisticated workstation computer system called Alias. Ku, owner of Quess Furniture in Toronto, Ont., and designer of high-end custom furniture, used Alias's computer imagery to refine the design for his elaborate wood-and-metal office furniture in lieu of developing expensive prototypes. He also used the image generated by Alias as a sales tool. With it he was able to sell his client on the furniture series before actually building the first pieces.

The process started not on a computer, but with pencil and paper: Ku drew many sketches before he arrived at his basic design. He then used a computer-aided drawing program (see "Computer-aided design" by Pete Conway on the following page) run on a personal computer to create a three-dimensional line drawing, also known as a "wireframe." Ku then used the CAD program's editing functions to modify the piece's curves and proportions and to refine any and all details.

For the next step, Ku contracted with Design Vision, a communications company in Toronto, to rent time on the Alias system. A complete set of CAD drawings was then used by a programmer to input all the initial coordinates that would define the furniture forms in Alias. It took the programmer approximately three days to input all the information before the machine could turn the wireframes into images with realistic surfaces and shadows. The actual running of the program took only about an hour. Then, refinements were made to the image as Ku and the programmer looked at the screen. Ku had brought along samples of the materials the furniture would be made from: pearwood, Australian lacewood, aluminum and colored metallic lacquer, and they tweaked the program to reproduce these colors and textures to match the originals. Once they were happy with the rendering,

Alias output the data to a special printer that created a photographic-quality image directly on a 4x5 color transparency.

Amazingly, Ku used only a fraction of Alias's potential for simulating reality. All aspects of the "Hawksmoor" furniture—wood grain, lacquer sheen and fine details—could have been rendered even more realistically, but for a much higher price. Some of the most sophisticated work done on the Alias system includes modeling for the animation sequences in last summer's Arnold Schwartzenegger movie, *Terminator 2: Judgement Day.* —S.N.

Panel optimization programs

While expensive workstation computers may be reserved for professionals, there is lots of personal-computer software on the market that's useful and affordable to most woodworkers. If you've ever built a kitchen using expensive hardwood-faced plywood for the carcases, you've probably spent hours trying different schemes to lay out the parts with the least waste. But put that pencil to rest: there are two low-priced computer programs that will help you develop an efficient cutting scheme. The first, Plywood Planner, which retails for $29.95, can economically lay out up to 50 pieces on a single sheet; its more powerful brother Casp'er (Computer Aided Sheet Planner) retails for $149.95 and can handle up to 250 pieces and 50 sheets. The programs, designed to run on an IBM PC, XT or AT (or compatible) were developed by Roger Drummond and are sold through The Woodworkers' Store (21801 Industrial Blvd., Rogers, Minn. 55374-9514).

Both programs come on either a 5¼-in. or 3½-in. floppy diskette and run with either a color or monochrome monitor (a standard graphics card is required). They share many basic features: You can specify the size of your plywood sheet (up to 145 in. sq. in Casp'er; 165 in. by 61 in. in Plywood Planner) and the thickness of the sawblade's kerf in thousandths of an inch, which the program figures into the layout. The dimensions of each piece, which must be rectilinear, are entered into a piece list; Casp'er allows you to note part descriptions and allows identically dimensioned pieces to be entered as a group (see the top photo at right). Fractions must be entered as decimal numbers, which can be

specified down to sixteenths of an inch or in metrics down to millimeters. After the piece list is done, either program computes and then displays a layout diagram showing each piece identified by number and economically arranged on the sheet, as shown in the bottom photo (subsequent sheets in Casp'er are displayed separately). Each layout diagram as well as a list of pieces for that sheet can then be printed out for use during cutout in the shop. Pieces the program can't fit on the plywood are transferred to another list. Casp'er's multisheet capacity is intended for the professional cabinet shop, cutting out parts for kitchens or large casework. Additionally, Casp'er allows storing the layout on diskette and includes more sophisticated optimization programs for adjusting the arrangement of pieces to best suit the job.

In an office full of computers, I did have a hard time finding a machine that had exactly the right internal configuration to run either program correctly. But once running, I found both programs easy to use. Since they are self-prompting (messages appear on the screen suggesting which keys to press to advance to the next step at

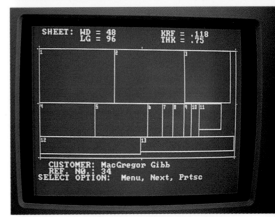

Casp'er, a panel-optimization program, produced the colorful parts list and cutting layout above. The user enters a list of plywood pieces and their dimensions (top photo), and then Casp'er economically arranges the pieces on a plywood sheet(s) and produces a layout diagram (bottom photo).

any given time), I could wade through the numerous program menus without having to delve into their skimpy manuals (Drummond has amended Casp'er's manual with a much-needed tutorial). When entering data in the piece list, I found it annoying to not be able to scroll backwards to fix a mistake; the piece must be re-entered correctly and the erroneous one deleted via commands from another menu. I also tried planning a whole kitchen's worth of parts with Casp'er and found it inconvenient that the program renumbers parts sequentially on each sheet—out of their original order on the original piece list. Therefore, you must print out each sheet's new piece list with its layout diagram—separate operations that I found time consuming. I also had to fiddle around quite a bit to get the best performance from Casp'er's optimizing functions. But the program does allow you to handle special situations such as finding out how big a sheet you'd need to fit all the pieces for a job. —S.N.

Computer-aided design
by Pete Conway

To work out the details of finished pieces before construction begins, I explore ideas through drawings. I use a personal computer set up with a computer-aided design (CAD) program. Besides being invaluable for developing a clearer idea of a piece's lines, proportions and construction details, a computer-generated drawing can help you sell a client on your ideas. And once your design is done, CAD programs that are part of many cabinet shop's software systems, such as Cabinetware or Cabinetvision, have peripheral programs enabling you to print out a precise bill of materials.

Software and hardware: A typical CAD system consists of both a CAD software program and the hardware needed to run it. Software ranges tremendously in price: Full-featured programs, like AutoCad and Cadkey, designed for advanced users like engineers and architects, can cost $3,000 or more. However, for less demanding users, such as hobbyists, simpler CAD programs and generic drawing and drafting software are available for less than $100. Each program has its own compatibility requirements, not only regarding the brand, model and memory capacity of the computer, but also the printer, monitor and

other peripherals. (Ask your software dealer about compatibility, as well as future program upgrades.)

While most inexpensive CAD programs will run on a very basic computer, more complicated drawings, like the three generated on AutoCad shown on the facing page, will require more elaborate hardware. Such a system, which will set you back anywhere from $1,500 to $3,000, should have a powerful central processing unit (CPU). In the IBM and compatible world, that means an 80286 or 80386 chip, and at least 640K of random-access memory (RAM). For large or complicated drawings, you need a hard disk drive, which allows you to access and store your drawings faster. A numeric coprocessor chip (sometimes called a math coprocessor) installed in the CPU considerably speeds up its ability to do the calculations necessary to render complex drawings.

You'll need a mouse for making the multitude of cursor motions that create and alter your drawings, as well as for selecting program functions. CAD programs can run on a color or monochrome monitor, but in either case, the computer should contain an EGA, VGA or better graphics card, or else curved parts of your screen drawings will be too jagged and crude looking. Color also allows you to assign various hues to different parts of a complicated drawing, for better clarity. If you wish to import designs from paper drawings or plans, you'll want to add a digitizing tablet, which allows a drawing to be laid over a pad with an electronic grid in it and traced with a pen-like stylus (you can also use the pad to draw freehand). For highest-resolution printouts of plans or drawings, plotters are best. These are devices that use ink-filled pens to print on large sheets of paper. But some programs are also capable of producing reasonable looking drawings on less expensive ink jet or dot matrix printers.

Drawing with CAD: I often use my CAD system to prepare accurate plans of cabinets and furniture and dimensioned drawings for parts to be constructed. I've found that the computer allows me to draw my ideas, using the mouse or digitizing tablet to create lines and curved forms on the screen and then to edit them as I see fit. Editing includes tasks such as moving sections of a drawing around the screen, changing the size or proportion of a form, adding or deleting parts, and typing in titles, instructions and dimensions. Certain CAD editing functions can save a tremendous amount of time, such as when drawing a symmetrical cabinet: I draw only half the

cabinet and then instruct the program to create a mirror image for the other half. This not only saves time, but also helps avoid mistakes. When you do make a mistake, the program allows you to delete all or part of your design (thank heavens for that!). Some CAD programs allow you to work in layers, like transparent overlays. You can draw the carcase of a cabinet as one layer, the plinth as a second layer and raised panel doors as a third. I've found this can make decifering a complicated structure easier, and it allows me to produce a detailed drawing of just that one component if need be. But CAD programs aren't magic. You cannot expect the software to produce a detailed drawing unless you first tell it what you want. And telling it what you want involves familiarity and experience using the program—just like woodworking, you have to practice.

Once an overall drawing is fleshed out, CAD programs give you the ability to zoom in on one area in much the same way that a zoom lens on a camera enlarges part of a scene. This allows you to refine minor details of a larger drawing, say the joinery of a case piece, to work out the fine points of construction. Another powerful feature of CAD programs is their ability to work in exact scale and automatically dimension the lengths of parts. And once you've proportioned a cabinet in the drawing to your liking, you can print it out in feet and inches (decimal or fractional), metric or in other scales. The ability to create a life-size drawing also allows you to use the printout as a template or pattern.

Three-dimensional drawings: While all basic CAD programs produce designs in two dimensions, most advanced CAD programs also allow drawing in three dimensions (3D). I particularly like 3D illustrations because they allow me to examine a complex design from a variety of viewpoints. With the CAD program I use, called AutoCad, I can evaluate a design from as many as four different viewpoints that appear on the screen at one time. Further, if I make changes on an individual view, the changes automatically affect the other views, thus altering the overall design. Since objects in a CAD drawing are only outlined in wireframe, solid areas, such as a tabletop or seat of a chair, are implied; the program has the ability to hide lines wherever parts overlap, to create the effect of solid surfaces. □

Pete Conway is an assistant professor at the United States Air Force Academy and an avid amateur woodworker.

From *Fine Woodworking* (January 1992) 92:62-66

Hepplewhite Card Table

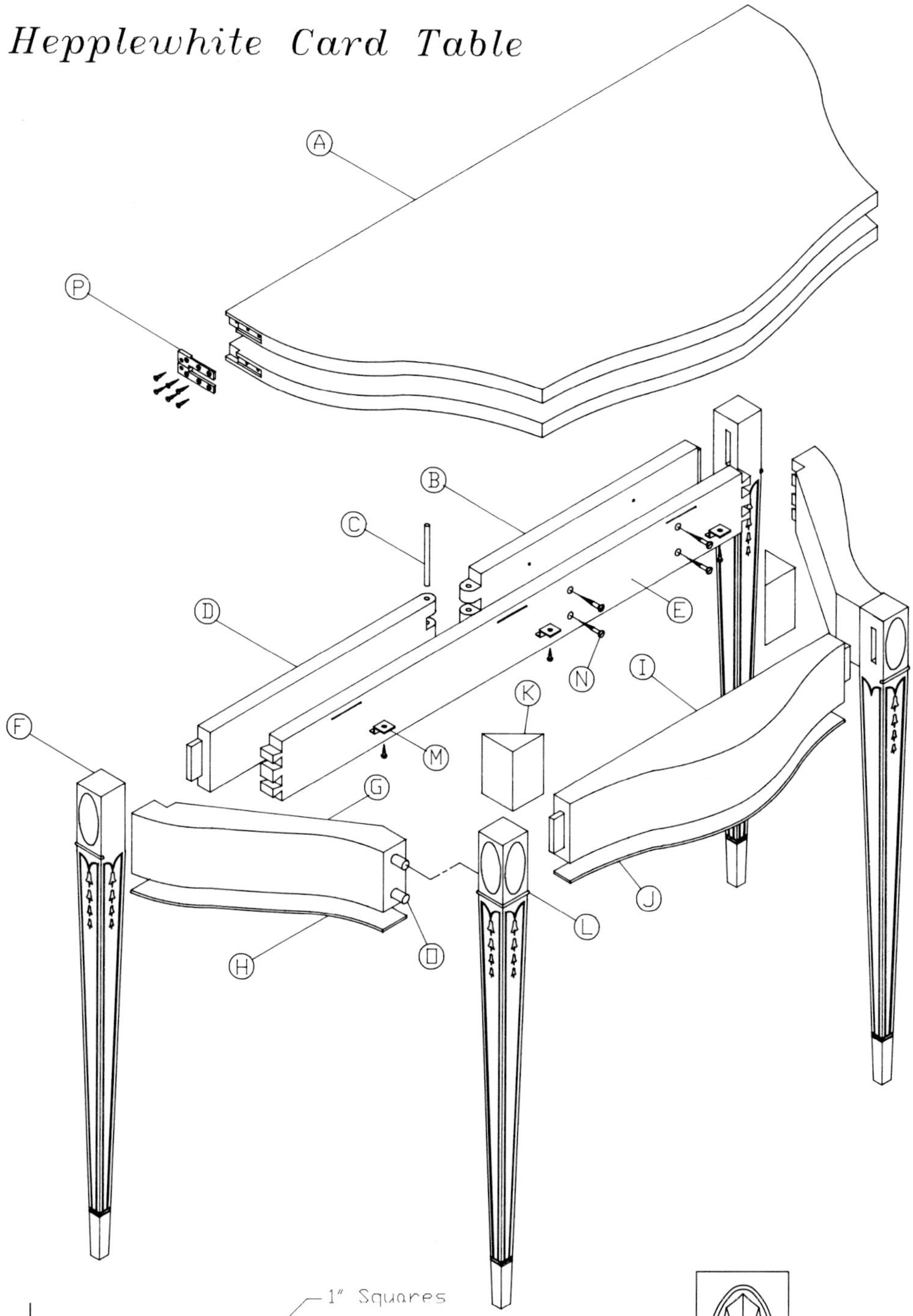

Labels: A, P, B, C, D, E, I, K, N, F, M, G, J, H, L, D

Top & Apron Detail

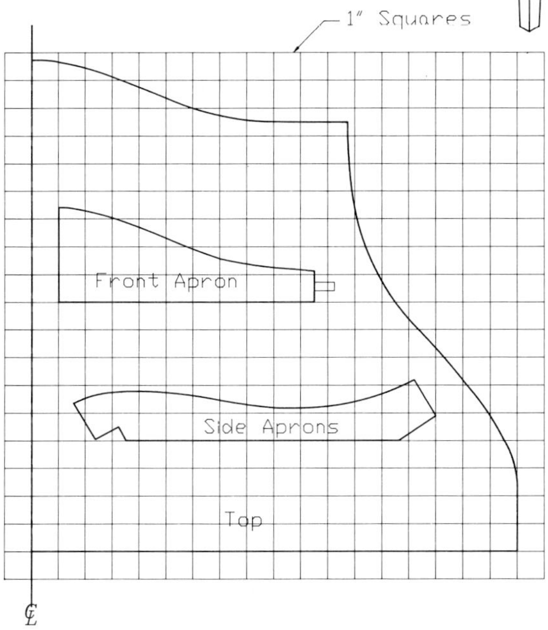

— 1" Squares

Front Apron

Side Aprons

Top

Ȼ

Inlay Detail

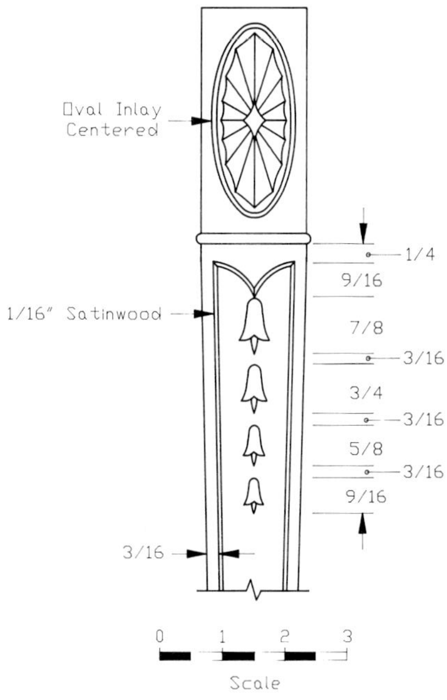

Oval Inlay
Centered

1/16" Satinwood

1/4
9/16
7/8
3/16
3/4
3/16
5/8
3/16
9/16

3/16

0 1 2 3
Scale

Drawings: Courtesy of Frank Pittman

Card table CAD

A mechanical draftsman for 30 years, Frank Pittman never thought a computer could replace his T-square and pencil. But he finally broke down several years ago and spent six weeks learning how to use a computer and AutoCad, a very powerful CAD program used by architects, engineers and other design professionals. Pittman, who teaches wood technology and furniture construction classes at Western Kentucky University, used AutoCad to create the drawings of the Hepplewhite card table reproduced at left. He and his students also use the program to create drawings of other furniture items and plans for possible production items. Before actually building the card table (see "Building a Gate-Leg Card Table," *FWW* #86), Pittman also created plan and elevation drawings and joinery details (not shown).

Pittman says that while developing a complicated presentation-quality drawing in CAD, like the exploded view above, can take quite a bit of time, it is no slower than drafting it in pencil and then inking it in. The speed of drawing with CAD is at least partially due to the ability to quickly duplicate like parts, such as the table's legs, and copy them to other locations. Pittman also finds the ability to manipulate the proportions of a part, without having to redraw it each time, to be a great design tool. One of the most difficult and time-consuming tasks in CAD is to create a free-form curve, because most CAD programs require you to define the curve via coordinates: You plot points on the screen that the line will pass through, and then command the program to connect the dots. A special function then smooths out the curve.

After the computer work was done, Pittman printed all the drawings shown here on paper using a relatively inexpensive plotter capable of printing on sheets up to 11 in. by 14 in. For the part drawing (below, left), he superimposed a scale grid over a plan view of one quadrant of the top and apron parts. Pittman then created a full-size pattern by redrawing the parts full scale on large grid paper. For the table's inlays, he printed four copies of the detail, shown below right, at full size, and then glued each pattern directly to a leg as a guide for cutting out the flowers. When designing complicated pieces requiring miter joints that meet at odd angles, Pittman will print out a paper drawing of an angled joint and, instead of trying to measure the angles, will use the drawing as a template for setting a saw's miter gauge or building a router jig.   —*S.N.*

The Maxym robot is a mechanized-milling machine run by a personal computer. Shapes can be programmed easily and quickly by drawing them on a digitizing tablet (shown in front of the computer). Then the machine employs a regular router and spiral end mill to perform the desired task. Here, the Maxym robot has been programmed to cut out a curved chair part as an experiment for Thos. Moser Cabinetmakers.

Woodshop Robots

While attending the Woodworking Machinery and Furniture Supply Fair in Anaheim, Cal., last fall, i was astounded at the number of small computer-numerically controlled (CNC) routing machines, that were both sized and priced to be practical for small- and medium-size shops. These machines are comparable to their behemoth brothers that are part of computer-aided manufacturing (CAM) systems used by factories and large production shops to churn out hundreds of identical parts economically. But small CNC machines employ a single—instead of multiple—router head, aren't as heavy in construction and typically can't produce very large parts. And they definitely don't compare in price: The heavyweights start at around $100,000, while some small CNC systems sell for as little as $10,000 including software (but not the computer needed to run them).

The milling head on a CNC router is designed to move in two axes for cutting out and shaping on flat surfaces, and three or more axes, for shaping complex three-dimensional forms. They're capable of astounding (and repeatable) accuracy—typically within 0.001 in. The heads' motions are directly controlled by the com-

Although this Thos. Moser continuous-arm chair is traditional in design, part of its manufacturing may soon be done by the Maxym robot, which would carve and sand the chair's seat.

puter, which sends instructions to sets of servomotors. The operator programs the computer with numerical coordinates (this is where the CNC name comes from) that determine the path in which the head travels, such as to rout a rabbet or mill a groove in a cabinet side, to round over an edge on a tabletop or to shape a curved chair part. Many machines accept a standard router as the milling head.

Small CNC routers are even being used on custom jobs. This is partially due to im-

provements in software that circumvent the tedious coordinate plotting, making the new systems more "user friendly" and quicker to program when routing complex or curved shapes. Some systems even allow routing patterns to be imported directly from a CAD program. Some of the jobs that small CNC systems seem especially suited for include: signmaking; carving small objects, special hardware and trim; cutting out, routing, boring and shaping furniture parts; and producing multiple parts for limited-production items.

One of the most impressive CAM machines I've yet seen is the Maxym Robot (pictured in the photo at left), manufactured by USA Robot in Saco, Maine. The company's owner, David Jack Hanson, first became involved with CAM systems when he and a partner decided to produce children's music boxes and clocks. They soon faced a situation where their orders far exceeded what they could make using regular woodworking machinery: they needed 12,000 parts per month from 190 different patterns. After failing to find a CNC machine to fit their needs, Hanson asked a friend with extensive computer and electronics background to help build a robot. But their first model, up and running after only a month, was difficult and time consuming to program, so they wrote a special graphics program that allowed them to draw or trace the desired pattern on a digitizing tablet to control the robot's motions. This fit Hanson's idea of using a robot as a creative tool, not just for repetitive operations.

When interest in their robot system grew, Hanson formed a company to manufacture the robot he named Maxym. Among his clients is Thos. Moser Cabinetmakers, a company that is researching the use of a Maxym for both prototype development and production. Because Moser produces large quantities of custom furnishings for architectural applications, the company often needs to quickly produce prototypes to work out manufacturing details and to present to potential clients. Moser also plans to employ the Maxym for actual production work, carving and sanding the deep-saddle seats on one of its standard-series continuous-arm chairs, like the one shown in the bottom photo above, a process that's now done by hand. Maxym will do the routing and sanding after the chairs are assembled, which will require careful programming so the milling head can work around the chair's spindles. —*S.N.*

Sandor Nagyszalanczy is managing editor at FWW.

Top photo: J. York; bottom photo: Courtesy of Thos. Moser Cabinetmakers

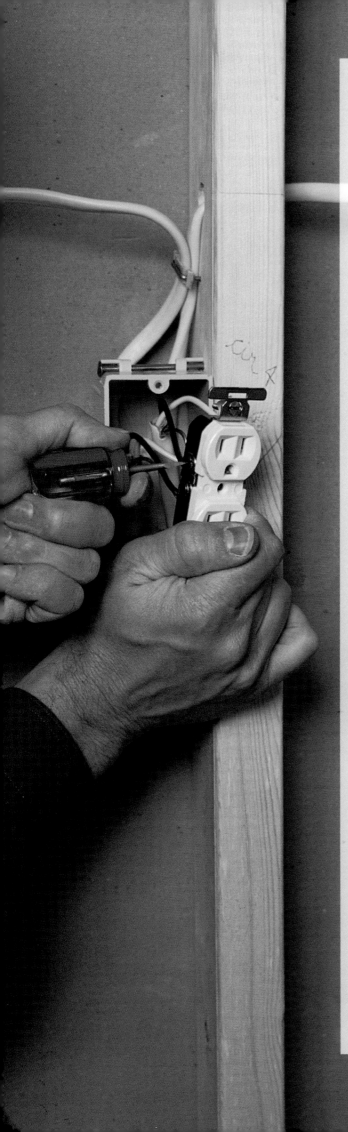

Wiring a Home Shop

Additional circuits and outlets get your motors running

by Grant Beck

Electricity is the lifeblood of power machinery, but if you work in a converted garage or basement shop, chances are that blood isn't flowing very well. It seems small shops never have enough power outlets, and no matter how well laid out the shop is, there's rarely an outlet within reach of a powertool's cord when you need it. Fortunately, rewiring is a job almost any woodworker can handle, with a little knowledge and a good dose of caution.

Although this article won't tell you exactly how to wire a shop from scratch, it will take you through the steps necessary to add new circuits and outlets to an existing electrical system. In addition, I will give you an overview of what to consider when determining your wiring needs, both for now and for the future. Even if you decide to hire an electrician to do the work, you'll still need to define your electrical needs and provide him with a layout drawing, so you'll get the job done correctly and economically.

Before you begin, here's a sobering reminder: When improperly handled, electricity can kill you. Therefore, do not attempt any of the procedures described in this article unless you are completely sure of what you are doing. Also, please read the sidebar on p. 47 on electrical safety. If you have any doubts, hire an electrician; it may seem costly, but the price is negligible compared to what you'd pay if the worst happened. Another important point: Making just about any change to an existing electrical system requires a permit from your local government planning office, but most municipalities will let homeowners do their own work.

How many circuits and outlets do I need?

The first step in planning additional circuits and outlets for your shop is to figure out how much power you'll need. To start, make a list of how many amps each stationary machine in your shop uses, along with what voltage that machine runs on, 110v or 220v single-phase (this article won't cover 3-phase power). The motor's size and voltage are found on its information plate. To calculate how many amps your breaker box must carry to run your shop, I follow this simple rule of thumb: add up the amperages of all the machines and divide by two. If your shop is on the same electrical service as your home, you may have to hire an electrician to help determine if your existing service can handle your shop or if you need your service upgraded and a larger box installed.

Once you've determined each tool's power requirements, you'll need to figure out where the stationary machines will be located or where power tools will be used, and make a drawing of your shop, like the typical shop sketch below. Draw in the location of the circuit breaker box, your workbench, doorways and windows, and label each machine with its amperage and voltage.

Before locating the outlets, you must determine the number of separate circuits you'll need. I've found that because most small shop's circuits are wired with 12-gauge (ga) wire, the general rule to follow is that a circuit with a 20 amp breaker should not carry a load of more than about 15 amps. Without this buffer, normal operation might trip breakers, as motors can draw more than their specified amperage upon start-up. In one-man shops, where only one tool is to be used at a time, a single circuit may have outlets for several power tools or machines, even if their individual power requirements exceed 15 amps. In a multiple-person shop, machines that might be run simultaneously should have separate, dedicated circuits (only one outlet per circuit). If the machine doesn't use the full capacity of the circuit, a spare outlet on the same circuit can be handy. For instance, circuit #7 in the drawing powers the lathe and has an extra outlet that could be used for plugging in a right-angle sander for power sanding a spinning turning. Workbench areas should have several outlets to allow

multiple handtools to remain plugged in. If there's a chance that several of these tools will be run at the same time, an outlet on a separate, dedicated circuit should be included (see circuit #10 in the drawing) and used with higher-amperage power tools, such as a plunge router, circular saw or a bench grinder.

Large machines with more powerful motors in the 1-HP to 3-HP range, such as tablesaws, planers and shapers, also require dedicated circuits. Most electrical codes require this as well. If a motor can be wired to run on either 110v or 220v, wire it for 220v operation. The reason is that doubling a motor's voltage causes its amperage requirements to drop in half. Therefore, you can use 12-ga wire to run circuits to 220v motors in lieu of switching to heavier (and more expensive) 10-ga wire to satisfy a 110v motor's higher-amperage requirements.

Location of outlets

While you may be tempted to locate your outlets so that each is closest to the machine it services, it's a good idea to spread them out as uniformly as possible to accommodate future needs. A few extra 110v outlets, evenly spaced around the room will allow you to use portable tools away from the workbench or connect new machines in the future.

As mentioned earlier, in the area near your workbench you will need more outlets placed closer together than in the rest of the shop. However, regular outlets cannot be moved if you decide to relocate your bench. But you can get around this problem by mounting an outlet strip on the workbench, as shown in the photo

Typical shop electrical layout

⏀ indicates 110v duplex outlets   ⏀ indicates 220v single outlets

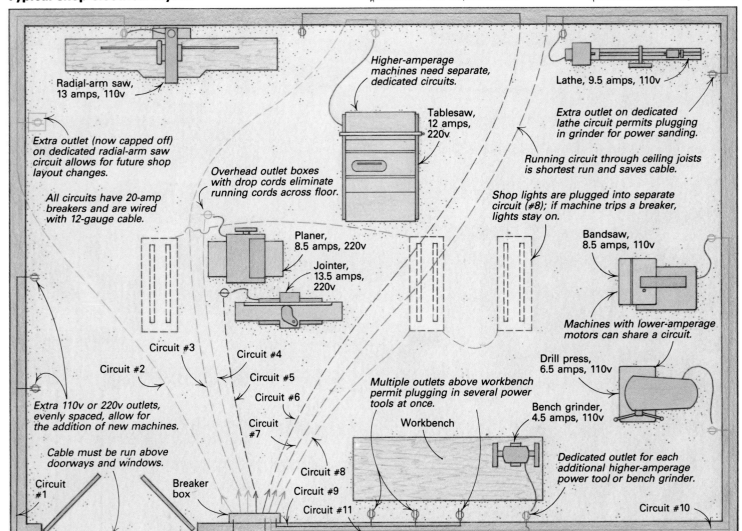

Radial-arm saw, 13 amps, 110v

Higher-amperage machines need separate, dedicated circuits.

Tablesaw, 12 amps, 220v

Lathe, 9.5 amps, 110v

Extra outlet on dedicated lathe circuit permits plugging in grinder for power sanding.

Extra outlet (now capped off) on dedicated radial-arm saw circuit allows for future shop layout changes.

Running circuit through ceiling joists is shortest run and saves cable.

All circuits have 20-amp breakers and are wired with 12-gauge cable.

Overhead outlet boxes with drop cords eliminate running cords across floor.

Shop lights are plugged into separate circuit (#8); if machine trips a breaker, lights stay on.

Planer, 8.5 amps, 220v

Bandsaw, 8.5 amps, 110v

Jointer, 13.5 amps, 220v

Machines with lower-amperage motors can share a circuit.

Circuit #3

Circuit #4

Circuit #2

Circuit #5

Circuit #6

Drill press, 6.5 amps, 110v

Extra 110v or 220v outlets, evenly spaced, allow for the addition of new machines.

Multiple outlets above workbench permit plugging in several power tools at once.

Circuit #7

Bench grinder, 4.5 amps, 110v

Cable must be run above doorways and windows.

Workbench

Circuit #8

Circuit #1

Breaker box

Dedicated outlet for each additional higher-amperage power tool or bench grinder.

Circuit #9

Circuit #11

Circuit #10

Photos: Sandor Nagyszalanczy; drawings: Vince Babak

A multiple-outlet power strip is an economical way to add extra outlets to a workbench, and it speeds up work because you can leave several portable power tools plugged in at a time. Most power strips have a built-in circuit breaker, in case there's an overload.

at left. Due to the large number of outlets on a power strip, it probably should be fed from a dedicated wall outlet (most strips have their own built-in circuit breaker). To increase the flexibility of your wiring plan in case you want to rearrange your shop, you can wire two or more outlets on the same dedicated circuit, and then fit only the one in current use with an outlet; cap off bare wires with wire nuts and install a blank cover over unused outlet box(es), as illustrated in the drawing of circuit #2. In case a new machine is brought in or the layout changes, the extra outlet can be made active and the currently active one capped off.

Outlets in the ceiling are fine for machines like the planer and jointer, where the hanging cord doesn't get in the way. If you ever work with big sheets of plywood, avoid dropping an overhead line to the tablesaw, because sooner or later it'll be in the way. Don't place outlets in the floor, even if it seems most convenient. These outlets can fill up with sawdust and become a fire hazard. Locating outlets on the wall about 42 in. above the floor will keep them above most workbenches and accessible behind stationary tools.

The lights in a shop should be on a dedicated circuit so that you won't be plunged into darkness if you overload a power tool and trip a breaker. So if you add new lights in your shop, wire the new lights on a separate dedicated circuit; don't tie them into the existing

The shocking truth about electrical safety

by D.L. Rogers

Before crawling out on a tree limb, you can evaluate the potential risk: Is the height 6 ft. or 60? Is the limb alive or dead? Is the ground below you soft turf or a pile of bricks? However, no one can determine the risk of electrocution at any given moment when working on live electrical wiring. This household friend that lights your shop and powers your tools can kill according to an obscure set of rules that should be understood by anyone who uses or works with it.

Electrocution is possible because electricity can pass between any two conductive objects: If you have your feet on the ground and touch an electrical part, you are offering the current a path through your own body. Normal skin oils and perspiration are good electrical paths through the pores and into your body, which is full of highly conductive fluids (electrolytes). These electrolytes are constantly changing; hence, you can't determine exactly how conductive your body is at any given moment.

Electricity sometimes kills by severely damaging body tissues and altering the electrolytes, which your muscles (including your heart) depend on for operation. This type of electrocution can be caused by large doses of either AC or DC power. However, the most insidious and lethal conse-

quences of electricity can arise from relatively low levels of AC current.

A shock below 100 milliamps (ma) may cause no sensation at all or a very painful sensation, often resulting in a drained or nervous feeling. But an electrical current of about 100 to 200ma (the amount of current it takes to power a dim nightlight) may override the heart's electrical signal. This can change the heart's normal rhythmic beating into a weak flutter known as ventricular fibrillation. In this state, your heart can't circulate your blood, and you may die unless emergency medical technicians arrive in time to restore your normal heartbeat.

Ironically, receiving a larger shock isn't always fatal. Above 200ma one may experience paralysis, excruciating pain, unconsciousness and tissue damage. Obviously, the higher the current the greater the tissue damage (which can be the sole cause of death if extensive enough). Therefore, someone may survive a high-amperage electrical shock with the loss of a foot or an arm, while a much weaker shock may cause fatal heart failure.

All of the above should convince you that working on electrical wiring is not a task to be taken lightly. Fortunately, a few precautions should keep you out of trouble: First, *never* work on live electrical wiring. Always turn

off the electricity at its main distribution box, and as an added precaution, put a sign on the box telling others not to turn anything on without checking with you. If you're unsure of how to turn the power off, you can't handle the rest of the job either, so consult a professional electrician. Some people will tell you, "Sure you can work on a 110v-electrical circuit while it's hot—just don't touch the black wire and the white wire at the same time." While you can get away with this most of the time, being careless only once can lead to disaster. Second, whenever you're wiring up a new tool or machine and must plug it into an old-fashioned two-prong receptacle, don't cut the ground pin off the plug. Instead, use a three-prong adapter and connect its ground screw according to directions. Finally, if you're installing new circuitry in your shop, consider Ground Fault Circuit Interrupter (GFCI) breakers or outlets. While considerably more expensive, GFCI devices will break an electrical circuit in a few milliseconds when a ground leak of less than 50ma—well below electrocution potential—is detected. You'll be mildly shocked, but you'll live to tell about it.

Dan Rogers is an electrical engineering consultant in Spring, Tex.

lights unless they are on a dedicated circuit (see circuit #8 in the drawing). As a rule, don't exceed 1600 watts on one 20 amp circuit.

Wiring supplies

Once you've arrived at a feasible layout, you may decide to do the wiring work yourself. After you've obtained a permit (check with the building desk at your local city or county planning office), you'll need to purchase the following items: cable, circuit breakers, outlet boxes and outlets with corresponding outlet covers. In addition, you'll need wire nuts to splice wires together, cable staples and clamps to secure wiring to walls and studs, and cover plates to conceal unused outlets.

The most convenient way to wire a non-commercial small shop is to use non-metallic sheathed cable (one popular brand is Romex). Such cable comes in a variety of gauges and configurations; 12/2 AWG (American Wire Gauge) has two insulated 12-ga wires—a black and a white one—along with a bare ground wire, all enclosed in a plastic jacket. For 220v runs up to 15 amps, the same cable comes in 12/3 AWG. This has an additional red insulated wire because 220v circuits require an additional hot wire. For wiring circuits to handle even larger loads, you'll want to use 10/2 AWG or 10/3 AWG, which contains higher-capacity 10-ga wire.

When calculating the amount of wire you'll need, be generous. Allow enough at the breaker box to reach any area inside, and allow an extra 6 in. at each outlet (both going in and coming out if the wire will feed subsequent outlets). Finally, add a few feet to each circuit run because when installed, the cable will dip and sag and, therefore, the required length will be a little more than the measuring tape revealed earlier.

Generally, when wiring with 12-ga cable, plan to buy a 20-amp breaker for each new circuit. To determine the type of circuit breakers you need, check your breaker box (breakers that fit one make of box won't fit another). Although they're considerably more expensive, you might wish to install special Ground Fault Circuit Interrupter (GFCI) breakers on circuits that take power outdoors or to damp areas. These have a special circuit that trips the breaker to prevent electrocution any time there's an improper leak of electricity to ground. If you have an older home that has a fuse box instead of circuit breakers, you'll probably have to hire an electrician to upgrade the entire system.

The type of outlet box you choose will depend on the walls of your shop. If you have exposed studs, buy the boxes—either metal or plastic—that come with nails attached for hammering them onto the studs. If the walls are finished, you will need boxes that have

What about extension cords?

To gain a few extra feet of mobility while using a portable power tool, you might be tempted to use a short extension cord, like the one the bedroom lamp plugs into. But all extension cords are not created equal. If you use the wrong cord, you can damage your tool or even burn down your shop.

There are two major things to remember when selecting an extension cord: wire size and cord type. The chart on this page shows common wire sizes and their current carrying capacity and cord types. The amount of current your tool uses will be noted on its specification plate. If it is listed in watts instead of amps, just divide the number of watts by the tool's voltage to determine the amps. Using a wire smaller than what is needed for your tool can cause the tool and cord to overheat. And if there is a worn spot in the cord, excess heat will find it fast. A burnout in the cord can start a shop fire while a burnout in the tool means costly repairs. The rating for cord type— heavy, medium or light duty—should be printed on the cord's jacket; if it is not, assume that the cord is an SPT-1 or SPT-2. Cords not rated for exterior use should not be used in wet conditions or strong sunlight.

Once you have selected the cord you need, buy the proper plugs and

connectors. They should be rated for at least as much current and voltage as the cord and be sized to fit the cord. Twist-style connectors are often a good choice for running portable power tools, especially if you work on a ladder where the tool coming unplugged is inconvenient or dangerous. Wire the plugs in the same configurations as the outlets that feed them.

If you plan to run an extension cord to a bench or stationary tool, you must route it carefully and secure it to walls and ceilings properly. Avoid passing the cord over any sharp or narrow edges that could cut through the insulation. Keep the cord in place with either insulated cable staples or support loops made in sizes to fit most cords. Do not bend the cord over nails since this often results in broken wire strands within the cord, which you cannot see.

Extension cords are a common culprit for trips and falls in home shops. If you must pass an extension cord across a walkway at floor level, make a simple wooden bridge, as shown in the photo on this page, by ripping a 30° bevel in both edges of a board that's at least 4 in. wide. Then, plow a dado on the underside to act as a raceway for the cord. To make the bridge more visible, paint it bright red or yellow. —*G.B.*

A wooden floor bridge protects an extension cord from damage while preventing shop occupants from tripping over it.

Extension cord amperage ratings

Wire gauge	Amps @ 50 ft. cord	Amps @ 100 ft. cord
18	10	7
16	13	10
14	15	13
12	20	15
10	30	20

Extension cord types

Cord type	Applications	Duty rating
SPT-1, SPT-2	Lamps, small appliances	Light*
SPT-3, SJ, SJT,	All purpose	Medium†
SJEW-A, SJOW-A, SJTW-A	All purpose weatherproof	Medium†
S, SE, ST	All purpose	Heavy‡
STW-A, SOW-A, SEW-A	All purpose, weatherproof	Heavy‡

* Cord should not be moved, stepped on or abused.
† Cord can be moved around on smooth surfaces; it can withstand some abuse.
‡ Cord can be dragged around, stepped on, etc.

pinch-type grabbers that lock into the paneling on dry wall. For cement or masonry walls wired with either a flexible or rigid conduit, you'll need metal boxes with ½-in. knockouts. Some 220v outlets require special boxes, so make sure you get one that matches your outlet. And since there are many styles of outlets available, make sure they match the correct voltage and amperage for the application. Most 110v tools use standard three-prong outlets. Twist-style outlets that prevent plugs on overhead outlets from falling out are available for either 110v or 220v plugs.

Wiring the circuits

The best way to install and wire your outlets depends on the construction of your shop and variations in your local electrical codes. In a shop with unfinished walls (exposed studs), first nail the out

A raceway is a practical way to run new outlets along a concrete wall. By removing the metal cover, as shown here, new circuits can be wired and outlets moved or added at any time.

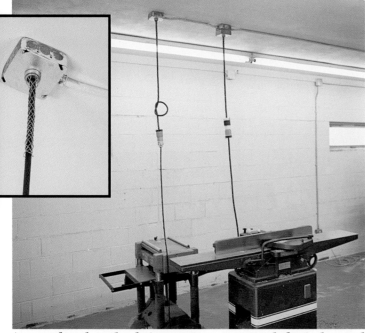

An overhead outlet brings power to a tool that's located away from a wall, and eliminates the need for the cord to run across the floor where it might be in the way. Special strain-relief hardware (see the detail) secures the drop cord, and twist-fitting plugs and receptacles on the cords keep plugs from falling out.

let boxes according to your layout drawing. To rout the cables, you must drill a hole through each wall stud between the breaker box and the outlet (a ½-in. hole is about right for 12-ga cable). Routing cables across the ceiling, through the joists will save wire, because you can pick the shortest route to the desired outlet. When running the wire through wall studs, place holes 4 in. to 6 in. above or below the outlet boxes, and center them to prevent the cable from taking a screw or nail when the walls are sheetrocked. Wherever the cable must go around a corner, drill three holes: one into the face of each of the corner studs on the adjacent walls, and a third drilled diagonally into the corner to intersect the other two. This last hole cleans up the inside corner created by the first two holes, allowing the cable to round the turn. When routing the cable down the length of a stud or joist, keep it centered and staple it about every 3 ft. Feed each circuit's cables through the holes and into the boxes. Secure each cable with a staple near the hole before going on to the next box. Leave at least 6 in. hanging out of each outlet box, and leave enough cable at the source end of each circuit to go into the breaker box, but don't put it in for now.

If you have finished walls, you'll need to rout wires into the walls by drilling down from the attic through the top plate or up from the basement or crawl space through the bottom plate. If you have concrete or masonry walls, you'll have to install conduit or some type of surface-mounted raceway for the wires. Raceway systems, such as the one in the photo at left, cost many times more than conventional wiring but are convenient and flexible. If you choose a raceway, be sure to check the system's current capacity: Many raceways are designed only for home or office use with low-amperage items like lamps or computers.

Installing the outlets

With the cables in place, you are ready to strip the ends of the wires and install the outlets. Outlets normally have a strip gauge molded into the body to show how far back to strip the wires, but if not, strip the wire ¾ in. Wire each outlet as specified on its package, or check a basic wiring guide. On a three-prong 220v system, the white wire may not be used; if not, fold it back out of the way as you install the outlet (do the same with that wire in the breaker box). After wrapping the wire around each screw and tightening it, install the outlet by folding the wires accordion style. Finally, install the outlet plates or covers. Cords dropped from overhead boxes require special strain-relief hardware, as shown in the photos at left.

Installing the breakers

The last step to completing your new circuits is to install the breakers. *First, make absolutely certain the power to your box is off. If you're uncertain about this (or any other step), delegate the job to a professional electrician.* After removing the cover, snap the new breaker in place. Next, you'll need to punch out appropriately sized knockouts in the breaker box to allow the cables to be routed in. Feed the cables into the panel, pull them snug and tighten the cable clamps at the knockouts. Now strip the ends of the wires and connect each circuit: The black wire goes to each corresponding breaker (black and red on 220v circuits), all white wires attach to the neutral bar and ground wires normally go to a separate bar. Put the cover back on the breaker box, and turn off all the breakers. Then with the main power on, turn each circuit on one at a time. This will tell you immediately if there's a problem, such as a short, and which circuit it involves. Now you're ready to test the outlets, and get back to your woodworking projects. □

Grant Beck is an electrical engineer in West Jordan, Utah.

Dust and the Woodworker
Examining the respiratory hazards

by Kirk Kundtz, M.D.

In 15 minutes of use, this disc sander filled a shop's atmosphere with a cup of powdery dust, the size that can negotiate your lung's smallest airways. The Occupational Safety and Health Administration (OSHA) recommends that your short-term exposure limit (STEL) be less than one rounded teaspoon of dust in a 24-ft. by 24-ft. shop in 15 minutes. OSHA's permissible exposure limit (PEL) for an eight-hour shift is about one-half of a teaspoon of dust suspended continuously in the same shop's atmosphere.

What serious woodworker doesn't know the pleasure of wiping a delicate film of very fine dust off a well-waxed jointer bed? I like reaching into a tablesaw base and spilling out arm loads of wood dust onto my knees and the surrounding floor. In fact, I don't mind dust in my hair, in my beard and in my pockets. And I've not only come to love the feel and sight of wood dust, but the satisfying aroma as well. I was first tempted to start woodworking when my best friend built a cedar porch swing for me—the air in his shop was filled with the rich scent of the wood. Since then, I've built my own shop and filled the air with dust from a dozen different woods, including sassafras, walnut, redwood, mahogany, teak, cherry, maple, oak and poplar.

Yes, the woodworker in me enjoys wood dust, but the doctor in me is suspicious because the dust so often irritates my eyes and lungs. My concerns led me to the hospital library to research woodworking's effects on the respiratory system. What I found was both surprising and a little disconcerting. A computer search of medical literature revealed more than 250 articles pertaining to the hazards of woodworking. The articles covered a wide range of problems, including traumatic injuries, skin disorders and cancer associations, but most dealt with how wood-dust inhalation affects the lungs.

How much dust is harmful?—Wood comes off tools in many different shapes and sizes, including broad, flat shavings; long, thin splinters; small chips; and coarse and fine powdery dust, such as that produced by the disc sander shown above. Hand-sanding produces fine dust. But power sanders, the big guns in the sanding arsenal, are the tools most responsible for creating lingering dust clouds in the shop. Powdery dust consists of the smallest particles and represents the greatest health hazard to the lungs. This fine powdery dust not only floats in the air for a long time, but it can be inhaled very deeply.

Dust particles can be classified into two groups: those smaller than 10 microns in diameter and those larger than 10 microns (one micron equals one millionth of a meter). The smaller particles are respirable: they are little enough to negotiate the tiny airways that reach deep into the lungs. Particles bigger than 10 microns tend to get trapped in the larger airways.

Wood dust, as inviting as it may be, is no friend to the woodworker. Given the fact that most of us are not going to sacrifice woodworking to save our respiratory system, the question arises: How much wood dust is too much? Two variables that must be considered are the amount of dust you breathe and how long you breathe it. If you spend just a few hours per week in the shop or if you work mainly on small projects that do not demand much sawing and sanding, you probably do not have to worry about bronchitis, pneumonia or nose cancer. If, however, you spend long hours on big projects that require extensive ripping and sanding, you should be cautious, especially in light of the small amount of dust that researchers and government regulators say is the threshold limit for ambient dust (beyond which lung disease begins to develop).

According to a 1981 report published by the American Conference of Governmental Industrial Hygienists, the maximum level of airborne respirable particles should average no more than five milligrams of dust per cubic meter of shop space in eight hours. Other studies suggest that this level is too high and recommend a maximum of two milligrams of dust per cubic meter. These studies propose that more than two milligrams of wood dust per cubic meter of shop space may damage your lungs.

What do these limits mean to you? Let's suppose your shop is 27 ft. long by 21 ft. wide and the ceiling is 9 ft. high, so it is roughly 170 cubic meters. According to the stricter guideline of two milligrams of dust per cubic meter, you should limit airborne dust to less than 340 milligrams. This is one-third of a gram, which I discovered equals slightly less than one-quarter of a teaspoon of dust. A full sandwich bag weighs almost 50 grams, which is enough to exceed the threshold limit of a 25,000-cubic-meter shop. This is all very disconcerting and even the authors of the cited study conceded that, though ideal, this strict (two milligram per cubic meter) standard is not very realistic.

A guide to your respiratory system—Dust's affect on your lungs, however, is realistic, but you must first understand your

From *Fine Woodworking* (July 1990) 83:72-75

Getting out of the dust

by Theodore J. Fink, M.D.

Getting rid of dust in a woodshop is like trying to eliminate salt from your diet, which is impossible because almost everything you eat or drink contains sodium. So the goal is not to totally eliminate dust, but to minimize your exposure. This can be accomplished with a three-phase dust-control plan that includes: decreased dust production, wood-dust capture and personal protection.

Decrease your dust production: Your woodworking techniques and tools determine the quantity and size of dust particles you produce. The larger the particles, the less hazardous the dust. Large particles settle quickly, are more easily captured by dust-collection systems and are not respirable. The finest dust particles, which are the most hazardous, tend to escape most collection methods. If you shine a beam of light through a dark, presumably clean workshop, the airborne particles you will see are those larger than 20 microns in size. Respirable dust (under 10 microns) is invisible.

You can reduce very fine wood dust by minimizing the need for sanding. By cutting rather than scraping when turning wood and by planing and scraping rather than belt-sanding, you will produce shavings rather than dust. All sawblades, planer blades and bits should be sharp, because dull blades produce finer dust. You should select the proper blade and feed rate to produce smoother surfaces when sawing. When bandsawing scroll work, you can get a finer finish requiring less sanding by using a blade with more teeth per inch (t.p.i.) and with standard tooth form (not a hook tooth). When ripping with a hook-tooth blade, be sure it has a large-size gullet that will accommodate large particles and use a fast feed rate. To decrease the amount of finish-sanding, be sure stock is precisely dimensioned by planing and jointing before assembly.

Dust capture: Despite your best efforts, you will make dust. Therefore, you should attempt to capture the dust before it becomes airborne. The most efficient method includes a dust-collection system hooked directly into stationary tools (see *FWW #67, p. 70*). Also, when buying small power tools, such as sanders and power planes, select those equipped with dust-collection bags. Although these are commonly called "dustless" and greatly reduce the amount of dust put into the air, they fail to capture some of the very fine dust.

Whenever wood is machined, a wide assortment of particle sizes is produced and to each particle a positive electrical charge is imparted. This is especially important for

3M's model 8500 dust mask, on the right, should be used "for comfort only," and isn't approved by the National Institute for Occupational Safety and Health (NIOSH). The Gerson 1710 and 1725, in the center, are approved for dust and some mist protection. The 1725 has an easy-breathing valve. The NIOSH-approved Willson 1200 series cartridge respirator, on the left, comes with replaceable particle filters, and an assortment of cartridges is available that protect you from a variety of hazardous chemical vapors and mists.

the smallest particles, which, because of low mass and positive charges, remain suspended in air for hours after production. Eventually these fine particles do settle, but because they repel each other, they are easily resuspended in the atmosphere when swept with a broom. Thus, it is much better to vacuum dust whenever possible.

Skin and eye protection: Coveralls that can be taken off before leaving the shop protect most of your skin. The coveralls should be cleaned regularly and dust remaining on skin and hair should be washed off immediately after leaving the shop.

Standard safety goggles provide some eye protection from fine dust, but if you are using a very irritating wood or one to which you have developed an allergy, an airtight full-face mask or diver's (underwater) goggles may be necessary.

Respirators and dust masks: The amount of exposure to the skin and eyes is minuscule compared to the surface area in the respiratory tract. Furthermore, all the respiratory surfaces are moist and very reactive to foreign substances. Thus, the most critical personal protective equipment is the dust mask or respirator.

These items, which must cover nose and mouth, vary widely in cost, comfort and effectiveness. The most comfortable, least expensive *and* least effective is the lightweight molded mask that is commonly held in place by a single elastic band, such as the 3M 8500 (shown above on the right) or the Gerson 1501 (not shown). Although these masks filter out up to 95% of airborne dust, air leaks readily around their edges. Neither mask is approved by the National Institute for Occupational Safety and Health (NIOSH).

3M's Model 8710 mask (not shown) and the Gerson 1710 mask (shown above, second from the right) filter in excess of 99%

of respirable dust. Both have two wide elastic straps for a tight, form fit, yet they're still quite comfortable, lightweight and disposable. And they are durable enough for extended use. Both are adequate for fine-dust protection, but not for harmful vapors.

If you need protection from paint, varnish or other harmful vapors, as well as dust particles, NIOSH recommends a cartridge-type mask, such as the Willson 1200 respirator (shown above on the left) or a similar model from 3M, U.S. Safety or North Safety Equipment. The Willson comes with replaceable particle filters and you can purchase an assortment of cartridges that protect you from a variety of hazardous chemicals.

Masks and respirators are only as good as their fit, and a tight fit may be difficult if you have a beard. The air helmet, such as the Airstream Dust Helmet (or similar battery-powered air-purifying respirator/hardhat combinations), may be a solution for bearded woodworkers.

Respirable dust remains suspended in the air for hours and it's invisible. Therefore, once you put on a mask or respirator for a dust-producing operation in the shop, leave it on for the rest of the workday.

As a mask or respirator is used, retained wood particles clog its pores and breathing becomes more difficult. As this happens, the effectiveness of dust capture by the mask actually improves, provided there are no air leaks around the mask. When you notice the increased breathing difficulty, it is time to change filters or the mask.

Before using any respirator or dust mask, always be sure to read and follow all instructions and warnings supplied by the manufacturer and NIOSH. ☐

Dr. Fink is an internist in Shelburn, Vt., a consulting physician for Digital Equipment Corp. and an amateur woodworker.

respiratory system so that you realize just how injurious dust can be. The lungs are extraordinary organs that continually bring fresh air into very close contact with your body's circulatory system. Structurally, the lungs are like sponges with millions of tiny air pockets. Their ultimate purpose is to remove carbon dioxide from the blood stream and replace it with fresh oxygen from the atmosphere. This process is called gas exchange. The air pockets are called alveoli, shown in the drawing on the facing page, and gas exchange takes place within them. When you breathe in, the alveoli fill with air and oxygen passes through their ultra-thin walls and into the surrounding blood. At the same time, carbon dioxide from the blood passes into the alveoli, where it is expelled during exhalation.

The flow of air in the lungs takes place through a set of airways that spread out very much like the branches of a tree, as shown in the drawing. The tree trunk corresponds to the trachea, the first large branches are the bronchi and the smaller branches are the bronchioles. In this analogy, the alveoli are like the leaves of the tree.

In addition to moving air in and out of the body, the lungs must keep themselves and the air clean, warm and moist. This job is accomplished by the "mucocilliary transport" system, a term for the mucus-producing tissue that lines the "bronchial tree" (see the drawing). We are all familiar with mucus, though we may not be familiar with its purpose. Not only does it serve to moisten the air, it also protects the underlying tissue from drying out. In addition, it acts like flypaper to catch the microscopic dust and dirt in the air we breathe. Once these dust particles are trapped, they must be discarded. This is done by the other part of the mucocilliary transport system, the ciliated epithelial cells. These cells have hundreds of tiny little arms that literally sweep the dust-laden mucus up and out of the lungs. In addition, a backup mechanism, the "alveolar macrophage," serves to clean out dust that gets into the alveoli. This system consists of cells that wander around in the alveoli like little street cleaners, sweeping up particles that threaten to interfere with the crucial gas-exchange system.

How does dust harm these organs? – In the healthy person, occasional dust particles in the lungs is not a serious problem because the lungs have built-in defense mechanisms, such as the mucus that lines the airways, that halt harmful substances like dust. The dust-laden mucus is then expelled from the lungs by the sweeping-motion cells lining the airways, as well as by coughing. Unfortunately, however, chronic inhalation of wood dust may damage the lungs' cleaning systems. When this happens, a vicious circle begins as more dust collects and further damages the lungs. The body then responds as it does to skin injury – it mobilizes an inflammatory response. That is, the bronchial airways become red, swollen and painful. Swelling decreases the diameter of the airways and produces shortness of breath, induces coughing and increases sputum, which is saliva and other discharged matter from the respiratory passages. A number of studies have shown that these symptoms are common in active woodworkers: those that spend long hours in the shop. Other studies have shown that woodworkers tend to develop lung problems similar to those found in patients with chronic bronchitis and emphysema – diseases associated primarily with cigarette smoking. Inhaling wood dust, while probably not as harmful as smoking, can be dangerous.

Perhaps the most documented effect of wood-dust exposure is nose cancer. Dozens of studies in more than 10 countries have shown an increased rate of this relatively rare form of cancer among woodworkers. Medically it is known as "nasal adenocarcinoma." Mucus-secreting glands in the noses of woodworkers tend to become cancerous at a rate 1,000 times greater than non-woodworkers, apparently because of the dust. Fortunately, this type of cancer is relatively rare even among woodworkers (only about one in 1,500 active woodworkers will ever develop it), and the time lag between exposure and the onset of symptoms is as much as 40 years.

Finally, wood dust can cause respiratory illness because it contains many types of allergens and toxins. These range from chemicals deposited on the tree from the outside, such as pesticides and fungal spores, to chemicals created by the trees themselves, such as alkaloids, saponins, aldehydes, quinones, flavonoids, steroids and resins. Individuals respond differently to these various toxins, but the symptoms are universal: coughing, sneezing, increased phlegm and sputum production, runny nose, red eyes and, in extreme conditions, bronchitis, pneumonitis, and asthma. These symptoms are found in woodworkers more often than in the general population.

You are probably more familiar with some toxins and allergens than with others. Perhaps woodworkers are most aware of the allergen called plicatic acid, a substance in red cedar that is responsible for a condition known as red-cedar asthma. This very debilitating condition occurs in about 5% of people who work with red cedar. Another similar condition is maple-bark disease, a severe form of asthma probably caused by fungal spores found in maple bark. Two other North American woods considered to have significant allergenic effects are boxwood and sequoia redwood.

Clearly, the concern about dust is not just academic and all of us woodworkers must be aware of these insidious problems. Most of us don't hesitate to use goggles, push sticks and blade guards, but how many of us use face masks and dust collectors regularly? Not many, I'm afraid. Dust masks can be uncomfortable and dust collectors are expensive, but both are well worth the investment. As with many other items I've bought for my shop, I've agonized over spending money on a dust-collection system, but I'll probably wonder how I ever got by without it once I use it. □

Kirk Kundtz is a resident physician in internal medicine at Mount Sinai Hospital in Cleveland, Ohio, and is an active woodworker. Thanks to Drs. Lawrence Martin and James Edmonson for assistance in preparing this article.

Sources of supply

Dust masks and respirators are manufactured by:

Louis M. Gerson Co., Inc., 15 Sproat St., Middleboro, MA 02346; (508) 947-4000.

Glendale Protective Technologies, 130 Crossways Park Drive, Woodbury, NY 11797; (516) 921-5800.

Mine Safety Appliance Co., Box 426, Pittsburgh, PA 15230; (412) 967-3000.

North Healthcare, 1515 Elmwood Road, Rockford, IL 61103; (815) 877-2531.

North Safety Equipment, 2000 Plainfield Turnpike, Cranston, RI 02921; (401) 943-4400.

Racal, Airstream Division, 7305 Executive Way, Frederick, MD 21701; (301) 695-8200.

3M/Occupational Health & Environmental Safety Division, 220-3E-04 3M Center, St. Paul, MN 55144-1000; (800) 328-1667, (612) 733-8029.

U.S. Safety, 1535 Walnut St., Kansas City, MO 64108-1312; (816) 842-8500.

Willson Safety Products, Box 622, Reading, PA 19603; (215) 376-6161.

The respiratory system

Alveoli

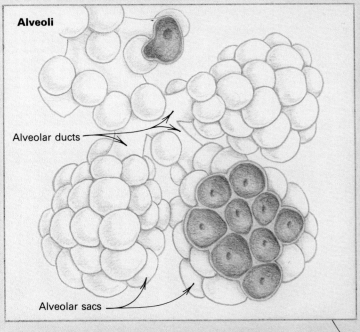

Alveolar ducts

Alveolar sacs

Enlargement of bronchial wall

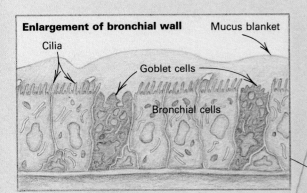

Mucus blanket

Cilia

Goblet cells

Bronchial cells

Cross section of normal bronchi and one showing chronic bronchitis

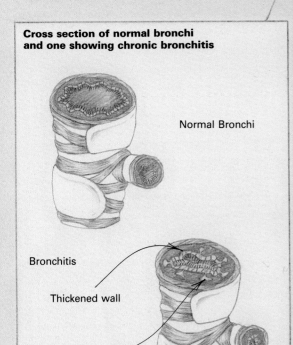

Normal Bronchi

Bronchitis

Thickened wall

Mucus-secreting gland

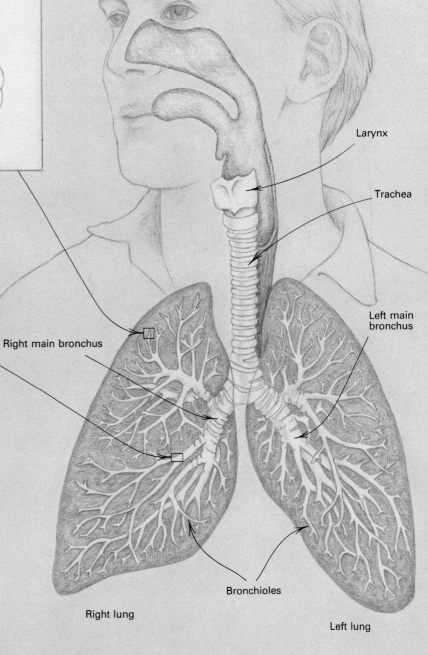

Larynx

Trachea

Left main bronchus

Right main bronchus

Bronchioles

Right lung

Left lung

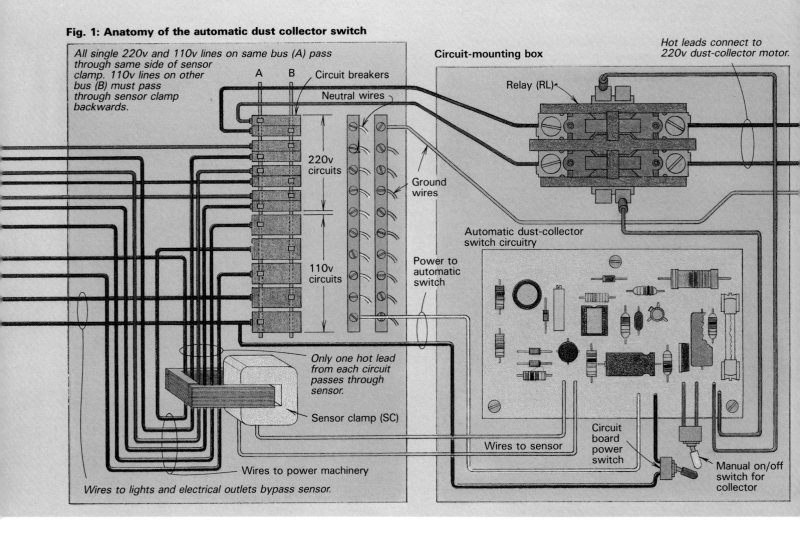

Fig. 1: Anatomy of the automatic dust collector switch

All single 220v and 110v lines on same bus (A) pass through same side of sensor clamp. 110v lines on other bus (B) must pass through sensor clamp backwards.

A   B   Circuit breakers

Neutral wires

220v circuits

110v circuits

Ground wires

Power to automatic switch

Only one hot lead from each circuit passes through sensor.

Sensor clamp (SC)

Wires to power machinery

Wires to lights and electrical outlets bypass sensor.

Circuit-mounting box

Hot leads connect to 220v dust-collector motor.

Relay (RL)

Automatic dust-collector switch circuitry

Wires to sensor

Circuit board power switch

Manual on/off switch for collector

Dust Collector Switch
An electronic sensor automatically turns the trick

by Robert Terry

Since I feel very attached to my lungs, I have a dust collection system installed in my shop so I'm not constantly breathing sawdust. But several things bothered me: It wastes money to continuously run a 2-HP collector motor during working hours, so I usually run it only when I'm working at a particular machine. But in my large shop, that can involve a lot of footsteps back and forth to the collector's switch. Then too, my young helpers frequently forget to activate the blower and consistently forget to turn it off. To alleviate these problems, I designed an electronic controller that automatically switches my dust collector motor on and off, regardless of which shop machine I use. The device doesn't need to be wired to any of the individual machines directly, and it's easy to construct even if you don't understand electricity and you've never

built an electronics project before. If you decide to build the collector switch from scratch, the parts will cost you about $60.

The automatic dust collector switch, which I'll abbreviate as ADS, is a device that senses the flow of electric current. Its basic anatomy is shown in figure 1. A sensor clamp (SC) is placed in the shop's breaker box with the wires that power all of the shop machines hooked up to dust collection threaded through it. The clamp sends electrical impulses to the ADS's voltage detection circuit, which operates a relay wired to the dust collector motor. When a shop machine is switched on, the controller detects current in its wires and then trips the relay, activating the collector's motor. Shutting off the machine tool causes the reverse effect, switching the collector off.

From *Fine Woodworking* (January 1988) 68:62-65

Fig. 2: Printed circuit board

At right, full-scale pattern for etching the printed circuit board, shown in gray with the copper side up. The dark lines show the location of components and connections on the reverse side. Note polarity of components. The part codes correspond to the parts list shown at the bottom of this page.

Below, the author mounted his automatic dust collector switch in a junction box next to the main breaker box in his shop. The unit can monitor any number of machine circuits and detects AC current from 0.5 to more than 60 amps. The lower limit is adjustable.

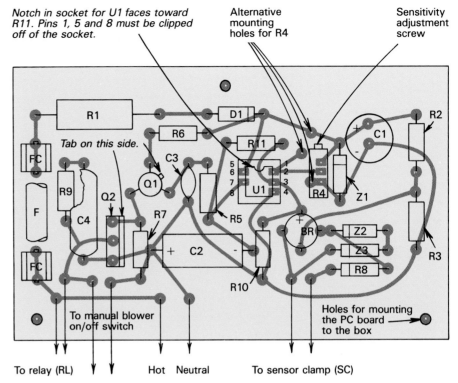

Notch in socket for U1 faces toward R11. Pins 1, 5 and 8 must be clipped off of the socket.

Alternative mounting holes for R4

Sensitivity adjustment screw

Tab on this side.

To manual blower on/off switch

Holes for mounting the PC board to the box

To relay (RL)　　　　Hot　Neutral　　To sensor clamp (SC)

The heart of the ADS is its printed circuit board. Mounted to this board are all the electronic components, as well as a 2-amp fuse to protect the circuit from overload. The diagram for the printed circuit board is shown full-size in figure 2, copper-side up. You can use it as a template to transfer the circuit pattern onto the board and to prick-punch all 72 holes. Etch the circuit, following the instructions provided in the printed circuit board kit (see parts list), except place the circuit board *copper-side up* in the acid and rock the tray gently from side to side as the board etches. With a #57 (0.043-in.-dia.) drill, bore all of the holes you punched earlier, and enlarge those for the fuse clips (which solder directly to the board) and wire leads.

Clean the circuit board with steel wool and kitchen scouring powder before soldering on the components. Use resin-core solder and a low-power, pencil-type soldering iron. Position components as shown in figure 2, observing the polarity and orientation of the components as marked. The socket for U1 should have pins 1, 5 and 8 clipped off before mounting. Raise R1 and D1 up slightly from the board—these produce heat and need air to circulate around them. So as not to overheat sensitive components Q1, Q2, and BR, temporarily attach small alligator clips to the component's leads to serve as heat sinks while soldering. Plug in the integrated circuit chip U1 only after you have finished soldering. Solder on the 22-gauge wire leads where they connect to the printed circuit board (see figure 2).

The controller's sensor clamp is made from an AC/DC power transformer that's been disassembled and altered as outlined in figure 3. The first lamination is difficult to remove, but it'll be discarded so don't worry if you mangle it. With a cold chisel, reshape each lamination by laying it on a piece of mild steel and chopping out the E's center to form a C shape. Deburr the new C-shaped pieces before reassembling the sensor. Use as many of the laminations as practical: The total is not critical for the sensor's sensitivity. Cut off the pins on the low-voltage side of the transformer and solder wire leads to the two remaining 110v pins (labeled 120VAC on the transformer).

Mount all the basic components of the ADS, except for the

Parts list		
Diagram Code	**Description**	**Radio Shack Part Number**
F1	Fuse AGC, 2 amp	270-1275
C1	Capacitor, (electrolytic), 470mf/35V	272-1030
C2	Capacitor, (electrolytic), 100mf/16V	272-1016
C3	Capacitor, .022mf/50	262-1066
C4	Capacitor, .1mf/600	***
R1	Resistor, 3.3K/2W	**
R2	Resistor, 10K/0.5W	271-034
R3	Resistor, 4.7K/0.5W	271-030
R4	Potentiometer 50K/20 turn	****
R5	Resistor, 22K/0.5W	271-038
R6,R7,R9	Resistor, 100/0.5W	271-012
R8	Resistor, 1K/0.5W	271-023
R10	Resistor, 100K/0.5W	271-045
R11	Resistor, 470K/0.5W	271-053
Z1	Zener Diode, 12V/1W	276-563
Z2,Z3	Zener Diode, 5.1V/1W	276-565
D1	Diode, 1N4003	276-1102
U1	Op-amp, 741	276-007
Q1	Transistor, 2N2646	**
Q2	Triac, 6A/400V, 2N6347A	**
BR	Rectifier, 1.4A/50PIV	276-1151
RL	Relay, 30A, 3 HP, DPST	1A639*
SC	Transformer, 120VAC/12.6/300MA	273-1385A
SW	Switch (2), SPST, 120VAC, 2A	**
P	IC socket, 8-pin	276-1995
FC	Circuit-board-mounting fuse clips (2)	Littlefuse 102071**
--	P.C. board kit (includes 2 boards)	276-1576
--	Metal junction box, 6x6x4 in. with cover	**

* Available from W.W. Grainger, Inc., 5959 W. Howard St., Chicago, IL 60648.
** Check local electronics store for availability.
*** Available from Sprague Electric Co., 149 Marshall St., N. Adams, MA 01247 (part no. 6PS-P10).
**** Available from Beckman Instruments Inc., Electronic Technologies Group, 2500 Harbor Blvd., Fullterton, CA 92634 (part no. P89PR50K).

Fig. 3: Constructing the sensor clamp

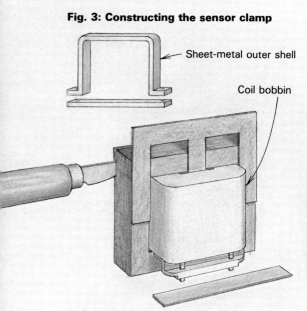

Sheet-metal outer shell

Coil bobbin

1. Pry off and discard the transformer's outer shell and separate the outer laminations with a knife. Carefully slide each two-piece lamination out of the coil bobbin and set aside.

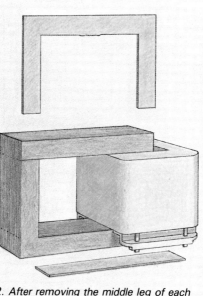

2. After removing the middle leg of each E-shaped lamination (turning it into a C shape), reassemble the pieces around the coil bobbin as shown. Insert C pieces into alternating sides of the bobbin.

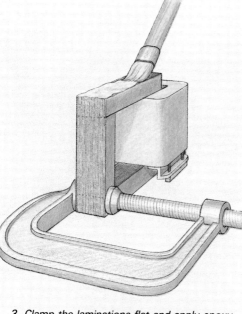

3. Clamp the laminations flat and apply epoxy to the edges to glue the assembly together.

sensor clamp, in an electrical junction box, because the circuit runs on AC power. The printed circuit board is mounted component-side-up on spacers to keep it from touching the box. Orient the board so the screw-end of R4 is close to one side of the box, then drill a hole large enough to allow adjustment with a small screwdriver. The ADS's power switch and manual on-off switch mount directly to the top or sides of the box and should be wired after mounting.

Before hooking up the ADS to your dust collector system, you must test and adjust the unit. Pass a single wire from a lamp cord powering at least a 150-watt floodlight (which draws about 1 amp), through the sensor clamp. With the floodlight lit, the ADS's power on and manual switch off, turn the adjustment screw on R4 until the contacts of the relay just pop open. At this setting, the ADS will switch the collector on when any electric load above 1 amp passes through the sensor clamp—a low enough threshold to react to almost any motorized machine.

Mount the ADS near the main breaker box in your shop (see photo, previous page) and wire the relay and line going to the collector motor as shown in figure 1 (note that in this drawing the circuit board has been oriented for clarity—you should turn

yours so you can adjust the potentiometer screw through the box side as noted earlier). Find a convenient place in the breaker box to locate the sensor clamp, and pass one lead from each circuit that supplies power to shop machines through the clamp. Note that only one of two hot wires leading to motors operating on 220v needs to be threaded through. To avoid phasing problems, note the direction that wires must pass through the sensor clamp. Avoid passing 110v lines leading to outlets used for power handtools or shop lights, because the 1-amp threshold of the controller will respond to these non-dust-control power users. While rewiring, *make absolutely sure the power to the breaker box is turned off*, and if you feel uncertain, hire an electrician.

Restore power and check to see that each of the monitored machines turns the dust collector on and off. □

Robert Terry is a retired electrical engineer and home-shop woodworker in Palm Beach, Fla. He offers a ready-to-solder parts kit, including an already-etched printed circuit board and relay, for $46.25 excluding shipping. For details, send a SASE to Techaid, Box 3272, Palm Beach, Fla. 33480. Rick Liftig provided technical editing assistance for this article.

Building automatic gate valves

by Reid Samuelson

Most dust collectors I've seen are inconvenient or impractical for a small shop, at least for the way I work. I constantly move from machine to machine, often using one for only a few seconds, before going back to the bench to do some hand work. I built an automatic collector switch similar in function to Robert Terry's. My system, however, goes one step further: I built and installed solenoid-operated gate valves that

open and close blast gates supplying vacuum to only the individual machine that's in use. Unlike regular blast gates that you must remember to slide open or closed, automatic valves are always in the right position at the right time—no unexpected piles of shavings from forgetting to open a gate before taking a pass on the planer.

The basic anatomy of the automatic blast gate is illustrated in figure 4. A simple

wooden box houses an AC-powered solenoid, latch mechanism, and a hinged and counterweighted door that functions as the actual valve gate. The box has two holes that tightly fit to the ends of the dust-collection ducts coming from the machine and going to the collector. The valve is normally in the closed position with the door up and latched, preventing air from entering. When the machine is switched on, current from the motor switch activates the solenoid, which pulls the latch up and releases the door. The collector's suction pulls the door open and allows the passage of wood chips and sawdust. When the machine is switched off, the power to the solenoid also cuts off, allowing the latch to drop to the locking position. No longer held open by suction, the door is pivoted back to the closed position by a counter-weighted arm, re-latching itself.

To construct the automatic blast gate, first cut all parts for the valve box, latch and door out of plywood. Proportion the size of the unit according to the diameter of the collection ducts in your shop. To make the hinge/counterweight arm, bend a steel rod and braze it to a steel plate that will be screwed to the bottom edge of the valve door. The rod sticks out and bears on hinge plates mounted on the box sides. The plates are made from short lengths of flat steel and smooth out the hinge's pivoting action.

If you have helpers in your shop and typically run several machines at the same time, you'll need to make the hinge rod very thick and strong, so it can be used as a handle to manually close individual blast gates when desired. This is because, with several machines running at the same time, suction keeps the valves open at each machine until the last machine is switched off, shutting down the dust collector.

Screw on the latch hinge and mount the solenoid on the box's top, attaching a rod or stiff wire to connect the latch to the solenoid's plunger. When power to the solenoid is switched off, the closing door lifts the latch slightly as it returns to the lock position.

Now locate the oversized holes that pass the hinge rod through the box's sides. There should be about $\frac{1}{4}$ in. above the bottom of the box. If the pivot point is right at the bottom, dust and chips may accumulate and prevent the door from closing. Pass the ends of the hinge rod through the sides and assemble the valve box around the door, nailing or screwing and gluing it together. I don't think a gasket is needed to seal the door, but to keep the vacuum leakage low, the door should be larger than the duct port by at least $\frac{1}{2}$ in. on all sides and it should seat flat against the inside surface of the box.

A lead counterweight about the size of a pecan is drilled to fit the rod and slid over the end, about 4 in. from the bend. You'll have to experiment to find the exact weight and placement.

Depending on whether your machine's motor runs on 110v or 220v, I recommend using a Dormeyer series 1000 AC solenoid or its equivalent (both the 110v, model

#1000-M-1, and 220v, model #1001-M-1, are available from Grainger Inc., 5959 W. Howard St., Chicago, Ill. 60648). It may take some fiddling with the wire's length and the latch mechanism to get the door to lock and unlock properly, but it's very important that the solenoid plunger is allowed its full stroke or it will constantly draw current and burn out prematurely.

Connect the power cord to the motor wires inside your switch box so flipping the switch on will send 110v or 220v to the solenoid. Run the wire to the solenoid, making sure no connections are exposed.

When I was buying the electrical gear for the valves and collector controller, the clerk in the electronics store asked what I was planning to make. When I said it was a device for my dust collection system, he responded, "I've heard of some strange collections, but *dust*?" I was about to explain but then thought how much fun he'd have telling about the weirdo he'd met who collects dust. □

Reid Samuelson is a retired electrical engineer and amateur woodworker. He lives in Eastford, Conn.

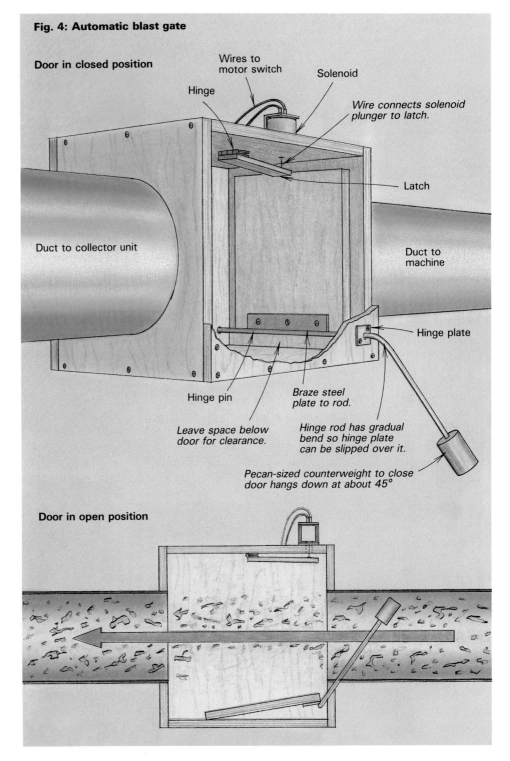

Fig. 4: Automatic blast gate

Door in closed position

Wires to motor switch

Hinge

Solenoid

Wire connects solenoid plunger to latch.

Latch

Duct to collector unit

Duct to machine

Hinge plate

Hinge pin

Braze steel plate to rod.

Leave space below door for clearance.

Hinge rod has gradual bend so hinge plate can be slipped over it.

Pecan-sized counterweight to close door hangs down at about 45°

Door in open position

Setting Up Shop

Three pros give advice on outfitting a first shop

W hat tools do you need to set up a good basic shop to make functional furnishings you can be proud of? That's the question I posed to three accomplished woodworkers—and teachers of woodworking. Independently, each affirmed the importance of both accurate, reliable power tools and high-quality hand tools in the modern woodworking shop. Though sometimes contradictory, the advice they offer is surprisingly consistent. And where it varies it's often because of their different backgrounds and the kinds of work they do.

Peter Korn was a professional furnituremaker for 12 years and taught furniture design at Drexel University for four of those years before becoming director of the woodworking program at Anderson Ranch Arts Center in 1986. He has written numerous magazine articles and newspaper columns on woodworking, and his book, *Working with Wood: The Basics of Craftsmanship*, was published by The Taunton Press in April. Korn left Anderson Ranch last December to start his own woodworking school, the Center for Furniture Craftsmanship, which is in Hope, Maine. The school offers two-week courses for basic and intermediate woodworkers.

Mario Rodriguez is a cabinetmaker and 18th-century woodworking consultant. He's been making 18th- and 19th-century reproductions for the past 12 years, specializing in Windsor chairs. He has been adjunct assistant professor of woodworking for the Fashion Institute of Technology's antique restoration program for the past five years and has lectured at the Brooklyn Museum, the Cooper-Hewitt Museum, Sotheby's, the Royal Oak Society and for other groups interested in Early American woodworking. He also teaches at Warwick Country Workshops in Warwick, N.Y. Subjects taught have included planemaking and use, dovetailing and veneering.

Mark Duginske, a contributing editor to *Fine Woodworking*, is a fourth-generation woodworker. His books include *The Band Saw Handbook*, *Band Saw Basics*, *The Band Saw Pattern Book*, *Precision Machinery Techniques* and most recently, *Mastering Woodworking Machines*, which was published by The Taunton Press last year. He has also done two videos, one accompanying his most recent book and the other called *Mastering Your Bandsaw*. His restoration work on the Frank Lloyd Wright home and studio in Oak Park, Ill. has been featured on *This Old House* and PBS's *Frank Lloyd Wright* special.

Although workshops are as individual as their owners, there's a common thread of good sense in the suggestions these three teachers and woodworkers have to offer. If you think we've forgotten something, though, or if you'd just like to comment on the subject of setting up shop, drop me a line. I'd be glad to hear from you.   □

Vincent Laurence is associate editor at Fine Woodworking.

***It takes time, money and good sense** to outfit a complete shop, but the principles involved are simple: Buy the best you can afford, cultivate hand-tool skills and acquire machines to perform those tasks for which they're best suited—the brute work of getting stock square, true and to size.*

Peter Korn: Building a foundation for a lifetime of craftsmanship

Every year I teach classes in basic woodworking, and every year the students want to know which tools they should buy to set up their first workshop. The answer, of course, depends upon what they want to make and how. I teach the skills necessary for building fine furniture, emphasizing the use of machinery for milling rough lumber foursquare and hand tools for cutting joinery and smoothing surfaces. Machinery and hand tools are complementary aspects of a contemporary fine furniture workshop.

Whether you're setting up a home workshop or starting a small woodworking business, you should acquire the same basic equipment. In neither case should you stint on quality. Good tools may not ensure good work, but poorly made, undersized or underpowered tools will adversely affect both your results and the pleasure you take in the work. Unlike most consumer items, whose obsolescence is engineered in, good woodworking hand tools and machinery will last a lifetime and beyond; if you buy the best from the start, you'll only have to buy once. In general, I consider Delta and Porter-Cable to be the minimum acceptable standard against which the quality of other power tools should be measured.

Power tools

If I could have only one piece of machinery in my workshop, it would be a bandsaw. This versatile tool can do anything from the brute work of resawing a 6-in. hardwood beam into planks to the delicate work of cutting the curves for a cabriole leg. With a bandsaw, handplanes and a little sweat, rough lumber can be milled perfectly foursquare. A 14-in. bandsaw is the standard size for most home and small professional shops. You should expect to pay around $700.

The truth is, though, I wouldn't consider getting started without a tablesaw, jointer and thickness planer if I could possibly afford them. Straight, flat, square stock is vital to well-crafted furniture, and these three tools work together to make the milling process easy.

The tablesaw is useful for many other tasks as well, such as making dadoes, tongues, tenons and miters. I recommend buying a good 10-in. tablesaw with a 3-hp motor, such as the Delta Unisaw, which will cost you around $1,500. If you try to save money by purchasing a smaller saw

"Machinery and hand tools are complementary aspects of a contemporary fine furniture workshop."

or a weaker motor, you will be itching to upgrade in no time at all.

I started my own shop with a 6-in. jointer, but if I had to do it over again, I would purchase an 8-in. jointer or an even wider one. Those extra inches of cutterhead width significantly reduce the number of boards you will have to flatten with handplanes or saw apart, joint and re-glue because they are too wide for the jointer. A good 8-in. jointer will run you approximately $1,500.

My first planer was a 12-in. Parks, sold by Sears in 1952. I found it abandoned and in pieces in the corner of someone's shop in 1977. While it's not a huge machine, it's been fine for me as a one-off furniture-maker. If I were buying a planer today, I'd stay away from the myriad of lightweight, portable offerings and get something built to last. I've heard good things about the Makita, Hitachi and Delta DC-33 stationary planers. Expect to pay upward of $1,300 for a solid 13-in. planer.

I've also heard good reports from students about some of the better jointer/planer combinations, such as the Robland and the Minimax, but I haven't tried them. Combination jointer/planers may be a good idea for woodworkers with little shop space and/or limited budgets, but

separate machines provide an element of convenience I would hate to forego. I am constantly moving back and forth from jointer to planer, so pausing to change one into the other would slow me down considerably. Though I've only used separate machines, I also suspect that they hold their settings more dependably than do the combination machines.

A drill press, for accurate, straight boring of holes, is the final piece of stationary power equipment essential to a woodworking shop. The size of the drill press isn't all that important, and variable speed isn't really necessary either. Any drill press will do as long as its run-out is minimal, it has an adjustable depth stop and the table is square to the quill. A satisfactory drill press can be had for $300.

Other stationary power tools that are useful but secondary in importance are a lathe, a radial-arm saw or chop saw, a compressor and a belt/disc sander. A vacuum system makes a shop more pleasant to work in, but a dust mask and a broom probably make more fiscal sense—especially when you're just getting started.

Other power tools

Among smaller and portable power tools, I would purchase a grinder, drill and router straight off. A circular saw, jigsaw and biscuit joiner can wait, as can palm, belt and random-orbital sanders.

A grinder is indispensable for keeping chisels and planes sharp. You can get a cheap one for about $50, but if you can afford to—and they're substantially more expensive—you should buy a grinder that spins at about 1,750 rpm, rather than the standard 3,200 rpm to 3,400 rpm. A slower grinder is less likely to overheat steel and destroy its temper.

A router is perhaps the most versatile tool in the shop. A small router with a ¼-in. collet is perfectly adequate for a small shop. My first choice would be Elu's 1-hp variable-speed plunge router, which features a soft start. It is a sweet little machine—just a pleasure to use, and at about $170, it is a very good buy.

My first portable power drill would be a ⅜-in. variable-speed, reversible model. One of its main functions would be to drive drywall screws when building jigs and fixtures in the shop. Milwaukee makes some of the most reliable drills, but they're also among the most expensive—about $120 for the model I recommend.

From *Fine Woodworking* (May 1993) 100:58-62

Hand tools

While you may not think of it as a hand tool, the workbench is where most of your handwork takes place. It may well be your single most important tool. A good workbench should have a flat top, be sturdy enough to take a pounding and not wobble. The bench should also have both tail vise and shoulder vise or the equivalent. If you can't afford to buy a good European workbench (about $1,200), building your own bench should be one of the first projects for your new shop. You can find the bench hardware for about $115.

I've found the following hand tools to be indispensable. I've explained briefly what each is used for as well as what you should expect to pay for a good tool, assuming you shop smart.

Folding rule and a tape measure. My favorite measuring device is a 6-ft. Lufkin Red End carpenter's rule with extension slide. It's durable, handy and accurate. $18 (for the folding rule) and $14 (for the tape).

Square. I use several squares regularly: a 4-in. engineer's square, a 6-in. try square and a 10-in. try square. If I had to settle for only one square, it would probably be either a 10-in. or 12-in. try square. $25 (for a 10-in. try square).

Sliding T-bevel. Indispensable for marking out dovetails and angles. $14.

Mat knife. For many purposes including marking out joinery. $4.

Chisels. I recommend buying a set of durable, plastic-handled bench chisels, such as Marples Blue Chip, in sizes ¼ in., 5⁄16 in., ⅜ in., ½ in., ¾ in. and 1 in. $45.

Handplanes. The first two I'd get are a block plane and a jack plane. The block plane is for planing joints flush, planing across end grain, fairing convex curves, and breaking edges. The jack plane is for flattening wide roughsawn lumber and for smoothing machined surfaces. $45 (block plane) and $73 (jack plane).

Marking and mortising gauges (or a combination gauge). For marking mortises, tenons, dovetail shoulders and for marking stock to be resawn. $34 (for a combination gauge).

Hand scraper. For smoothing surfaces. Sandvik makes the best. $7.

Backsaw. For cutting joinery. I use a small, inexpensive saw with a 10 in. by 1⅝ in. blade. Its 21 tiny teeth per inch leave a very thin kerf. $13.

Coping saw. For removing waste when cutting dovetails and for sawing interior curves. $14.

Awl. For marking pilot holes. $7.

Wooden mallet. For driving chisels. $14.

Hammer. For a multitude of uses. $16.

Twist drill bits. From 1⁄16 in. to ½ in., by 64ths. $48.

Brad-point bits. From ¼ in. to ½ in. by 16ths, plus ⅝ in. and ¾ in. $40.

Half-round rasp and wood file. For smoothing curves and shaping edges. $16 and $14.

Mill bastard file, 8 in. For scraper preparation and for odd bits of metal filing. $6.

Water stones, 1,000-grit and 6,000-grit. For sharpening chisels and plane blades. $47 for the pair.

Clamps. I recommend buying six 2½-in. C-clamps, six 12-in. quick-action clamps, six 24-in. quick-action clamps, and six 4-ft. bar clamps. About $275.

Although $6,500 or so (a rough total) may seem like a lot of money now, it is almost a negligible sum when amortized over a lifetime of pleasure, productivity and value. Buying good tools to start with and making sure that they're the right tools for the job, will get you off to a good beginning on your career as a craftsman.

–Peter Korn

Mario Rodriguez: Quality hand tools and a few machines—a good start

When you decide to set up shop, you're immediately faced with decisions about space, equipment and tools. As your skills and experience grow, so will your collection of tools. But, to get you started, here's a good basic kit.

My suggestions are heavy on hand tools because I believe in a strong foundation of hand skills. But a combination of hand tools and machines enables a woodworker to achieve speed *and* practice a high level of craftsmanship.

Stationary power tools

Bandsaw. If I could have only one or the other, I'd choose a bandsaw over a table-saw. Bandsaws are cheaper, take up less floor space, can resaw and cut curves and are considerably quieter than the tablesaw. With a good, well-tuned machine, the quality of cut is excellent. And while it's true that a bandsaw's rip capacity is limited to its throat size, a resourceful woodworker can work around that. You can get a good bandsaw (the Delta 14 in., for example) for as little as $650.

Jointer. Buy the best and largest jointer that you can afford. A jointer is useful for cleaning up edges cut on the bandsaw, straightening and squaring edges for gluing, and for flattening boards. The Delta 6 in. sells for about $1,100.

Sliding compound miter saw. This saw is invaluable for clean and accurate crosscuts and miters. The sliding-arm feature lets you crosscut up to 12 in. wide (like a small radial-arm saw). Look for a model that takes a 10-in. blade instead of an 8½-in. blade. Not everyone carries 8½-in. replacement blades. I like Makita's version, which sells for around $450.

Portable power tools

Router. You can do it all with this tool: dado, rabbet, mortise, joint or shape an edge, or follow a template. Porter-Cable's ⅞-hp router is a good value at $110.

Drill, ⅜ in. In addition to using it to drill

holes, you can also use it for driving screws, light grinding and polishing. A basic unit can be had for $50.

Hand tools

Chisels. Buy a good set of wooden-handled bench chisels (¼ in., ½ in., ¾ in., 1 in.) and a ¼-in. mortise chisel. Wooden handles are more comfortable and more visually appealing than plastic, and if ever they split or get chipped, you can replace them with little effort. I prefer traditional Western chisels (mine are made by Sorby) as opposed to Japanese chisels, which I think require too much work, especially if you're just getting started in woodworking. If you can afford to, buy a 2-in.-wide bench chisel in addition to the four smaller ones. Its extra-wide blade is ideal for paring tenons. A set of four Sorby chisels costs about $80, the mortise chisel about $30 and the 2-in. paring chisel about $40.

Sharpening stones. I prefer waterstones because they're cleaner than oilstones. I use 800-, 1200-, 4000- and 6000-grit stones.

Combination square, 12 in. This tool will mark out stock at 90° and 45° and can double as a ruler and a marking gauge. Buy the best you can afford: Starrett and Browne & Sharpe are both good brands. You can find the Starrett for about $50.

Engineer's square, 3 in. This is great for marking out and checking small parts and edges. It's smaller and handier than the combination square and generally more accurate. You can get a 3-in. engineer's square for around $5.

Sliding bevel. This is an essential layout tool used for setting and copying angles. Shinwa makes a compact and inexpensive version (about $10).

Hammer. A good 13-oz. claw hammer is ideal for general cabinet work and is useful for installation work as well. I use a one-piece, leather-handled Estwing, which costs about $18.

Carver's mallet. This is useful for driving joints home and for chopping out mortises. I like a medium-sized turned lignum vitae mallet. Expect to pay about $15.

Marking gauge. I use a compact version made by Reed, which, unfortunately, is no longer in production. It's simple, keeps its setting and has a removable (and replaceable) blade for easy sharpening. Starrett makes a very similar gauge (their #29A) for around $30.

Marking knife. I use a pointed chip-carving knife for marking joints. Its slim, pointed tip lets me scribe a good line even in very tight spots, and the shape of the blade allows me to apply pressure for a deeper cut when needed. Less than $10.

"A craftsman's training should be based on a strong foundation of hand skills."

Folding rule, 6 ft. I prefer a ruler over tape. I find it more accurate for cabinetwork, particularly when measuring inside cabinets and checking diagonals. Lufkin's Red End is the best and costs about $18.

Dovetail and tenon saws. For cutting small pieces, I use an 8-in. dovetail saw with a turned handle and 18 teeth per inch (t.p.i.). I use a 10-in. brass-backed dovetail saw with 14 t.p.i. for cutting dovetails and tenons. Japanese saws will also do a great job, but they can require delicate handling, and replacement blades are often expensive. Expect to pay about $10 for the dovetail saw with the turned handle and about $40 for the brass-backed model.

Block plane. I recommend the Lie-Nielsen block plane, either the low-angle or the regular. Solid, compact and well-made, it's the best block plane on the market. A block plane is useful for planing small parts, flushing surfaces and planing end grain. It sells for $75.

Smoothing plane, #3. A smoothing plane is used for final planing of surfaces as well as for shooting edges on short pieces and for fairing joints. I don't care for any of the smoothing planes on the market for under $100; they're just not made as well as they used to be. I think a reconditioned Stanley, pre-1940, is your best value. I got mine from Tom Witte, an antique tool dealer (P.O. Box 399, Mattawan, Mich. 49071; 616-668-4161). Expect to pay from $60 to $85 for a good used #3.

Rabbet plane. There are several planes that fit the bill, but the Stanley #93 is the most versatile because its front half can be removed to convert it to a chisel plane. This plane is used to trim rabbets, plane into corners and trim joints flush. It costs about $80.

Cabinet scraper. I use Sandvik scrapers. They're inexpensive, work well and last forever (I still use one I bought over 14 years ago). Scrapers are good for smoothing hardwood and veneered surfaces, either before or in lieu of sanding. You can get a Sandvik scraper for about $6.

These tools are just a beginning. I've tried to keep the list short both to keep your initial outlay of cash from getting out of hand and because it's a good idea to become comfortable and familiar with the basics before adding to your collection. Just remember: Buy the best tools you can afford, take care of them and keep your blades sharp.   —Mario Rodriguez

A basic kit of hand tools doesn't have to cost a fortune or take up a lot of space. Here, with some changes and additions, is Mario Rodriguez's basic kit. The chisel handles (and the brass-backed dovetail saw's handle) are all replacements made by Rodriguez.

Mark Duginske: Buy the basics, and know when not to compromise

Setting up shop takes money, but it also takes time, thought and energy: a room full of tools doesn't make a shop. It's important to reach a point of critical mass, though, having all the tools you need to do a job adequately. And while you don't want junk, you're better off with a shop full of inexpensive tools that allow you to get the job done than only one high-quality tool that leaves you stuck. At the same time, I believe, you're better off buying a good tool and buying it once. The trick is to know when a tool is good enough.

Tablesaw

The tablesaw is at the center of more shops, both figuratively and literally, than probably any other machine. This is partially because of the now ubiquitous use of sheet goods, which the tablesaw alone among stationary woodworking equipment is able to cut down to size. But it's also because the tablesaw can rip stock far more cleanly than the bandsaw and more safely than the radial-arm saw.

Your choices for under $1,000 are the Taiwanese contractor's saws (sold under more names than I can keep up with) and the Delta contractor's saw. The Delta is well-made, easily adjustable and it holds its adjustments well. The problem with the Taiwanese saws is their inconsistency. Some are fine out of the box, but I've also seen one on which it was impossible to align the blade with the miter-gauge slot without disassembling the saw and filing out the trunnion holes. On other Taiwanese tablesaws, I've seen the finish on the inside of the miter-gauge slot as rough as a file. If you take the time to expand your miter bar to fit the slot tightly (either with a prick punch or by peaning the bar), the adjustment will wear away very rapidly by the rough side wall. If you're going to buy a Taiwanese saw, buy it from a local dealer, and check it out before any cash changes hands.

Two of the best used tablesaws are the Inca 259 and Delta's old 9-in. contractor's saw. Both are excellent machines; if you see one for a reasonable sum, jump on it. Another excellent used saw is the Delta tilting arbor saw, which had cast-iron wings like the Unisaw, but an open base like the contractor's saw.

Bandsaw

If you can afford only one really good tool, make it the bandsaw, especially if you'd like to do restoration work or any kind of

"Setting up shop takes money, but it also takes time, thought and energy: a room full of tools doesn't make a shop."

work that requires curve cutting. There are only two choices for an affordable first-rate bandsaw: the Inca 340 and the 14-in. Delta. Both are fine pieces of equipment and each has its strengths. The Inca weighs only 60 lbs., which makes it quite portable. Also, with its optional micro-adjuster, it's well-suited for joinery, such as cutting tenons and dovetails. The Delta's strength is its resaw capacity, which, with the optional riser block, is 12 in.

As for used tools, I'd look for a 14-in. Delta or an old Sears with a tilting table.

Saws for crosscutting

If you're doing more carpentry-type construction or you're just doing a lot of crosscutting, particularly of long pieces, then you should consider buying a radial-arm or a sliding-compound miter saw, which has replaced the radial arm for most contractors and for many—if not most—woodworkers. The sliding-compound miter saw has no rip capability, but it can crosscut up to 12 in. on most models and can cut accurate 45° and other miters as well as compound angles. These saws are portable, and their simple design keeps them surprisingly accurate.

Jointers and planers

The Ryobi and some of the other small planers have transformed the small shop

by bringing the price of a planer into the range of most woodworkers' budgets. Along with a 6-in. jointer and a contractor's saw, anyone can afford to dimension his own stock now. Bring a reliable straightedge with you to check the beds when shopping for a jointer. A jointer is a precision-oriented tool, and its beds must be flat and parallel.

A combination jointer/planer is another affordable way to set yourself up to prepare stock. Hitachi, Inca and Robland make very good jointer/planers.

Gadgets and gimmicks: beware

Hand-tool skills and basic power-tool savvy are a woodworker's best foundation. A disturbing trend I've noticed in the past few years, primarily at woodworking shows, is the number of beginning woodworkers buying gadgets and gimmicks rather than investing in solid, basic tools. Granted, the basic power tools represent a more significant investment, but these jigs, fixtures and whatnot that promise to deliver flawless joinery with no effort are only distractions that insulate novice woodworkers from acquiring basic hand skills and mechanical knowledge.

The combination of hand-tool skills, a router and some medium-sized, well-tuned decent equipment will allow you to do just about anything. You may not get it done as quickly as if you had each one of Delta's industrial tools, but you will be able to do a variety of quality work without spending a ton of cash on equipment.

Buying tools is only part of becoming a woodworker. The other ingredient is skill, which is purchased with time and determination. Each tool—whether power or hand—has its own learning curve. The current trend—to learn machine woodworking before developing hand-tool skills—is backward. Compounding this problem, or perhaps causing it, is that we as a culture are so goal-oriented that we have to make things right away rather than playing with a tool and getting to know it. It's possible to develop the same kind of intimacy with power tools as you develop with hand tools, but it doesn't happen when you're in a mad rush to finish a project. Traditionally, knowledge was gained by continuous repetition during an apprenticeship period. Today, experimentation and practice are the best ways to learn. But there are no shortcuts—no matter how much you're willing to pay.

—*Mark Duginske*

Drill Press Primer

Anatomy and use of a woodworker's standby

by Bernie Maas

Using a metal rule, Maas double checks each hole's edge distance for the series he bored with a machine-spur bit chucked in his drill press. A fence, clamped to the table with a hold-down, keeps the workpiece aligned while the machine's depth gauge (next to the feed lever) ensures that the holes are uniformly deep.

If your solutions to boring holes have been a wrist-cracking brace and bit and an ear-straining electric drill, then you'll break into a smile when you crank up a drill press. Originally devised for metalworking, the drill press offers the same professional results for woodworking: consistently accurate holes. While the press is a premier hole maker, its name belies its ability to do other work, such as mortising. In contrast to most stationary machines, the press is a quick study, and it's quiet and fairly safe to use.

Basically, there are two types of drill presses: benchtop and floor standing. Bench models range in height from 22 in. to 46 in., while floor models can be anywhere from 52-in. to 76-in. tall. Drill-press capacity or throat size—the largest circular workpiece you can bore a central hole through and not hit the column with—is often expressed as *swing* or *diameter*. Bench models usually have a swing from 8 in. to 12 in. Floor models range from 10-in.-dia. machines up to 21-in.-dia. monster presses. I prefer the floor-standing

models in the 11-in. to 16-in. range because they can be positioned in tight spots without occupying valuable bench space, and this size is ideal for most woodworking jobs.

Drill-press parts and their purposes

The drill press is made up of four basic parts (see the drawing on p. 65), which are clamped to a polished steel column. From the bottom up, there's a base (foot), a movable table, a safety collar, and a head. Both the table and base are usually cast iron and ribbed for strength and rigidity. The base is big enough to stabilize the machine, and usually features bolt-down holes. The table, adjustable up and down, has a smoothly machined flat top that's either square or circular. Commonly, there's a split ring and a screw handle to lock the table to the column. Some tables have slots to clamp fixtures; some tilt for angle work, but all have a central hole so that you won't easily run a bit into the metal top. The safety collar is locked to the column just beneath the head to sup-

port the head in case it accidentally slips. Finally, there's the head itself, a cast unit that houses the most important parts: the motor, pulleys, pinion shaft, quill and electricals. Most drill presses have sealed-bearing motors ranging from $\frac{1}{4}$ HP to $\frac{3}{4}$ HP. The drive belt is tensioned by shifting the motor on its bracket. When properly tensioned, the belt should flex about an inch midway between the motor and spindle pulleys.

The quill assembly—The heart of the head is the quill, which is the sleeve that contains the spindle. The quill allows the spindle shaft both to revolve (drill) and to reciprocate (press) simultaneously (see the drawing detail on p. 65). Ball bearings at each end retain the spindle within the quill and keep it centered and free to rotate. Rack-and-pinion gearing, controlled by the quill handle (feed lever), moves the quill up and down. Quills usually have a vertical stroke of 3 in. to 4 in., although some travel 6 in. An adjustable clock spring returns the quill

Selecting spindle speed

Heat is the enemy of bits; you need to get your bit in and out of a workpiece before friction heats it up. To do this, your drill press has to generate the correct number of RPMS. Most presses will run between 400 RPM and 5500 RPM. Speeds are adjusted by altering the position of the drive belt. The press will run fastest when the belt couples the smallest spindle pulley with the largest motor pulley. To help determine the best speed to use for the bit you've chosen, refer to the chart below.   —B.M.

Bit type/size☆	Recommended speed (RPM)*
Machine spur	
1/8 - 5/8	3,600
over 5/8	1,800
Multi-Spur	
1/2 - 2	1,200
2 - 3	900
over 3	600
Forstner	
3/8 - 5/8	1,800 - 2,400
11/16 - 1	1,400 - 1,800
1 1/16 - 1 7/16	900 - 1,200
1 1/2 - 3	250 - 600
Spade†	
1/4 - 1 1/2	1,000 - 2,000
Powerbore†	
3/8 - 5/8	1,800 - 2,500
3/4 - 1	1,200 - 2,000
Twist	
1/16 - 3/16	2,400 - 4,700
1/4 - 7/16	1,250 - 2,400
1/2 - 3/4	700 - 1,250
Plug cutter	
Under 1/2	2,400
1/2 - 1	1,800

☆ Don't use long (over 6 in.) thin-shank bits over 1,000 RPM

* Slower RPMS (when range is given) are for hardwoods. Actual spindle speed will be influenced by step-pulley sizes and density variations within the wood. Generally, the larger the bit and the harder the material, the slower the speed.

† Speeds over 2,500 RPM will likely burn workpiece.

to its up position. From time to time, the spring and quill should be lubricated through their oil holes, but unless you're desperate for entertainment, don't try to take apart the spring assembly.

You can lock the quill or preset the depth to which it can advance. On the left of the head is the quill-lock handle. On the right is the depth gauge, usually a simple rod-and-nut arrangement. To set the depth gauge, lower and lock the quill at the desired depth, and snug the gauge's bottom stop nut against the lug on the head. Then unlock the quill, return it to the starting position, and lock the gauge's top nut against the bottom one.

The chuck—Fixed to the lower end of the quill is a three-jaw chuck, sometimes called a Jacob's chuck (after its inventor). While 3/4-in. and 3/8-in. chucks are not uncommon, most presses have 1/2-in. or 5/8-in. chucks. A chuck's size designates the maximum diameter shank that it will take; minimum capacity is usually 1/16 in. Some chucks have springs that automatically eject the key, so it can't be left it in the chuck accidentally. For the best grip possible, tighten all three of your chuck's key holes, especially when boring large holes (over 1 1/2 in.). Large bits exert considerable torque, sometimes stalling while the chuck continues to spin. This chews up the chuck and galls the bit shank so that it won't run true.

Drill-press safety

The drill press is not inherently dangerous, but it deserves respect and warrants some precautions. The greatest hazard is spinning work. Large bits muster enough torque to rip work from your grip, smacking it into your knuckles or worse—launching it at bystanders. Besides causing injury, a whirling piece of wood can bend a bit or the spindle. Boring a hole off center can also whip work around. Misalignment occurs when the bit grabs a hole's edge or when small or unwieldy stock dances out of line or becomes cocked due to vibration or table tilt. Chips and debris left on the table also can allow a piece to drift dangerously off center.

In order to avoid these hazards, always keep the floor around the press clear and the table clean and well lit. To prevent work from spinning when boring small holes, brace it against a clamped block or fence, and when using bits over 1/2 in., clamp the work down. In addition, you can use a hold-down (available from Enco Manufacturing Co., 5000 W. Bloomingdale, Chicago, Ill. 60639) to prevent work from lifting when you withdraw bits (see the photo on p. 63). Through the following good shop practices, you'll avoid other hazards, such as flying

pieces, entanglement and cutter contact: Never leave the key in the chuck; wear eye protection; tie back long hair and don't wear jewelry or loosely hanging clothing. Remember that the chuck and bits revolve clockwise—keep your hands and body clear of them and anything else that might spin.

Feed rate, pressure and speed

When boring wood with a drill press, the spindle speed, feed rate and the pressure you apply determine the quality of the hole. Too much pressure on the feed lever causes rough cuts or jammed and broken bits. Too slow a feed rate can burn the work and overheat the bit. Feed steadily and evenly. A fast or choppy stroke can cause drift, thus elongating a hole. Boring at the correct rate and pressure produces uniform shavings, about .040-in.-thick. If you're coming up with dust, either the feed is too slow or the bit is dull. If your bit is advancing slowly but is requiring a lot of pressure, then your speed is too fast or your bit is dull. Refer to the chart at left for recommended speeds for bits. With a little practice, you'll know when you've found the best combination of feed rate, pressure and speed.

Boring with a drill press

Before you do any boring, cover the drill-press table with an auxiliary table of 3/4-in. plywood. The auxiliary table supports the fibers on the underside of your work and may save you from running an expensive bit into the cast-iron table. Additionally, if a bit slips as you're chucking it, it'll only drop a few inches onto plywood instead of diving 4 ft., point first, into the cast-iron base. A fence is another drill-press helper. I clamp a fence to the table to help keep the work from spinning and to align a series of holes, such as bracket holes for shelving. My fences are made from straight lengths of 1x2 hardwood with a 3/16-in. chamfer on the bottom edge. The chamfer acts as an escape hatch for chips, which otherwise will pack against the fence, throwing off its registration.

To bore a hole, put your auxiliary table down first, and then adjust the table to a comfortable height. After selecting the right bit for the job (see the sidebar on p. 67), mount it in the chuck and set the spindle speed for the size and type of bit you are using (see the sidebar at left). If the bit has a center lead point, ding a center hole in your work with an awl or punch. For plug cutters and Forstner bits, which don't have lead points, lay out the circumference of the hole with a circle template (found in most art-supply stores). If you're boring an angled hole, lay out the hole's upper limit (where the boring will begin). And remember, the perimeter of an angled hole is an ellipse.

Most holes will be shallower than your press's stroke, but if the hole depth exceeds the stroke of the machine, you can use a bit extension shaft or drill as deep as you can, and then raise the table or block up the work until you get to the depth you need. If the hole depth is less than the stroke and shallower than the thickness of the workpiece, adjust and lock your quill travel. Keep in mind that the chip ejectors for both Forstner and Multi-Spur bits work best in shallow holes. In deep holes, the chips wad up, making it tough to back out the bit. Avoid wadding by raising these bits periodically to evacuate the waste. But don't retract a Multi-Spur bit completely from the hole, and then feed the spinning bit back in again because the teeth will likely grab the hole's edge and ruin the face of your work. Instead, stop the machine and feed the bit back into the hole. Restart the motor and continue boring.

If you have to bore completely through the workpiece, there's a good chance you'll split the underside. You can avoid this by drilling only deep enough for the lead point to come through and then back drilling from the other side. To do this, first, lower the bit (with the motor off) and sink just the point into the auxiliary table. Lock the quill at this position and set the depth gauge to bore only this deep. Release the quill lock and fire up the machine. Get a good grip on your work or clamp it down, and bore until the depth stop bottoms out. Then turn the work over and look for the tiny pilot hole made by the point. If you back drill carefully, you'll wind up with a splinter-free hole. This method won't work with a Forstner bit because it doesn't have a lead point. So instead, set the depth stop to where the bit's rim barely brushes the underlayment. Then carefully bore down from the topside. Lower the bit gently until you feel the bit just break through.

To use a fence when boring a series of holes, first set the workpiece on the table. With the motor off, lightly tack your bit's point into a hole's center and lock the quill. You don't have to align the fence parallel to the table's edge because only one point—the bit's center—must be the correct distance from the fence. Snug the fence against the work (chamfered edge down and toward the bit), and clamp the fence to the table. Make sure the clamp pads are on a flat spot under the table, not against a rib where they might vibrate loose. Release the quill lock, start the motor and bore the first hole. Slide the work along the fence to bore the rest of the holes in a row, as shown in the photo on p. 63.

Fixtures and table vises

There are dozens of drill-press fixtures that you can make. A few that I like are a V-block

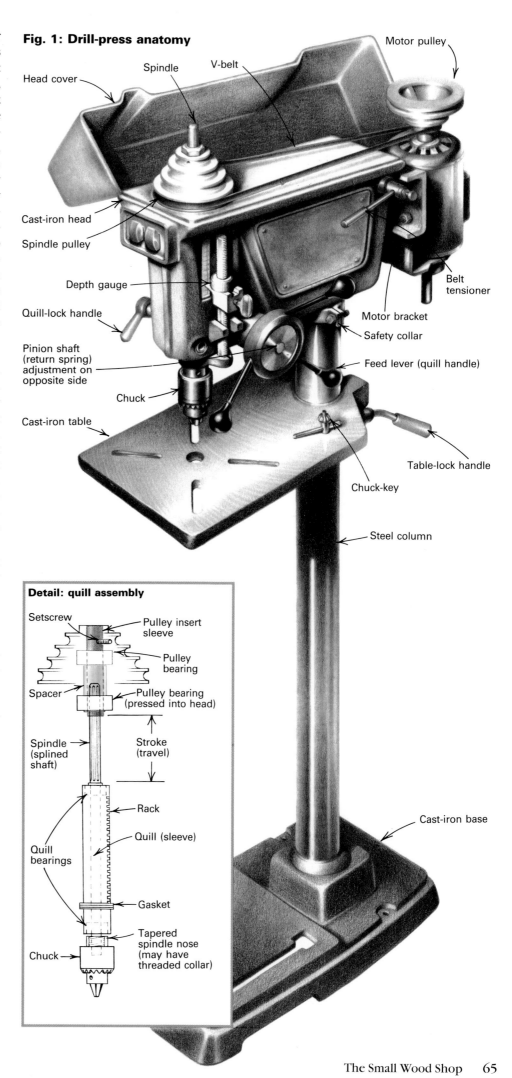

Fig. 1: Drill-press anatomy

Head cover

Spindle

V-belt

Motor pulley

Cast-iron head

Spindle pulley

Depth gauge

Quill-lock handle

Pinion shaft (return spring) adjustment on opposite side

Chuck

Cast-iron table

Belt tensioner

Motor bracket

Safety collar

Feed lever (quill handle)

Table-lock handle

Chuck-key

Steel column

Cast-iron base

Detail: quill assembly

Setscrew

Pulley insert sleeve

Pulley bearing

Spacer

Pulley bearing (pressed into head)

Spindle (splined shaft)

Stroke (travel)

Rack

Quill (sleeve)

Quill bearings

Gasket

Chuck

Tapered spindle nose (may have threaded collar)

When boring angled holes for splayed legs, Maas uses ramps like the pair in the foreground (above). A pocket-hole fixture (left, background) makes sloped (75°) holes for recessed screws. The steel vise (right, background) serves as a tilting table, which can precisely hold small pieces.

A V-block cradles a dowel being bored with a Forstner bit (left). To make the cradle, the author cut 45° chamfers on two edges of a foot-long 2x4, ripped the 2x4 in half and glued the halves together.

(cradle), a pocket-hole fixture and a riser block (ramp). A V-block (see the photo above left) allows you to bore almost any cylindrical workpiece. If you try to bore a hole in a dowel freehand, the dowel will roll, and you will have a devil of a time getting the hole where you want it. But you can stabilize the dowel by cradling it in a V-block. To make a V-block, simply cut a 45° chamfer along two edges of a 1-ft. length of 2x4; then rip the piece in half, and glue the halves together to form a 90° cradle.

A pocket-hole fixture comes in handy when you need to make angled holes for screws that fasten an apron to a tabletop's underside or screws that join stiles to rails in a cabinet face frame. The fixture is L-shaped and like the V-block, forms a 90° cradle (see the photo above right). But a pocket holer tilts the workpiece at about a 75° angle. When using a pocket holer, always bore the large hole (land) that recesses the screw head first. Then bore the hole for the screw shank most of the way through before turning the work over to back drill. If you want your pocket holes in a neat line, add a fence to the setup.

You'll also need holes that are angled to the work surface when socketing splayed legs for a stool. If your press has a tilting table, you can bore the angled holes directly. Whenever I do this, however, my lumber, clamps and ruler end up on the floor. A good solution is to build a riser block or ramp, which is simply an inclined auxiliary table. To make a project-specific ramp, just cobble together some plywood scraps to form the table angle you need as well as a base with a clamping ear. A variation of this has a hinged table, so you can bore at almost any angle, much like a tilting table. The photo above right shows a couple of ramps that my students have made over the years.

A steel drill-press vise (see the photo above right), sometimes called a milling vise or an angle vise (also available from Enco), mimics a tilting table. But, because they have machined jaws with intersecting grooves to improve their grip, these vises let you precisely hold small objects, such as tubing and rods. They're also great finger savers. The more sophisticated vises have swiveling bases and cross slides, which allow you to hold odd-shaped pieces at very precise alignments to your drill-press spindle. Although some vises can be expensive, their accuracy and durability justifies the cost.

Other functions and accessories

The press can perform many secondary functions that are variations on boring, such as countersinking screw holes. You also can counterbore (superimpose a large hole over a smaller one) by clamping the work and using a Forstner or Multi-Spur bit. With a set of plug cutters (see the sidebar on the facing page) you can make cross-grain plugs for hiding counterbored screws, instead of using end-grain dowels. With a fence and a Forstner or Multi-Spur bit, you've got a basic mortiser; just bore interlocking holes and chisel the resulting slot square. A hollow-chisel mortising bit and a drill-press yoke will let you do both operations at once (see *FWW* #83, pp. 52-56).

For some drill-press users, a set of drum sanders for smoothing curved edges is also a must. But because drum sanding exerts substantial side pressure, you're likely to cause premature wear on the chuck, spindle or bearings. This is true for drill-press grinding and routing, too. Furthermore, drill-press routing isn't very effective because the press can generate only about one-fifth of the necessary speed. And without a guard and anti-kick-back pawls, the procedure is dangerous. For these reasons, I leave sanding, grinding and routing to the tools designed specifically for those functions and save the drill press for the boring operations that it does so well. □

Bernie Maas is an associate professor of woodworking at Edinboro University of Pennsylvania.

Sources of supply

Information on sharpening methods and recommended speeds for bits is furnished by the following bit manufacturers.

Machine spur and Multi-Spur:
Forrest City Tool Co. (a division of Textron Corp), 620 23rd St. N. W., Hickory, NC 28601.

Forstner:
CONVALCO, 102 Washington St., PO Box 1957, New Britain, CT 06050

Spade:
Irwin Co., 92 Grant St., Wilmington, OH 45177

Powerbore:
Stanley Tools (a division of Stanley Works), 600 Myrtle St., New Britain, CT 06050

Twist drills and plug cutters:
Vermont American Tool Co., PO Box 340, Lincolnton, NC 28093.

Common woodworking bits

Multi-Spur

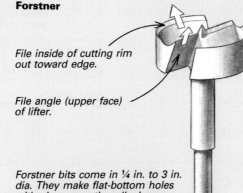

File relief of tooth at factory angles; avoid shifting its tip.

File lifter's upper face rather than the lower clearance angle.

Brad point

If properly sharpened, lifter shears after tip cuts hole's edge.

Multi-spur bits come in ⅜ in. to 4 in. dia. and are your best choice for holes larger than 1 in. They have brad points to seat and lead them into wood. They use saw-like teeth arranged in a circle to cut the outside of the hole and recessed lifter tips, which shear off and eject the wood chips. Bits can start holes at almost any angle, bore overlapping holes (good for mortises and rabbets) and start holes on curved surfaces or cylindrical workpieces.

Forstner

File inside of cutting rim out toward edge.

File angle (upper face) of lifter.

Forstner bits come in ¼ in. to 3 in. dia. They make flat-bottom holes with glass-smooth walls. Large Forstner bits usually have tiny cone-shaped lead points. Ersatz-Forstner bits have long lead points but won't make flat-bottom holes. The bits combine an outside razor-edged circular band, which cuts wood fibers with an interior pair of lifters that hog out material. Because lifters and cutters act on the same plane, these bits are increasingly grabby with size. Bits can bore angled holes, overlapping holes and holes on curved surfaces.

Powerbore

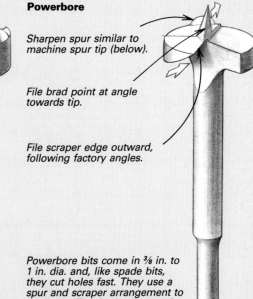

Sharpen spur similar to machine spur tip (below).

File brad point at angle towards tip.

File scraper edge outward, following factory angles.

Powerbore bits come in ⅜ in. to 1 in. dia. and, like spade bits, they cut holes fast. They use a spur and scraper arrangement to cut holes. They're less expensive than other brad-point bits and they make cleaner holes than spade bits.

Plug cutter

File upper angle of lifter.

File outside of rim toward cutting edge.

Plug cutters come in sizes from ¼ in. dia. to 2 in. dia., and come in lengths from under an inch to over 3 in. They use a cutting rim to scribe a hole's edge and a lifter to remove chips. Plug cutters can make a custom plug for almost any counterbored hole, whether to cover a screw head or to inlay some decoration.

Spade

Grind both edges of lead point.

Set tool rest to grind scraper edge(s) at a 5° to 10° rake angle.

Spade bits come in ¼ in. to 1½ in. dia. They're made for quick, rough holes. They have long, sharp-edged lead points, and either one or two scrapers. Bits work well in endgrain, and if you need a hole with a different-shaped bottom, just grind the spade to the profile you need. If you need an in-between sized bit, you can grind its outside diameter down to size.

Machine spur

Brad point

File relief and flute lifter (avoid "belly").

File spur toward tip from inside.

Machine-spur (brad-point) bits come in ¹⁄₁₆ in. to 1¼ in. dia. These are the best all-around hole makers for wood. They have two perimeter spurs that sever wood fibers, and lifters scrape out the interior of the hole. Brad (diamond) point starts and leads the bit into the wood.

Choose the right bit and keep it sharp

Many of us have chucked twist bits in a drill press because they're cheap and handy. While twist drills can make holes in wood, they're really designed to cut metal. In contrast, screw-tipped bits, although made for wood (like augers designed for slow hand-boring), should never be used in a drill press. An auger in a press feeds itself too aggressively. The result is a torn-up hole or an unclamped workpiece whipping out of control. Luckily, there are better bit alternatives for boring crisp, precise holes in wood.

When I'm boring holes with a drill press, I usually use one of three bit types: machine spur (or brad point), Multi-Spur or Forstner. And although I don't use them as often—spade, Powerbore and plug-cutting—are three other bits that come in handy. All six types (shown in the drawing above) are designed to cut wood, so they are available from most woodworking-supply stores.

Basic bit care: Only run bits at their recommended speed, and don't toss them in a drawer. Instead, store them in an index, a cloth pouch, a rack or a compartmented wooden case. Also, douse bits with WD-40 every so often to discourage rust, and pol-ish the bit's flutes and spirals with steel wool to keep them running cool. To keep carbon steel bits surgically sharp, touch up their edges with auger-bit files. Don't worry about wire burrs left from filing; they'll be stropped away as you bore holes. For hardened-steel edges, like those on most spade bits, use a grindstone. If you want to sharpen your twist drills, see Ken Donnell's article in *Fine Woodworking* #82, pp. 72-74. Finally, if you think a bit has been used or honed beyond reason, don't despair, and don't toss it out. For a nominal fee, most bit makers will restore bits to their factory specs. —*B.M.*

Tuning Your Drill Press

How to find and eliminate vibration, play and wobble

by Robert M. Vaughan

To check for wobble in a chuck, place a dial indicator on the table with its plunger perpendicular to the chuck. Unplug the machine and turn the spindle pulley; the gauge will read any eccentricity.

W hether you buy a new drill press, a used one or you inherit one from granddad, you should periodically check its precision. Provided you've chucked in a straight, sharp bit, your press should run steadily, and it should bore clean holes. But there are basically three things that can prevent top performance in your press: vibration, play and wobble (runout).

Taking out vibration

Vibration usually originates at a press's drive system. If you feel vibration, open the head cover, turn the machine on and see if the pulleys idle smoothly and without noise, beyond the humming of the belt. If they don't, kill the power, remove the belt and check its condition. If the belt is brittle or has bumps or cuts, replace it. Next, hand spin the pulleys to see if they have any cracks or are out of round. Before replacing a pulley that wobbles, try retightening its setscrew. If there's rumble or growl when the pulleys are spinning, dirty or worn bearings are likely the problem and should be replaced (for more on this, see the article on pp. 83-85).

Removing quill side play and spindle end play

A press can develop side play between the head casting and the quill. To check for this, lower the quill and then shake it (not the chuck) from side to side to see how much slack there is. If the head casting is split at the front, there should be a bolt and locknut that will allow you to snug the halves together to take some of the play out. If your press has a solid head, then a remedy for side play is unlikely.

To check spindle end play, lock the quill, and try to move the chuck up and down. If there's end play, then the slack is probably between the quill and the collar above the upper quill bearing. To fix this, loosen the collar's setscrew, and slide the collar back to its original position. If you're lucky, a plate will be on the front of the head to access the collar. If not, the feed lever and the pinion will have to be removed along with releasing tension off the quill's return spring. This procedure is tricky and somewhat dangerous, so if your machine's instruction manual doesn't cover how to disassemble the spring assembly, have a professional do the work.

From *Fine Woodworking* (May 1992) 94:60-61

Wobble and how to find it

A wobbly chuck usually results from poor techniques. For example, you get a bit hung up in a workpiece and it swings around and bangs the column; or you let a workpiece dance around on the table while you're drum sanding the inside of a tight curve.

To detect and measure wobble, you'll need a dial indicator mounted on a magnetic base. First, chuck in a precision rod of known straightness. I use a ½-in.-dia. by 2-in.-long hardened, ground-steel dowel. Next, put the indicator's base on the table or column, so the plunger is touching the end of the rod. With the press unplugged and the head cover open, hand turn the spindle pulley and watch the indicator to pinpoint maximum fluctuation. Stop turning when the rod is at its farthest from the plunger. Wrap a piece of masking tape around the chuck, and mark a reference point above the plunger with a felt-tip marker. You can also check the outside of the chuck in this way (see the photo on the facing page). If I get more than .003-in. at the tip of the rod or more than .002-in. on the chuck, I feel it's time for some corrective action.

Correcting wobble with a smack

Rather than replacing your machine's most expensive parts (quill, spindle and chuck), you may be able to smack wobble out (see the bottom photo). Since a shock force knocked things out of alignment, an equal-and-opposite blow (within reason) can line things up again. Move the arm of the indicator out of the way, and then mount a hefty steel rod in the chuck and put on your safety glasses. Position the chuck so you can smack the rod directly opposite your mark. Your first tap should be a light one—similar to driving a ⅝-in. brad into soft pine. Chuck your precision rod, reposition the plunger and rotate the spindle to observe any change. Repeat until you've got less than .002-in. wobble.

Chuck removal

Occasionally, you'll have to remove a chuck to install a mortising yoke or to clean and repair the chuck. The backs of most chucks (including the key-and-scroll Jacob's type and the hand-tightening Albreicht type) have a tapered hole, which mounts either onto a matching tapered stud on the spindle nose or onto an adaptor that connects to the spindle. Chucks that mount directly to the spindle nose are usually held on either by a plain friction-fit or by a combination of friction and a threaded collar with snap ring.

If there's a ring with holes around the top of the chuck, you can unscrew this collar to force the chuck down off the spindle. To turn the collar, most press manufacturers provide a spanner (similar to an open-end wrench). Stick the spanner's pin into a hole in the lock ring, and insert the handle of the chuck-key into a chuck hole. Grip the key for leverage and loosen the collar by turning the spanner clockwise (see the center photo). Keep turning, even though it'll feel like the collar is tightening again as it bears against the top of the chuck. If it doesn't break free, wrap a cloth around the chuck, and clamp it in a drill-press table vise. Then try to unscrew the collar.

Chucks without collars can often be popped off with an ordinary open-end wrench. First, lower the quill to expose the top of the chuck, and lock the quill. Then take a wrench that fits over the shaft between the chuck and the quill, and dislodge the chuck by snapping the wrench upward, as shown in the top photo. If the chuck doesn't come off, rotate the spindle a half turn, add some Liquid Wrench and try again. Your next options are to try either prying the chuck off with a set of Jacob's-brand removal wedges or taking the quill assembly out of the head and bringing it to a machinist or service center to have the chuck removed.

To remove a chuck from an adaptor, first use a drift wedge to dislodge the adaptor (with chuck). Then drill a hole in a block of

There are two ways to remove most chucks. For chucks without a collar (above), lower and lock the quill and insert an open-end wrench above the chuck. Snap the wrench upward to pop the chuck off. To remove chucks with threaded collars (right), grip a chuck hole by inserting the handle of the chuck-key, and turn the collar clockwise with a spanner.

The author uses a hammer to remove wobble (below). He taps a chucked steel rod and then rechecks for runout with a dial indicator and a precision rod.

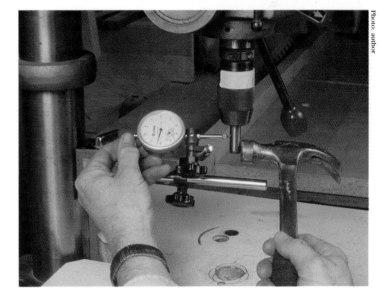

Photo: author

wood to accept the Morse-taper end of the adaptor. Split the block in two, and clamp it around the adaptor in a vise. Twist the chuck off with the key or a pipe wrench.

Chuck remounting

To remount taper-fit chucks, first clean the mating surfaces with a dry rag and press the chuck onto the spindle by hand. Next, retract the chuck's jaws and strike the bottom of the chuck squarely with a wooden mallet. Or reseat the chuck by lowering it evenly against a piece of plywood laid on the press's table. If the spindle's nose is worn, a couple of drops of cyanocrylate (super glue) can often hold it in place, and the resulting bond still can be broken easily when needed. Finally, check concentricity with the indicator and the straight rod again, and, if needed, fine-tune things with a few hammer taps on the heavier rod. You'll be amazed how light a blow it takes to align things. □

Robert Vaughan is a contributing editor to FWW.

To avoid gouging the wood, the author keeps the sander's platen flat on the board at the beginning and end of each stroke. He guides the sander, but lets the machine's weight provide the sanding pressure.

Flat or curved edges can be smoothed with a belt sander. Here, Becksvoort sands a table's edge and frequently checks the edge with a try square to make sure it remains square with the top.

Using a Portable Belt Sander
An abrasive approach to flat surfaces and smooth curves

by C.H. Becksvoort

The portable belt sander is a real workhorse in my shop. It grinds down humps and bumps, levels large surfaces in a fraction of the time it would take to plane and scrape them, and it smooths even highly figured woods like bird's-eye maple. It's a versatile tool for everything from removing paint to shaping cabriole legs. But a belt sander can also be a recalcitrant tool and difficult to live with. At its worst, it refuses to track correctly, and it gouges the wood, sputters and coughs while spewing clouds of fine dust. Over the years, I've come to terms with the tool and in this article, I'll show you how to handle the most common sanding problems and get good performance from your machine.

Belt-sander anatomy—All portable belt sanders work pretty much in the same way. The sander's motor powers the rear drive roller through a gear reduction drive. Most sanders are belt driven, but the better, heavy-duty sanders are chain driven. The front roller, which rotates freely, is spring-loaded to tension the sanding belt. A lever releases the tension whenever the belt must be installed or removed. Turning an adjustment knob swivels the curved front roller slightly and coaxes the belt to track correctly and ride dead center on the rollers. A rigid platen between the two rollers provides a flat sanding area. The belt itself is backed by a replaceable steel wear plate that rests on a cork cushion that is attached to the platen. Sacrificial steel or ceramic strike bars prevent the edge of the rotating belt from damaging the sander's housing.

Using the belt sander—A belt sander is a relatively safe machine, but there are a few common-sense precautions that you should observe while operating one. Belt sanders typically weigh from 8 lbs. to 15 lbs. and most require two hands to operate safely. Although a dust bag is a valuable accessory, it won't pick up all of the dust, so wearing a mask is a must. Always wear safety glasses. Most belt sanders are noisy and high pitched; if you expect a lengthy session, it's also a good idea to use ear protection.

Before beginning to sand, unplug the machine and clean the dust intake chute of any clogged dust and chips. Then, make sure the belt is installed properly. The arrows on the belt's cloth or paper backing should point in the direction of roller rotation. This ensures that the belt's bonded seam won't catch on the work and tear the belt. After you adjust the belt to track correctly, you're ready to sand.

Sanding belts are available in grit sizes from 36 through 180, but I only use 80- through 150-grit for sanding hardwood furniture. The coarse grits, from 36 to 60, are for removing paint, gross leveling and sculpting. Because grits above 150 tend to burn the wood,

From *Fine Woodworking* (September 1989) 78:80-81

It takes practice to handle a belt sander with enough precision to smooth small-radius, curved surfaces with the front roller, as Becksvoort is doing here.

I use an orbital sander or I hand-sand with finer grits for final smoothing. I'm partial to cloth belts, even though they are more expensive than paper, because they wear longer and tear less. I've also found that alumina oxide abrasive will out-last garnet, which sands aggressively but fractures easily and wears out rapidly. Deciding when to change belts is a trade-off between the cost of a new belt and the additional time required to sand with a well-worn belt. My rule of thumb is to change the belt when its surface feels like the next higher grit. I don't throw the used belts away; they're great for hand-sanding on the lathe. If you are working with a glued-up piece, it's important to scrape off residual glue that could gum up and ruin the sanding belt.

As with hand tools, the best way to develop skill and competence with a belt sander is to practice. With time, you'll develop confidence in the tool and discover that it is a real time-saver for a wide variety of sanding tasks. But don't start off by practicing on furniture; instead, use scrapwood. Here are some techniques to practice for smoothing large, flat panels and narrow frames, leveling irregular surfaces and shaping curved surfaces.

Smoothing panels–To smooth large, flat surfaces, it's necessary to keep the sander level, move the machine at a uniform speed and apply uniform pressure. As with most sanding operations, you should avoid sanding across the grain.

Be sure the workpiece is firmly anchored on a flat, horizontal surface, and positioned at a comfortable height. I usually secure the piece to my bench with the end vise and dogs, but alternative clamping schemes could be developed for each job. Next, place the sander flat on the panel and sand along one edge, parallel with the grain. The weight of the belt sander alone provides sufficient sanding pressure, so it isn't necessary to bear down. Besides, applying pressure is tiring and makes it difficult to maintain the consistency necessary to produce a uniformly sanded surface. It's more important to concentrate on guiding the sander in long strokes at a constant speed. I drape the sander's electrical cord over my shoulder to keep it out of the way as I move with the sander along the full length of the workpiece. I let the sander run no more than half its length over the end of the work; keeping at least one half of the platen flat on the stock, as shown in the left photo on the facing page, helps prevent gouges in the wood. Then, I pull the sander back in the opposite direction, overlapping the previous pass by one half of the width of the sanding belt. The process is repeated until the surface is completely sanded. If the surface is free of U-shape tracks at each end of the workpiece, you probably have the hang of it. Avoid any tendency to move the sander more slowly at the ends of the workpiece or you'll risk gouging or beveling the surface.

Leveling surfaces–The belt sander also can be used like a jack plane to remove bumps and high spots and to level a surface. My procedure is fairly simple. I start by holding a straight edge at one end of the board so it's perpendicular to the grain. Then, I put a pencil mark wherever the straight edge touches the wood's surface. I repeat this procedure every 2 in. along the full length of the board. The sander is used in the same way as described for smoothing surfaces, except that I concentrate on removing the high spots indicated by the pencil marks. To blend smoothly, I allow the sander to overlap a short distance into the adjacent "valleys." The whole process is then repeated, usually three or four times, until the board's surface is perfectly flat.

Edges and frames–Once you've gotten the hang of handling a belt sander and mastered the technique of smoothing large, flat surfaces, you're ready to tackle edge sanding. Like jointing an edge with a plane, the trick is to keep the sander stable on the center of the edge and to sand along the full length of the board. One thing that makes a sander different from a plane is that the sander continues to remove material on the backstroke, so be careful as you pull the sander back. Check the edge with a try square frequently to make sure the sander has not tilted up or down. It's important to keep the sander level and maintain that position as you sand. Even a curved edge, like the one shown in the right photo on the facing page, can be sanded this way.

Belt sanders are also useful for smoothing frame-and-panel doors. The panels, whether flat or raised, are most easily sanded before they are assembled into the frames. The frames also require special treatment because the grain directions of the stiles and rails run perpendicular to each other. I sand the rails first, but I'm careful to let the sander travel across the joint onto the stile only enough to flatten the joint. After the rails have been smoothed, the stiles can be sanded. It's important that the belt is tracking to the extreme edge of the platen: In this way, I can smooth the stile and remove any cross-grain scratches introduced when the rails were sanded, without crossing the joint and spoiling the already-smoothed rail. Here again, sand in long, even strokes; resist the temptation to slow down in the critical corner areas. Mitered corners, of course, will have to be smoothed with a pad sander.

The sanding techniques for frames can also be used to smooth the face frame of a chest of drawers or other furniture piece. It's more difficult because the frame members are usually shorter and narrower. Lay the carcase on its back so you can sand horizontally. A steady hand and control of the belt sander are required to keep the narrow surfaces flat and not introduce cross-grain scratches where the rails join the vertical stiles. When you are confident enough to take on a challenge, like sanding the face of a walnut dresser with an 80-grit belt, or using the front roller to sand curved surfaces as shown in the photo above, left, you'll be well on your way toward taming the beast in the belt sander. □

Christian Becksvoort, a professional furnituremaker in New Gloucester, Maine, is a Contributing Editor to FWW.

Belt/Disc Sander Upgrade

Minor modifications improve belt tracking and dust collection

by William Tandy Young

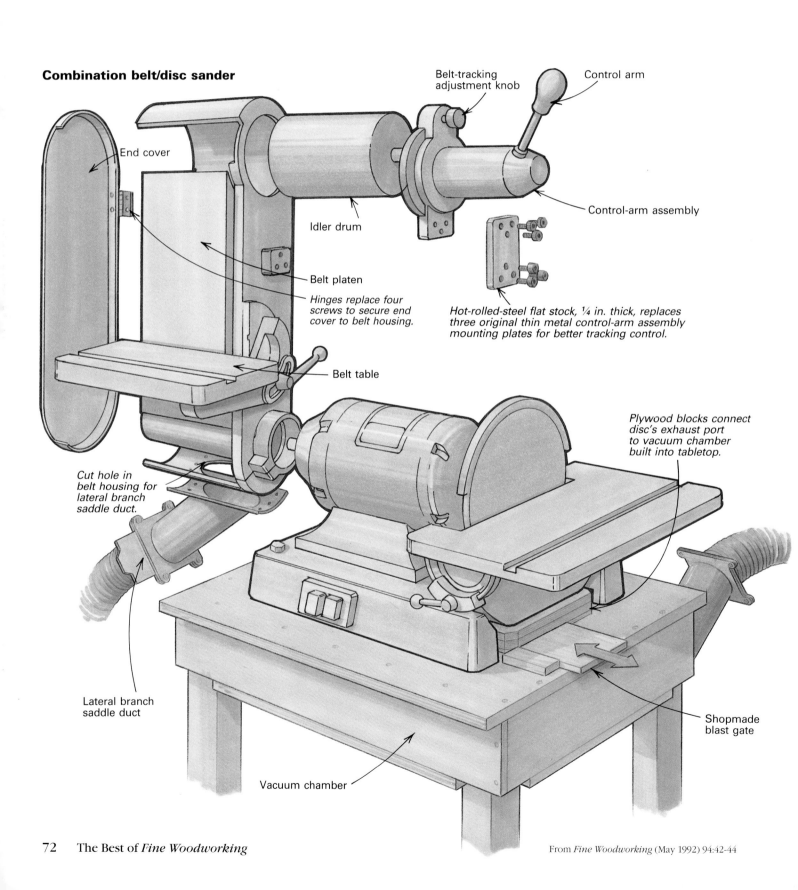

Combination belt/disc sander

End cover

Belt-tracking adjustment knob

Control arm

Control-arm assembly

Idler drum

Belt platen

Hinges replace four screws to secure end cover to belt housing.

Hot-rolled-steel flat stock, ¼ in. thick, replaces three original thin metal control-arm assembly mounting plates for better tracking control.

Belt table

Plywood blocks connect disc's exhaust port to vacuum chamber built into tabletop.

Cut hole in belt housing for lateral branch saddle duct.

Lateral branch saddle duct

Shopmade blast gate

Vacuum chamber

From *Fine Woodworking* (May 1992) 94:42-44

T he combination belt/disc sander is a tool that is probably not on many peoples' list of basic essentials. But the combination sander in our shop has grown to be a necessity that can help move work along in unrivaled fashion. The possibility of owning one of these versatile machines has in recent years been enhanced by the appearance of several modestly priced Taiwanese brands that have the potential for top performance.

The word *potential* is key because, like many inexpensive light-industrial tools, the Taiwanese sander shown in the photo at right, did not arrive at my doorstep perfectly designed and manufactured. However, because the machine had sound, basic components, such as castings, bearings and controls, I was able to get it to perform quite well with a certain amount of remedial upgrading. But be aware that any of these changes may void your warranty. I've taken a generic approach in my discussion of these upgrades because they apply to similar sanders offered by other importers.

Compensating for high speed

The first thing I noticed about the sander after setting it up was that the belt ran too fast for optimal woodworking. Indeed, both belt and disc functions can professionally burn endgrain on short notice. Because the unit is driven directly by an AC-induction motor, the only remedy for the excessive speed is to use sharp (fresh), high-quality abrasives and a light touch with the workpiece (both are good habits to develop anyway). There are advantages to mounting a direct-drive motor between the disc and belt sanders, however. This arrangement allows room for using the belt sander without interference from the disc cowling, as on some belt-driven machines, and the direct drive provides a disc sander that runs remarkably true and needs no further modification.

Belt-tracking modifications

Belt-sander tracking was the next issue I had to deal with. Lateral belt tracking on this machine is controlled with the spring-loaded control-arm assembly at the top of the belt housing, which is fitted with an adjustment knob for fine tuning. But the sandwich of thin metal plates that link the control-arm assembly (including the idler drum) to the belt housing are not stiff enough to ensure continuously true belt tracking. At the suggestion of a smart, neighborly machinist, I replaced these plates with a solid piece of ¼-in.-thick hot-rolled-steel flat stock that's 2 in. wide by 3¼ in. long (see the drawing at left). The plates and the control-arm assembly are easily removed from the belt-housing body by backing out six Allen bolts. Using one of the original thin plates as a template, I drilled slightly oversized bolt holes in the new ¼-in.-thick plate. The over-sized holes allowed some front-to-back adjustment so that the idler drum could be aligned with the platen and the drive drum.

Although tracking improved dramatically with these upgrades, I still found the belt-tracking adjustment knob to be extremely sensitive as a consequence of the basic system design. However, there are advantages to this design that more than outweigh the inconvenience of having to monitor the position of the belt during use. The main advantage is the ease with which the belts can be changed. You simply pull down the control arm (which relaxes the idler-drum tension) and slip the belt off the drums.

Hinging the end cover for easier belt changes

The only real hitch in the belt-changing process is the end cover of the belt housing. As shipped from the factory, the end cover was screwed to the belt-housing casting in four places and was rather laborious to remove for belt changes. So I simply hinged the cover to the housing, as shown in the photo above. I placed shims between the hinge leaves and the belt housing to compensate for the

To adapt his belt sander for dust collection, the author cut a hole in the bottom of the belt housing. He also connected the disc sander's exhaust port to the table, which acts as a vacuum chamber.

thickness of the cover lip, and I ground off the excess length of the sheet-metal screws (used to mount the hinges) inside the cover in deference to the well-being of the belt. I found that bending the lip of the cover a bit here and there created a friction fit to the housing that would hold the cover closed without a latch.

Because belt changes are speedy with the hinged cover, I don't hesitate to change grits or use dedicated belts for different materials. The belt drums on this sander are manufactured with ample crowns to aid in positive, steady belt tracking, but the crowns can distort the belt's flatness across its width after a period of time. Additionally, since belt tension is not adjustable with this system, the belt continually takes the maximum amount of spring tension manufactured into the control-arm assembly. I think of this as a graphic depiction of job stress and give the belt a rest every evening by removing it from the sander.

Belt-platen tricks for longer belt life

Removing the belt overnight will help increase its life, but no belt would last very long while cascading over the sharp leading edge on the belt platen of this machine. I carefully relieved the leading and trailing edges with a mill file. And, while I was at it, I eased all the unnecessary sharp edges throughout the machine.

Another trick to increase belt life and performance is to reduce friction between belt and platen by using graphite (commonly sold in pad and stick form.) Rather than attaching pads to the platen, I

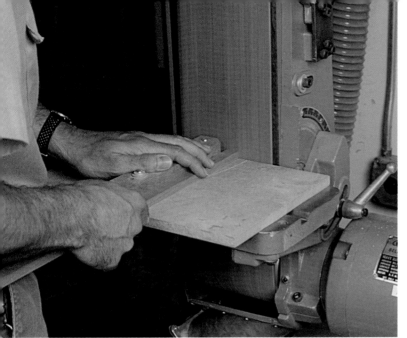

The author built two sliding tables: one with a 90° fence and one with a pair of 45° fences for accurate end sanding. The tables ride in the miter-gauge slots.

the rear, as shown in the photo on p. 73. A hole in the stand's top lines up with the exhaust port for the disc sander, and a stack of plywood blocks, with holes in their centers, slip over the exhaust port and connect to the stand. Included in the plywood blocks is a shopmade, plywood blast gate to control the vacuum.

To provide dust collection for the belt sander, I ran a branch off the main line into a lateral branch saddle duct fit to a hole that I cut in the bottom of the belt housing. The branch saddle is a dust-collection-system fitting available in various sizes. This one is designed to fit a 7-in.-dia. duct pipe and reduces to a 4-in.-dia. opening for a blast gate and hose. To cut the hole in the belt housing, I first removed the control-arm assembly, the belt table and the belt platen, as shown in the drawing on p. 72. Then by loosening two bolts, I removed the entire belt housing. I traced the branch-saddle opening and cut the hole in the belt housing with a metal cutting blade in a variable-speed sabersaw. I screwed the saddle on with self-tapping sheet-metal screws, and I used just enough flex hose to allow the belt housing to be rotated to its horizontal position. This fitting does a superb job of collecting dust and replaces my earlier inadequate attempt of connecting the vacuum to the end cover. The wooden plug on the end cover in the photo on p. 73 shows you where *not* to attach a vacuum hose.

sparingly rub a graphite stick (Process Engineering Corp., Crystal Lake, Ill. 60039-0279; 815-459-1734) on the platen as needed. Graphite should not be applied to the belt or to the drums because any buildup will reduce drive friction, affect tracking and over-stress the belt. After removing the belt and unplugging the sander, I periodically remove any excess graphite from the drums with paint thinner.

Adding dust collection

Once I had fine-tuned the sander, I used it more often, and, consequently, I discovered what a dust generator it is. Although my sander had an exhaust port under the disc, it had no port for the belt. Since I needed a stand for the machine, I built one with an enclosed box beneath its top that acts as a collection chamber for the disc sander. The main dust collection line enters the box from

Auxiliary tables for accurate sanding

The modifications described here have greatly increased the performance of my machine, but various jigs have contributed to really accurate sanding. For example, I made plywood tables like the one shown in the top photo at left that have strips screwed to their bottoms that ride in the tables' miter-gauge slots. One table has a fence that's 90° to the belt, and the other has a pair of 45° angled fences. Unfortunately, because of variations in the two miter-gauge slot locations, I need a different set of tables for the belt and disc functions, but when end sanding pieces for a precise fit, these tables are indispensable. □

William Tandy Young is a professional cabinetmaker and conservator in Stow, Mass.

Shopmade sanding belts

Epoxied butt joint ———————————— by Bill Skinnner

I've been making sanding belts for my stroke sander and smaller machines for more than 40 years. I use an angled butt joint reinforced with a strip of Kevlar cloth (similar to fiberglass but much stronger) glued to the back of the belt with Hexcel Epolite 2461 epoxy resin (see the photo at right). The belts joined with this system are plenty strong (I haven't broken one yet), and the butt joint allows me to run the belt in either direction. Kevlar cloth and Hexcel Epolite resin, which are commonly used by boatbuilders, are available from the Fiberglass Mart (12619 Highway 99 S., Everett, Wash. 98204; 206-743-0332). One quart of resin and hardener and ⅓ yd. of Kevlar cost about $40, which should do all the belts you'll ever use.

I cut the belt stock (cloth-backed only) about 4 in. longer than required for the finished belt and clamp it along a straight edge with the ends overlapped to yield a belt of the exact length needed. With a sharp knife guided by a straightedge, I cut through both layers of abrasive to create a perfect butt joint. An angled joint reduces bumping as the joint passes over the platen.

I reinforce the joint with a 1-in.-wide strip of Kevlar glued with a spoonful of resin/hardener. I put a piece of waxed paper under the belt and over the Kevlar strip and then clamp a short piece of 2x2 over the joint and let it set overnight. □

_____

Bill Skinner is a retired cabinetmaker in Everett, Wash.

Photo: Bill Skinner

Butt-joined sanding belts are easy to make, and they can be run in either direction. The author glues a strip of Kevlar cloth across the back side of the joint with Hexcel Epolite epoxy resin.

A Disc Sander on a Bandsaw

Getting double duty from a common shop tool

by Roger Ronald

With a few hours' work and about $20 worth of hardware, I added a disc sander to my Rockwell/Delta 14-in. bandsaw (see the top photo). When I bought the saw secondhand, the door for the sheet-metal box that covers the drive pulley and belt on the back of the saw was missing. The shaft protruded 2 in. beyond the pulley, a condition that gave me the idea for mounting a sanding disc there. Because sawing is done only from the machine's front, there is no interference between sawing and sanding functions. For safety reasons, it's best to keep all the moving parts, except the face of the disc, under cover—either the original belt cover or a shopmade box of wood or metal.

Mounting the sanding disc—To attach the ½-in.-thick disc to the shaft (see the bottom photo), I simply bolted a 3½-in.-dia. solid-steel pulley to the disc through three holes, evenly spaced around the pulley to ensure good balance. I chose a solid-steel pulley because it's easier to drill than cast iron and stronger than one made of sheet metal. If your bandsaw's lower shaft doesn't extend beyond the pulley, you could replace the pulley with one made from solid steel and drill the mounting holes directly in it; just make sure the bolts don't interfere with the belt groove.

I cut out the large sanding disc to have a diameter of 12½ in.; the smaller plywood disc in the photo acts as a spacer to keep the sanding disc clear of the sheet-metal box. The heads of the ⅜-in.-dia. mounting bolts are counterbored into the sanding disc's surface. I trued up the sanding disc and trimmed it to exactly 12 in. (to fit commercial adhesive-backed sandpaper discs) with a router after mounting the assembly on the shaft. I did this by clamping a router with a straight bit to a sturdy table and positioning the router so that the cutting edge of the bit contacted the edge of the disc. Then I rotated the disc by hand, moving the router in bit by bit until I had cut a perfect 12-in.-dia. circle. I sealed the plywood disc with a two-part epoxy coating to prevent splinters from pulling away from its surface when sandpaper is peeled off.

The tilting table—By adding a tilting table to a disc sander, straight-edge sanding is improved, large pieces are more manageable and sanding at precise angles becomes possible. Most of the table dimensions are arbitrary or will depend on the bandsaw. After bolting two uprights to the saw's base, I experimented with the placement of the table's pivot point until the table edge would stay close to the disc even when tilted. This point was 1 in. from the plane of the disc and ⅝ in. below the work surface. I used ½-in.-dia. bolts for the pivots, with flat washers between the wooden parts. The lock-adjustment handle is a 1¼-in.-dia. dowel with a threaded connector imbedded in its end. The connector draws a carriage bolt's square shaft tightly into the table-edge extension (see the bottom photo). □

Roger Ronald works out of a garage shop in Sachse, Tex.

This 14-in. bandsaw has a sanding disc mounted on its lower drive shaft. The table's front edge is beveled so that it can be tilted and locked at any angle up to 45° (above).

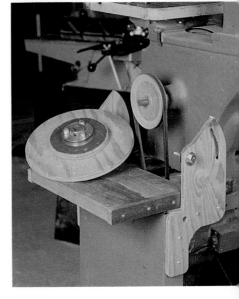

The author bolted a standard pulley to a plywood sanding disc, and mounted the disc on the bandsaw's drive shaft. The smaller plywood disc between the pulley and the large sanding disc is just a spacer. A bent nail in the end of the table-edge extension (far right in photo at right) points to an angle gauge written on a strip of paper that's taped to the upright's edge.

Machines on Wheels

*Hinges, handles and casters
make tools roll to save space,
but stay put when in use*

by Jim Boesel,
Drawings by Jim Richey

Moving tools around *is a fact of life
for woodworkers with restricted shop space. The setup
shown here, two lawn mower wheels mounted on the back of the
tool's base, works great for moving tablesaws. The handles are placed
at a good height for lifting and pivot out of the way when not in use.*

From *Fine Woodworking* (November 1992) 97:60-63

Every woodworker would love to have enough space so that every machine could be set up and ready to go at all times. In reality, most shops don't provide that luxury. As often as not, woodworking machines have to share a garage with, of all things, a car. And even if the shop space is sacred unto itself, tool collections have a way of outgrowing space the way kids outgrow clothes. For many woodworkers, the only solution is to move a machine into whatever open space is available when they need to use it and then stow it away again to make room for the next machine to be used. Unfortunately, most floor-model machines are designed to be heavy and stable; ease of movement is a minus not a plus, so woodworkers have had to figure out how to make machines mobile when necessary while keeping them stable when they're in use.

In a letter to the editor in *Fine Woodworking* #93 (March/April 1992), Charles Klaveness of Hempstead, N.Y., asked other readers for ideas about how to stabilize tools on wheels. In response, we received more than 20 letters with suggestions ranging from sources for commercial locking casters (see the sources of supply box on p. 79) to tried-and-true methods used in the theater to move scenery and props quickly and efficiently. Here is a distillation of the best of these ideas.

Tip onto two wheels

One of the most direct approaches was sent in by Dean Stevick of Herndon, Va. (see the drawing at left). Stevick attached two lawn mower wheels to the back of his tablesaw, so the tool still sits solidly on the floor but can be moved by lifting its front end. The wheels were mounted on an axle made from a ½-in.-dia concrete anchor bolt with a 90° bend in one end. The metal brackets that hold the axle were bolted to the saw's base. Stevick recommends the wheels be mounted no more than ⅛ in. above the floor when the machine is standing upright. And he advises against using this method on top-heavy machines like a drill press or bandsaw.

Mounting wheels on the back side of a machine works well as long as you can lift one end without too much difficulty. J. Rufford Harrison offered a similar method but added two oak handles that make lifting a heavy machine much easier on the back (see the drawing at left). The handles are bolted to the machine's base or stand so that they normally hang vertically alongside the machine and out of the way. When the handles are pivoted up to the horizontal position, they bump into another bolt that prevents further rotation and provides the leverage to lift the machine. The handles can be placed at a height that gives the most leverage and that makes it easy to roll the tool around like a wheel barrow.

Stabilizing swivel casters

The above method is fine if you have the room to manuever the machine forward and back on two wheels when making sharp turns, but what if you, like T.L. Manley Jr. of Coraopolis, Pa., have to turn your bandsaw on a dime to move it around a cramped shop? Manley mounted his bandsaw on four swivel casters for optimal manueverability and then bolted two straight-line toggle clamps to the angle iron used to mount the casters, as shown in the drawing at right below. The toggle clamps, or "thrust jacks" as Manley calls them, lift the weight of the tool slightly and act as brakes. Instead of using four jacks, one for each wheel, Manley used only two, but he has devised a way to lock the swivel mechanism on the other two casters to prevent any wobble at that end of the saw. He welded nuts on opposite sides of the caster base to receive small "crank" bolts that are sharpened to a point, so they will jam in notches ground in the caster's turntable (see the drawing at left below).

To align the wheels, he rolls the machine forward just before throwing the jacks down. This situates the wheels at a right angle to the force of the thrust when the saw is in use. Then he screws the crank bolts into the notches to eliminate any chance of the wheels changing position.

Another type of brake for a tool mounted on four casters was sent in by Pete Russell of Hilton Head Island, S.C. Russell simply

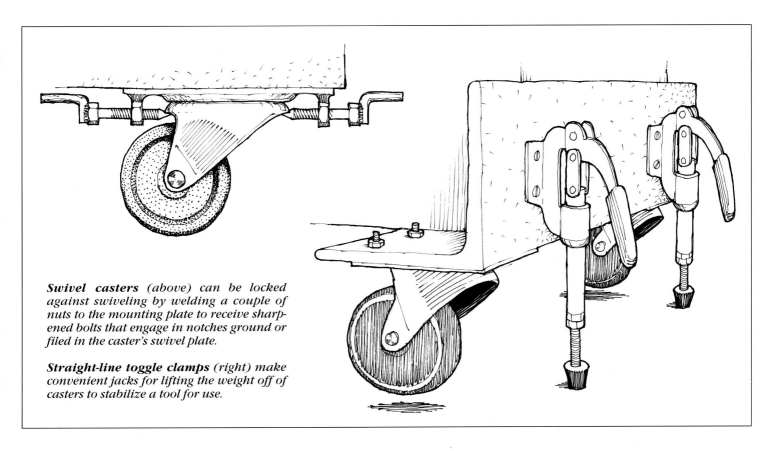

Swivel casters (above) can be locked against swiveling by welding a couple of nuts to the mounting plate to receive sharpened bolts that engage in notches ground or filed in the caster's swivel plate.

Straight-line toggle clamps (right) make convenient jacks for lifting the weight off of casters to stabilize a tool for use.

It doesn't take much to stop small diameter casters from rolling. Bent-wire stops slipped around each wheel (right) will do the job. Or raise the load off the wheels by driving opposed wedges against wedges attached to the underside of the machine's base (below).

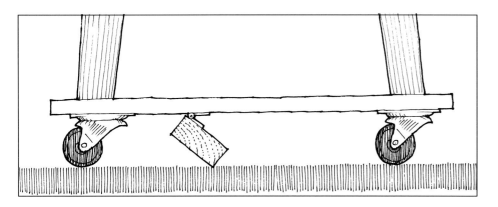

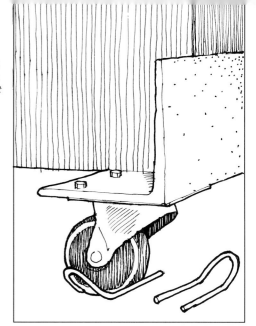

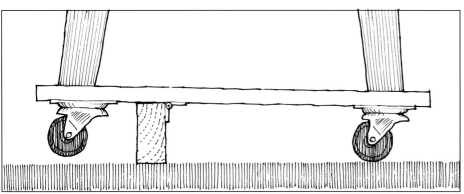

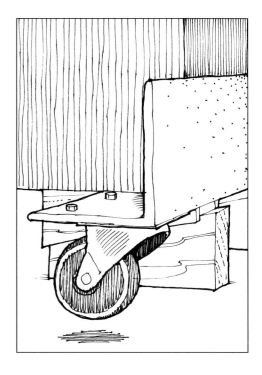

A 2x4 hinged to the bottom of a plywood platform will bounce along the floor when the tool is rolled in one direction. When you want to park the tool, just lift it slightly, and then rock it up onto the 2x4. Hinge the 2x4 so that the hinged joint resists the thrust of feeding material.

Hinged dollies are what stagehands use to move props and scenery. The basic method is to attach the wheels to a plywood plate and then to hinge the plywood to the base or legs of the machine. Two versions are shown below.

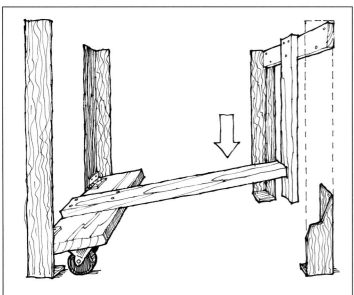

A simple latch activates this two-wheel dolly. The horizontal lever is screwed to the hinge plate. The vertical latch is screwed to a crosspiece or to the machine itself.

Pressing down on the lever deflects the latch. When the lever clears the latch, the latch springs back and locks the wheels in the down position.

hinged a 2x4 to a plywood platform (see the top left drawings on the facing page). When moving the saw, he pushes or pulls it front end first and the 2x4 bounces along the floor. When he wants to use the saw, he simply lifts the front end of the saw slightly and rocks it up onto the 2x4; the hinge joint jams to resist the thrust when feeding material from the front of the saw. If your floor is concrete, the weight of the saw provides enough friction to keep the 2x4 from sliding along the floor when the saw is in use. But Russell suggests that you could increase the friction, if necessary, by adding a rubber strip to the 2x4's bottom edge.

Hinged dollies facilitate a change of scenery

Hinges are also an integral element in the methods shown in the bottom drawings. According to a couple of the readers who sent in variations on this method, hinged dollies have been used for years to move theatrical scenery and props on and off stage in a hurry. Brian Ganter of Foxborough, Mass., mounts two heavy-duty casters on each of two pieces of plywood, which are then hinged to the machine's base or legs. A long arm is securely bolted to one of the plywood dollies so that it extends to the front of the machine and serves as a foot pedal. When you step on the pedal, you cause both sets of wheels to push down and to raise the machine an inch or two off the floor.

David Rogers of Thornhill, Ont., Canada, uses one two-wheel dolly with a simple spring latch to hold the wheels in the down position. The dolly is hinged to two legs as in Ganter's method, but the foot pedal (or lever) doesn't extend quite as far. Instead, the lever is just long enough to deflect the latch mechanism—a 1x2 extending down from a crosspiece attached to the other two legs of the machine's base. When the lever clears the 1x2 latch, the latch springs back and prevents the lever from moving back up. To lower the tool stand back to the floor, Rogers disengages the latch with a "deft little sideways kick, which leaves my foot in position to control the upward motion of the lever and to prevent the tool from dropping heavily."

Bob Thayer of Barnstable, Mass., another reader who credits his theatrical experience for similar methods, points out that leverage is increased by mounting the casters close to the hinge pivot point. He can lift his bandsaw equipped with hinged dollies with "only

finger pressure." Thayer also recommends two books, *Scene Design and Stage Lighting* by Parker and Smith (Holt, Rinehart and Winston, Inc.) and *Scenery for the Theatre* by Burris-Meyer and Cole (Little, Brown and Company), as good sources for variations on these methods.

A couple of low-tech approaches

Of course you could keep things really simple and just take Don Greenfield's advice. Greenfield, of Crofton, Ky., makes stops by bending a 9-in. length of ⅛-in.-dia. solid wire around a ¾-in. pipe clamp. He then takes the U-shaped wire and bends the curved end up at about 20°. Sliding one of these stops under each caster locks the wheels when the tool is in use, and the 20° bend makes it easy to pull them out when it's time to roll the tool away. Similarly low-tech is Scandia, Minn., woodworker Keith Hacker's idea for stabilizing mobile tools with wedges, as shown in the top right drawings on the facing page. □

Jim Boesel is a woodworker and writer living in Vancouver, Wash. Jim Richey, of Katy, Texas, edits and draws FWW's Methods of Work.

Sources of supply

The following companies carry casters or mobile bases for heavy machine tools. (The yellow pages for most large cities will also list caster suppliers.)

Delta International Machinery, 246 Alpha Drive, Pittsburgh, PA 15238; (412) 963-2400. (Locking mobile base.)

Garrett Wade Company, Inc., 161 Avenue of the Americas, New York, NY 10013; (212) 807-1155. (Rigid plate casters and locking swivel casters.)

Grizzly Imports, Inc., PO Box 2069, Bellingham, WA 98227; (206) 647-0801. (Locking mobile bases.)

HTC Products, Inc., PO Box 839, Royal Oak, MI 48068-0839; (800) 624-2027. (Locking mobile base.)

Payson Casters, Inc., 2323 Delaney Road, Gurnee, IL 60031-1287; (312) 336-6200. (Wide variety of locking casters.)

Shopsmith Inc., 3931 Image Drive, Dayton, OH 45414-2591; (800) 762-7555. (Retractable casters adaptable to any stand or base.)

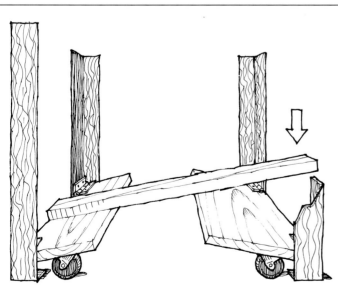

In this arrangement, a single lever can activate two sets of hinged casters.

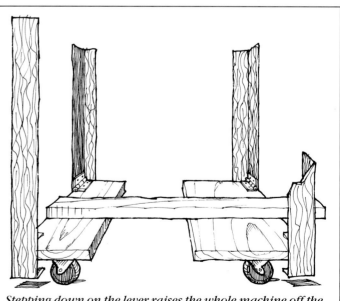

Stepping down on the lever raises the whole machine off the floor.

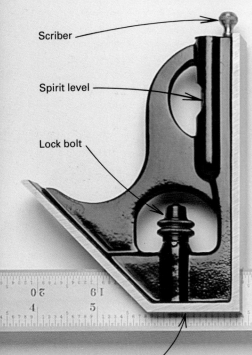

Scriber

Spirit level

Lock bolt

Square head

The Combination Square
A patternmaker's tips for getting the most out of this precision instrument

by Benjamin A. Wild

Center head

W hen I started my patternmaking apprenticeship 16 years ago, I was told to show up for work with a hammer and a combination square. I understood the need for a hammer, but I wondered why the square was so important. Besides the obvious use of laying out square and 45° miter lines, I soon found the combination square indispensable for accurately setting up and checking out machines as well as other layout work. Because a combination square is adjustable, it works quite well as a marking gauge and a height, depth and thickness gauge. It also transfers lengths of preset measure. Accessories, such as a protractor head for laying out angles and a center head for finding the center of round and square stock, extend the tool's usefulness. In addition to these techniques, I'll discuss some of the basic considerations for buying and using one of these versatile instruments.

Buy quality
When the boss saw the shiny, new, bargain-basement square that I bought, he threw it into the garbage. He then took me to the store and bought a Starrett square, protractor and center head set for me and deducted the cost from my first paycheck (L. S. Starrett Co., 121 Crescent St., Athol, Mass. 01331; 508-249-3551).

That Starrett square has fallen off benches, scaffolds and boats. The level vial is smashed, the scriber is lost and the paint is chipped. Recently, I put a 24-in. blade into it, set it on a surface plate (a precision ground granite table) and put it up against a 24-in. machinist's try square. I couldn't see light between the blades anywhere. After 16 years of hard use, it's as good as the day it was made. The cheap square, which I secretly retrieved from the garbage, went out of square and was thrown into Dad's toolbox years ago.

Quality materials and precision machining set the Starrett and other good squares, such as Brown and Sharpe's (Brown and Sharpe Manufacturing Co., Precision Park, 200 Frenchtown Road, North Kingstown, R.I. 02852-1700; 401-886-2000), apart from run-of-the-mill squares. The heads are forged and hardened; the rule

blades are made of hardened steel and are available in a polished or satin-chrome-plated finish. I recommend the satin-chrome finish because it reduces reflection and glare, making the rule much easier to read. As a bonus, the chrome plating protects the blade from rust and wears exceptionally well.

Starrett squares also have what the manufacturer refers to as "quick reading graduations," which are staggered graduations with the inch subdivisions numbered as well as the inches, as shown in the photo above. A variety of graduation schemes are available, from all fractional, decimal or metric to some combination of these divisions. The decimal graduations, because of their predominant use in the aerospace industry, have become known as aircraft scales. These scales are handy if you use a calculator for determining layout dimensions because you can measure directly in decimals without converting to fractions.

My personal preference for a square is Starrett's catalog number C33HC-12-16R. This unit has a square head and a center head, and the 12-in.-long, satin-chrome blade has quick reading 32nds and 64ths on one side and aircraft quick reading 50ths and 100ths on the other side. A 24-in.-long blade is convenient for many applications, but the 12-in.-long blade does the job 90 percent of the time.

The center head makes quick work of finding the center of round or square work. Simply butt the edges of the stock against the V of the head, with the rule extended across the end of the stock, and scribe a line. Rotate the tool approximately 90° and scribe another line. The intersection of these lines marks the center of the piece. A protractor head is a useful, optional accessory for machine setups and for transferring angles.

Care and maintenance of the square
With proper use and care, a good square can be passed on for generations, so I've developed some techniques to maintain the quality and accuracy of my square. When sliding the blade back and forth or taking it out of the head, I push on the lock bolt to re-

Photo: Susan Kahn

A quality combination square is an invaluable aid in any woodshop as a marking and measuring gauge, for scribing lines, for transferring measurements, and for setting up and checking machines. The various heads, used individually, perform specific functions and increase the tool's versatility.

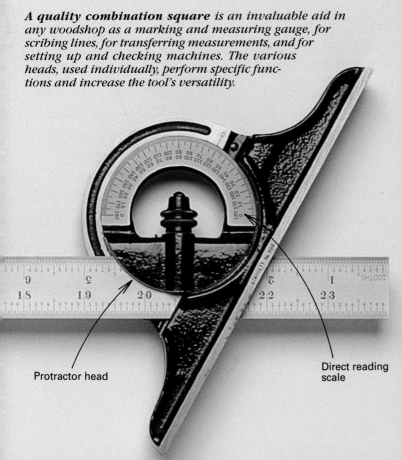

Protractor head

Direct reading scale

lieve the tension of the spring. This makes it easier to get the blade in and out of the head and prevents wear on the lock bolt and the head contact surface. To lubricate the blade, I use paraffin because it doesn't attract dust as oil will.

It's also a good idea to check the square's alignment every so often, especially after the square has been dropped or otherwise abused. Hold the square head against a jointed straight edge of a board with the rule extended across the surface of the board. Mark a line along the rule on the board's surface; then flip the square over so that the head is against the same straight edge, but the rule is on the opposite side of the line. Any gap between the rule and line will be double the amount that the square is off.

If the square is out of alignment, check the blade to see if it is straight and doesn't have any dings or burrs that might interfere with proper seating in the head. Burrs can easily be smoothed out by rubbing lightly with a flat sharpening stone. For more serious problems, contact the manufacturer for reconditioning.

Using the combination square

I learned one of the most important tricks for using a square from an old Southern craftsman, named Wes, while working at a Virginia boatyard. Pete, a young apprentice, was having trouble with out-of-square cuts and approached Wes for advice. Wes drawled out a couple of inquiries, "Did you mark the line straight? Did you cut directly on the line?" When Pete quickly responded "yes," Wes asked, "Pete, can you see straight?"

From that interchange, I learned to look at what I'm doing. I look to be sure the head of the square is tight to the edge of the workpiece. After marking a line, I look at it. If it looks wrong, I check it. I've avoided many mistakes with this simple procedure, and as I've gotten better as a woodworker, I've learned to trust my eye and recheck anything that doesn't look right.

When using a square, a bump or defect as small as ½ in. along the edge of the board, can cause the blade to be more than ⅛ in. out of square. To avoid errors, the combination square's head must be held tightly to the workpiece. I wrap my thumb around the curved part of the head with my palm pushing the head down and in against the edge of the workpiece. My index finger pushes down on the blade as far away from the head as I can comfortably reach. With this grip, I can slide the square along the board while keeping the head of the square pressed firmly against the edge. For the most accurate line, I place my knife or pencil on my mark, slide the square up to the marking instrument and then draw or scribe the line. (See the sidebar below for a discussion on marking lines with a knife vs. a pencil.)

The square as a marking gauge

The square can be used as a marking gauge by setting the desired length from the end of the blade to the perpendicular face of the head. Then, while holding a marking instrument against the end of the blade, slide the square's head along the edge of the board, as shown in the top left photo on the following page. This technique requires some dexterity and practice for best results. Because the wood's grain has a tendency to throw off the marking instrument, I only use this method for quick parallel lines when the layout is not critical. For more exact lines, I use a marking gauge.

The square as a thickness, depth and height gauge

My first rule of measuring is "don't, if you can avoid it." The ability to slide and lock the blade of a square lets me establish a consistent frame of reference that helps me avoid measuring in several different situations. Rather than measure the thickness of a board to plane another board to the same dimension, I use the square as a thickness gauge. I place the reference board on a flat table and

Accurate layout depends on a fine line

In any operation that requires handwork, the results are predicted by how clearly and accurately the line is marked. The clearest and most precise lines are made with a sharp knife that cuts the wood fibers. Lines scratched with an awl tend to be fuzzy, particularly across the grain. And a pencil line (no matter how sharp the point) is a lot wider than a carefully scribed line. The wide pencil line can lead to confusion about whether to work to the near side, far side or middle of the line.

To help make a scribed line more visible, I run a hard lead (4H) drafting pencil with the tip sharpened to a chisel shape along the score line. This darkens the line without affecting its accuracy. Sand paper (180-grit) glued to a piece of wood works well for sharpening the pencil.

My favorite layout knife is the X-Acto model with a large plastic handle, as shown in the top left photo on the following page. The thin X-Acto blades produce very clean lines. The thicker the blade and the deeper the cuts, the less accurate the line will be. And, if you make a mistake, a thin, lightly scored line is easier to sand away.

When scribing, make sure that your finger doesn't hang over the edge of the rule; I've found that most patternmakers have at least one scar as a result of having made this mistake. —B.W.

From *Fine Woodworking* (September 1992) 96:60-62

The combination square also can serve as a marking gauge. Simply hold a knife or pencil against the end of the blade while drawing the square's head along the edge of the stock.

As a depth gauge, the combination square can be used to check the thickness of planed stock, as shown here. The square also can check mortise and dado depths and the lengths of tenons and tongues.

Lay out evenly spaced divisions with the combination square by first setting the square to the desired increment. Then align the rule's end with the starting point, and score a mark at the square's head. Without lifting the knife, move the square along the board, butting the rule's end to the knife blade, and make the next mark at the square's head, as shown here.

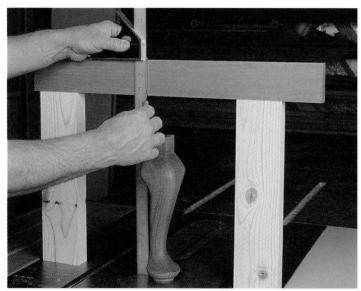

With a set of parallel uprights and a story stick, you can accurately lay out and transfer measurements from irregularly shaped objects. Mark the top edge of the story stick to be sure that it is properly oriented when transferring measurements.

hold the head of the square vertically on the board with the blade hanging over the board's edge, as shown in the near left photo. I then extend the blade to the tabletop and lock it in place. That set measurement can be used as a "feeler" gauge to judge the thickness of the board I'm planing. I've found that my sense of touch is much more accurate than trying to measure in these situations.

The height of a tablesaw blade or router bit can be set using this same technique. I set the square to the desired depth of cut using the comparative technique described above whenever possible or the rule's scale. Then, with the end of the blade resting on the saw table or router base, I adjust the blade or bit to the square's head. Again, feeling when the bit or blade just contacts the square's head provides a more accurate setting than trying to see the adjustment.

I've also used the square in this manner to check and compare tenon lengths to mortise depths and the tongue lengths on shelf ends to dado depths in carcase sides.

The square as a spacer

The square, set for a specific dimension, can be used to evenly space elements in a project, such as pickets in a fence, slats in a crib or dividers in a set of pigeonholes. I generally use a calculator when determining element spacing, and this is where the Starrett's decimal graduations come in handy. I can set the square directly from the calculator readout without the need to convert back to fractions thus eliminating another possible source of error.

Using this technique of laying out an element by referencing from the previous element or layout mark does introduce the possibility of cumulative error—an insidious mistake that quickly grows as the number of elements increases. However, in this situation, cumulative error can be minimized by aligning the blade end of the square with the reference surface and scribing along the perpendicular square head with a knife blade. After scribing the line, but before lifting the knife, I move the square down and butt the end of the blade against the side of the knife blade. I then scribe the next line against the perpendicular square head, as shown in the photo at left. I continue to leap frog the square and knife down the board until I get near the opposite end. Then I determine the amount of cumulative error and divide it among the last few increments to make the error all but undetectable.

Transferring points with a square

Lines or points are easily transferred from one side of a board to the other or even from piece to piece by setting the blade to the desired length. The key to accurate transfers is to establish datum surfaces that are straight, flat and square to each other and then always to measure from these datum surfaces.

This technique works fine for square projects, but what about curved surfaces? For irregular surfaces, machine shops have a coordinate measuring machine—a device that rides on a track above the part and measures the distance between points. For our purposes, however, a combination square, a story stick and a set of parallel blocks will accomplish the same thing. The story stick is held over the object by the parallel blocks and becomes the datum surface for measuring all the features of the object. Using the square, as shown in the photo at left, I transfer all the desired points from the object to the story stick. Marking a datum surface on the stick helps keep the stick from getting turned around. I can then transfer these dimensions from the story stick to create another piece or to make a drawing. □

Ben Wild, a former patternmaker, runs an apprenticeship program and teaches vocational training for the Rochester, N.Y. school district.

Ball Bearings in Shop Tools and Machines

When and how to replace these vital components

by Robert M. Vaughan

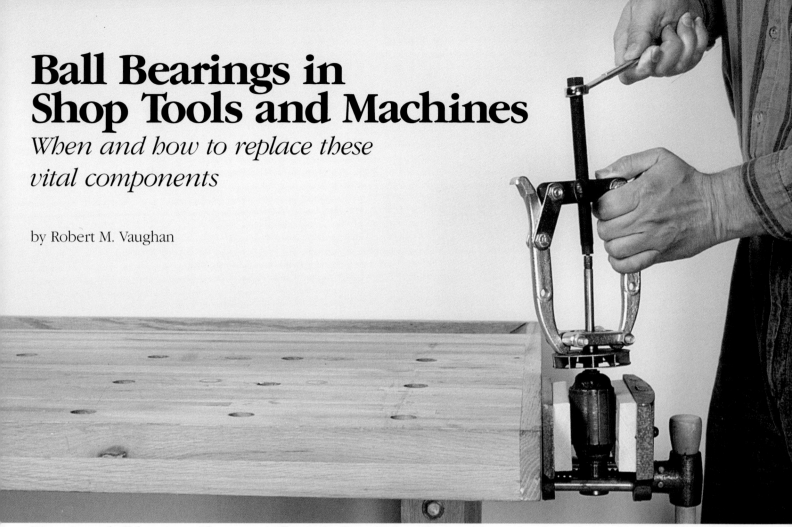

Removing a ball bearing with a gear puller is the first step in replacing worn-out bearings. Shown above, a bearing separator inserted between the bearing and the fan on a hand-drill motor's armature provides a means for the puller to grasp the bearing.

Ball bearings are among the hardest-working components in any woodworking machine or portable power tool. At rest, they are constantly under stress from tight V-belts, and under a load, bearings take an incredible high-speed pounding. In addition, sawdust packs around ball bearings, threatening to contaminate their inner workings or soak out the lubrication within. The fact that these precise, compact, antifriction components last more than a few working hours is amazing.

Eventually, all ball bearings succumb to the affects of heat, dust and friction that are part of normal tool use and need to be replaced. Fortunately, a bearing is designed to be the weak and replaceable link in the power transmission train in any piece of quality woodworking equipment. Unfortunately, you might not know when a bearing is good or bad, whether you can remove and replace it yourself, or what size and type of bearing you need to replace the old one with. Since ball bearings are used in a million different applications in woodworking alone, I can't cover all the situations. But I can give you some good tips on how to spot a bad bearing and on how to remove and replace a bearing, if you're inclined to do so.

Ball-bearing anatomy

While all machines, motors and running mechanisms have bearings of some kind, not all are ball bearings. Some machines have bronze-sleeve bearings or poured-lead babbitt bearings, but ball bearings are more complex than either of these. A basic ball bearing is comprised of an inner race, which is a sleeve that fits around a precisely ground area on the machine's shaft (called the bearing seat) and has a groove in which the balls roll; an outer race, which captures the balls in another groove and fits into the socket or housing on the machine; a cage, located between the two races that

keeps the balls evenly spaced; any number of hardened-steel balls; and a shield that keeps the bearing's lubricating grease or oil from leaking out and prevents dust and debris from contaminating the bearing. Variations in size, material, design and grade differentiate one bearing from another. Some bearings use double rows of balls, and some use rollers—straight, tapered or thin needles—in lieu of balls. Any ball bearing is capable of operating under a higher work load, running at a higher RPM and lasting longer without relubrication than less-expensive bronze-sleeve bearings. But state of the art or not, ball bearings still do wear out and need to be replaced, so you must be able to tell a good bearing from a bad one.

Diagnosing bearing problems

Figuring out whether or not your machine has a bad ball bearing isn't as simple as you might think because different problems will often produce the same symptoms. A difference in the feel or sound of a running power tool might indicate that a bearing has started to go bad, but not always. For example, loose pulleys on stationary power tools are infamous for mimicking the sound of bad bearings, and on portable power tools, bad brushes will do the same. Since fixing a pulley or brushes is easier than replacing bearings, check your machine carefully for loose or vibrating parts before disassembling it. Audible rumbles and clicks when a machine starts or coasts to a stop can indicate a lack of lubricant in a bearing and warn of an oncoming failure. When a machine's sound changes octaves—from a whispering baritone to a sore-throat soprano—you should suspect that the bearings are the problem. Any looseness in a power tool's shaft or arbor indicates a bearing-related problem, but not necessarily a bad bearing. A worn bearing socket, a common problem with portable power tools, usu-

From *Fine Woodworking* (September 1991) 90:49-51

ally results in a worn shaft. Excessive shaft wear can also occur when the ball bearing itself freezes up, but the shaft continues to rotate inside the inner race–usually requiring extensive repairs.

Some shop situations that seem unrelated to a machine's bearings can cause problems. For example, repairing a stationary machine with an arc welder can ruin the bearings; the massive current flow can cause the electric arc to jump the small gaps between the bearing's balls and the races, causing fine pitting and, eventually, premature bearing failure. A machine that's been submersed in water, such as in a flood, is another candidate for early bearing failure. Grit and debris can flow and settle into bearings and cause failure, sometimes after only a few hours of operation. Hence, any machine that has been in a flood should have all bearings replaced. If a machine's bearings continually go bad, examine other causes, such as a bent shaft, an out-of-round bearing seat or a worn bearing housing.

When you locate a bad bearing, your first tendency will probably be to relubricate it. However, the majority of ball bearings found in woodworking machines either are permanently sealed and lubricated or they are shielded bearings, which can be difficult to relubricate; in either case, replacement is recommended. Non-sealed bearings that lack shields are most often seated in housings with grease nipples, and these bearings should be lubed as part of the machines standard maintenance. Whatever you do, resist the temptation to spray a noisy bearing with a penetrating lubricant, like WD-40; it will eventually dry and leave an undesirable sludge film inside the bearing.

Extracting bearings

Removing and replacing ball bearings yourself can save time and money, but you must proceed carefully to avoid problems. Before old bearings can be extracted, a power tool or motor must be disassembled, and usually the arbor assembly must be removed from the machine. First and foremost, *unplug the tool or motor before beginning*. Keep in mind that disassembling a tool usually voids a still-valid warranty, and that unless you're careful and work in a clean environment, taking any machine apart can lead to other problems, such as losing or contaminating crucial parts or reassembling the tool incorrectly. If you don't have the proper tools, take the job to a reputable machinery-repair shop. Portable power tools can usually be sent back to the manufacturer for bearing replacement.

Once a bearing shaft or housing is exposed, you may have to remove snap rings, which are sometimes used to hold the bearing in place on the shaft or in the housing. Snap rings are best removed with special pliers designed to engage the holes on their ends. There are two separate kinds of snap-ring pliers: one for snap rings that have to be compressed for removal (used in bearing housings) and the other for rings that must be expanded for removal (used on a shaft). Trying to remove snap rings without these special pliers is extremely difficult, and you also risk damaging the seals or shields of a bearing.

After the snap ring is removed, the bearing will usually slip fairly easily from its housing, which is typically part of the cast body of the machine or motor. But if the bearing's inner race fits tightly against the shaft, a lot of force is required to remove the bearing from the tool's shaft or armature. I've used a couple of big screwdrivers and a vise to remove a few bearings, but I damaged the parts in almost every instance. The lesson here is use the right tools. Hydraulic H-frame or rack-and-pinion arbor presses are the best devices for either removing or pressing on bearings. However, a bearing (or gear) puller also works well, is affordable, is available at better auto-supply stores and bearing suppliers, and can also be rented. A good, all-around puller has two or three claws, which grip the bearing's outer race, and a center screw that bears against the end of the shaft and pulls the bearing out as the screw is tightened with a wrench. Sometimes the claws can't reach around the bearing, such as when a motor's cooling fan is in the way. In that case, you can use a bearing separator. This device consists of a split plate that is dished out to fit into tight places and is drawn together behind the bearing with two bolts. The bearing puller's jaws are then fit around the edges of the separator, and the puller is used as just described (shown in the photo on p. 83).

For light bearing-pressing work, like removing armature bearings on portable power tools, you can use a drill press as an arbor press. First, insert a hardened-steel dowel or pin all the way to the back of the chuck, and tighten the dowel in place. Then, support the ball bearing on either side with a couple of scraps of wood, and lower the drill-press quill to force the tool's shaft from

Pressing a new ball bearing on a machine's shaft is best done with a hydraulic or arbor press, but it can also be done with a pipe and a mallet. Above, the shaft (a table-saw arbor) is placed on a wood block on the floor. Then, a pipe fit over the bearing's inner race is pounded until the bearing seats.

A drill press can press on small ball bearings, like the end bearings on a router's armature (right). Pipe that fits over the bearings' inner race is mounted in the chuck, and pressure is applied by lowering the drill-press quill.

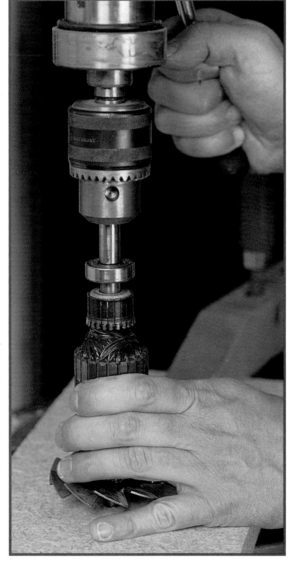

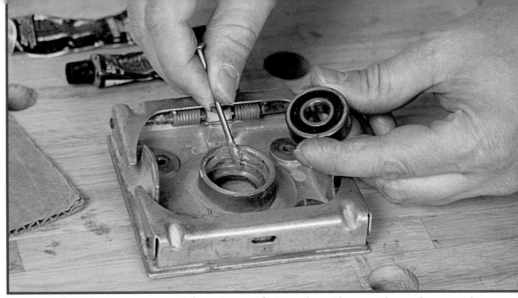

the bearing. However, reserve this method *for small bearings that press out easily*, and use it only with a high-quality drill press; the abuse could strip drill-press gears.

Buying replacement bearings

Ball bearings come in hundreds of types and sizes. Standard sizes for bearings are in metrics, except for a couple of inch-size series and a few metric/inch combination sizes. These specifications are also true of router-bit pilot bearings and other portable-power-tool bearings. Bearings also come in different grades, from one to seven, the latter being the most precise, durable and expensive.

When I'm ready to buy new ball bearings, I contact the machine's manufacturer or dealer so that I'm certain of getting the right replacement bearings. If the manufacturer or dealer doesn't stock the part (or if I need bearings quickly), I visit my local bearing supplier. (Check the yellow pages of your local phone book under "bearing suppliers" or "power transmissions.") I've purchased ball bearings from mail-order companies, such as W.W. Grainger Inc., 5959 W. Howard St., Niles, Ill. 60648; call (312) 647-8900 for your regional distributor. I've also gone to local skateboard shops, lawn-mower shops and other equipment-repair shops to get a replacement when in a pinch. Visiting a skateboard shop may seem farfetched, but skateboard-wheel bearings that sell for about $1.50 are the same size and type as the sealed bearings commonly used in portable power tools. And these bearings can cost $5 or more from a bearing-supply shop.

Each manufacturer has its own numbering and lettering system (marked on the bearing) to denote the bearing's dimensions, type of seals and grade. Bearings of the same external dimensions may seem interchangeable, but may not be. For example, ball bearings found in many tablesaw arbors and lathe headstocks contain a double row of balls; single-row bearings of the same size do exist, but aren't as durable. So before ordering a replacement, get a strong magnifying glass and read the numbers, letters and manufacturer's name on the side of the bearing. If bearing suppliers don't carry the same make of bearing, they can cross-reference your bearing's designation to their brand. I always bring the old bearing along; if I can't get an exact replacement, I can usually find a substitute that will work. Exact bearing replacement is usually recommended, but changing an older machine's open or shielded bearings to fully sealed bearings may be a good idea, such as on a tablesaw where sawdust has caused premature bearing failure. Without getting into a lengthy discussion of choosing higher-grade bearings (for information on this, consult SKF's booklet cited at the end of the article), let me just say this: Don't try to save money by buying bearings that are a *lower* grade than those the machine's manufacturer specifies. You'll face more frequent replacement with inferior bearings, and they can cause more serious problems, such as scored shafts.

Installing new bearings

Pressing a ball bearing on a shaft usually isn't as delicate as extracting a bearing, but it's still best done with a hydraulic or arbor press. In lieu of a press, a hammer and pipe will suffice if used judiciously. Select a pipe that just fits over the machine's shaft and that will contact only the inner race of the bearing. Make sure the pipe's ends are cut square and that any rough edges are filed smooth, lest they damage the bearing or shaft. Now, place one end

You can build up a worn-out bearing socket, such as the one shown here on the bottom plate of an orbital sander, with fortified epoxy. To do this, give the new bearing a light coat of wax, apply epoxy to the worn socket and set the bearing in place.

of the shaft on a hardwood block on a solid floor, slip the new bearing on the shaft, and fit the pipe down over the bearing's inner race. Tap carefully on top of the pipe with a hardwood mallet, a dead-blow hammer, or a regular hammer and a block of wood until you feel the bearing make solid contact with its seat (see the left photo on the facing page). When you first start tapping, be sure the bearing is straight on the shaft, or you could ruin the shaft, the bearing or both. For pressing lighter bearings onto portable-power-tool shafts, you can use a good drill press as discussed earlier (see the photo at right on the facing page); just substitute a piece of pipe for the pin in the drill chuck.

Occasionally, you'll find that a new bearing fits loosely on its shaft or in its bearing housing, indicating excessive wear in those areas. You can usually repair the worn areas with fortified epoxy (such as Loctite Weld brand, available at bearing- and machinist-supply stores), but I mix my own by adding finely shredded fiberglass from insulation to regular two-part epoxy. To build up a worn bearing housing in a router, for example, I first apply a thin coat of wax over the new bearing to keep it from gluing permanently in place. Next, I spread a layer of the epoxy on the inside of the worn housing (shown above). Then I reassemble the machine and let the epoxy cure. I've also used this technique to build up the bearing seat on lightly worn tool shafts; if you do the same, clean the shaft thoroughly with a solvent, such as lacquer thinner, before applying the epoxy. Loctite makes a more expensive compound called Quick Metal #660 (also sold at bearing- and machinist-supply stores) that works well for filling gaps up to 0.020 in.

More information

I've just skimmed the surface of ball-bearing problems and remedies encountered with woodworking machinery. If you face a problem not discussed here, you might try contacting a bearing manufacturer's technical-service department, although I prefer talking to a knowledgeable person at my local bearing-supply store. A booklet by ball-bearing manufacturer SKF called the *Bearing Installation and Maintenance Guide* is free at bearing stores and through SKF Bearing Industries Inc., 1100 First Ave., King of Prussia, Pa. 19406-1352; (215) 391-8000. Although primarily for maintenance engineers who service big machines, like newspaper printing presses, the booklet offers useful technical information that relates to the bearings used in woodworking machines. □

Bob Vaughan is a woodworking-machinery rehabilitation specialist in Roanoke, Va.

How to Install Bandsaw Tires

Getting them on is only part of the job

by Robert M. Vaughan

Stretching a new bandsaw tire over the rim of the wheel is a tough task made easier by the author's method, which employs both wheels as stretching forms. After pulling a loop of tire from between the pair of wheels, Vaughan inserts dowels one by one around the perimeter. The new tire can be slipped down over the wheel's rim after dowels have been inserted at each spoke.

Bad tires are the number one cause of poor bandsaw performance. I'm often asked to repair or adjust bandsaws as part of my machine-restoration business. Often, the tires on old machines are brittle or full of grooves caused by the tooth set of narrow blades, or they have deep cracks and missing chunks. Sometimes, the tires have been replaced but haven't been properly trimmed and recrowned, resulting in a bandsaw that vibrates and won't track blades correctly. No matter how much attention is paid to alignment and adjustment, a machine with bad tires simply won't perform well.

The way to restore an older bandsaw's smooth and accurate performance is to replace the tires. Although each bandsaw is a little different (some types of bandsaw wheels require factory-made tires that need special installation), fitting new tires usually can be done right in the shop by following the steps outlined in this article. The process includes removing the old tires, cleaning the rims and then stretching the new tires on and gluing them in place. Then the new tires should be equalized, trimmed and crowned and, finally, the wheels should be rebalanced.

Removing old tires and cleaning the rims

Getting off the old tires is sometimes easily done with two fingers. Other times, the cement tenaciously sticks to both the tire and the wheel. In either case, the process is simple enough, but a few extra steps can effectively reduce some of the wheel cleanup later. In the toughest instances, insert a razor knife between the wheel and the tire and pour in a slight amount of lacquer thinner, which will partially dissolve the contact adhesive that holds the tire to the wheel. Wait about 30 seconds, and then pry with a screwdriver to enlarge the opening. After inserting a small wooden wedge, pour in a little more thinner, and wedge the tire farther off the wheel. Continue this process until the tire comes off entirely.

Next, all of the old contact cement has to be removed from the wheel; otherwise, it will cause lumps and gaps in the bonding of the new tire. First, remove the wheels from the saw, a process that's usually only slightly more complicated than taking a V-belt pulley off a motor shaft. Typically, this involves just removing a single nut on the end of each axle and pulling the wheel off (if you're in doubt, consult your saw's manual). Clamp one of the wheels in a vise with padded jaws. Working in a well-ventilated area, lay a strip of old sock on top of the wheel and pour on lacquer thinner. Let the soaked sock set for a couple of minutes and the thinner will soften the old contact cement, so it can be scraped off. After using this technique all around the perimeter of the wheel, go around it again with a solvent-coated, stiff-wire brush to remove any dry and crumbly cement. A wire wheel in an arbor or chucked in an electric drill works quickly on cast-iron wheels but can ruin the tire-bonding surface on aluminum or plastic wheels.

Stretching on new tires

Solid-band tires, which are most commonly found on woodshop bandsaws, cost about $1 per inch based on the diameter of the wheel (up to 38 in. dia). I purchase mine from the Pennsylvania Saw Co. Inc. (PO Box 533, Emigsville, Pa. 17318-0533; 800-233-9381). Often, the tires on many small-wheeled bandsaws—12 in. dia. or less—can be manhandled onto the wheel without much difficulty. Just C-clamp the tire to the wheel at one point, and work your way around the rim. However, installing new tires on bandsaws with 14 in. or larger wheels is like trying to stretch your lips around a bowling ball. To fit correctly, most new tires are about 15 percent to 20 percent shorter than the circumference of wheel they're made for.

To install tires on large-spoked bandsaw wheels (the most common design) with relative ease, I've developed a method whereby the wheels themselves are used as a form for stretching the tires, so they can be slipped on. With both wheels removed and cleaned, as described above, lay them down on the bench, one on top of

From *Fine Woodworking* (July 1992) 95:50-53

the other. Next, insert a ring-shaped spacer (I use an old ball bearing, but you could easily turn one from wood) between the wheel hubs so that the rims of the wheels are separated slightly more than the width of the new bandsaw tire. Now, sandwich the new tire loosely between the two wheels, and, as a temporary axle, insert a dowel or rod through the wheel hubs and spacer. Finally, put another spacer under the bottom wheel to raise the assembly about ½ in. or more off the bench.

Before the stretching begins, you'll need to cut some short, sturdy dowels (the same number as the number of spokes on one wheel). I use old broom handles and cut them about 2 in. longer than the total height of the wheel sandwich. You'll also need three 12-in. lengths of mason's twine or strong cord to tie the dowels in place during stretching. Cut a fourth length of twine about 24 in. long; thread it through the new tire, and tie the ends into a loop for use later to stretch the tire.

To begin the tire stretching, fish out a loop of the tire from between the wheels, insert a dowel down through the loop and tie it to the wheel's rim (over one of the spokes) with a length of twine (see the photo on the facing page). Securing the dowel this way prevents it from rolling around the perimeter of the wheel each time the tire is stretched at a different spot. Repeat the stretching and dowel-insertion process about a third of the way around the wheel to form the second side of an equilateral triangle. For the third leg, pull on the string that's looped through the tire to help you

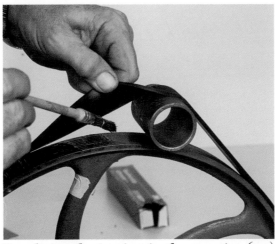

Equalizing the tension in the new tire (top) *will prevent a bumpy performance later. This is done by rolling a short length of pipe around the wheel several times.*

To cement a tire in place (bottom), *lift the tire off the rim with a pipe, and apply weatherstrip adhesive in one small area at a time, gradually working your way around the wheel.*

For cementing the new tires on, I use 3M's weatherstrip adhesive because it's convenient to apply right out of the tube, and I find it much stronger than the other adhesives I've tried. Starting near your masking-tape mark, lift the tire with your fingers, and insert the short pipe you used to equalize tire tension. Brush some cement on the exposed area of the wheel and the tire on one side of the pipe, as shown in the photo below. In the time it takes to apply the adhesive to both surfaces, the glue will get tacky, and the pipe can be rolled a short distance, so the cemented areas can bond (the tension of the tire should flatten any globs of cement that result from uneven application). Continue to apply the cement, working all the way around the wheel. When you get near where you started, there'll be a small area where you won't be able to apply cement, but don't worry about it; this small, unglued area won't be a problem. Now, let the glued tire dry for about 24 hours to be sure of a good bond.

Trimming and crowning

Now you're ready for the most important steps of this job: trimming the tires concentrically and shaping a crown on them, which are necessary for good blade tracking. First, remount the wheels on the bandsaw, and tighten the axle nut firmly. Make sure there is no slop or looseness in either wheel on the saw; otherwise, the crowning will give lumpy and bumpy results.

For trimming and crowning, I use a shopmade jig, shown in the drawing on p. 88. I've used this setup on bandsaws with 12 in. to 36 in. wheels. The

stretch the tire so another dowel can be inserted (see the photo on the facing page). Repeat this pulling ceremony with the remaining dowels. I've found it unnecessary to tie the last few dowels to the rim because the first three dowels hold things pretty much in place. Once all the dowels are in place, you should be able to work the tire down over the bottom wheel without much trouble. Then, working carefully, one dowel at a time, remove the untied dowels first, and then cut the strings, and remove the tied dowels. Finally, turn the assembly upside down and repeat the procedure to mount a new tire on the other wheel.

Equalizing the tire and cementing it on

Once in place, the new tires need to be equalized to even up unequal thickness in the rubber that may have resulted from stretching. With a wheel on its edge on the bench, carefully lift the tire in one spot and insert a short piece of pipe (about 2 in. dia.) with a dowel slipped through the center (see the top photo). Now roll the pipe around the perimeter of the wheel at least three revolutions to equalize the tension of the rubber tire. Keep track of the revolutions by marking a starting point on one of the spokes with masking tape.

jig, which is temporarily clamped to the saw, allows an electric die grinder fitted with a router bit to be pivoted into the tire. I use my Black & Decker die grinder because it runs at the same speed as a router, and it has a long, straight neck that's easy to mount. For a cutter, I use a ½-in.-dia. laminate trimmer bit with a ball-bearing pilot. I trim a V-shaped crown on all the bandsaw tires I install rather than the round crown typically seen on new tires. This V-angle is about 7°, which I find works well with any bandsaw blade but especially well on narrow (¹⁄₁₆-in. to ¼-in.) blades. I can't imagine ever going back to the more-difficult-to-grind round crown.

To make the trimming jig, start by bolting a pair of pillow blocks to one end of a hardwood bar. The pillow blocks hold a ¾-in.-dia. drill-rod pivot shaft, locked to the blocks with setscrews (some styles use locking collars). This allows the shaft to pivot but keeps it from sliding out. Bandsaw the grinder-mounting bracket to the shape shown in the drawing, and bore holes at each end—one for the shaft and one for the neck of the grinder. Kerfs sawn through these holes and bolts installed in T-nuts provide a means for locking the bracket to the shaft and the die grinder to the bracket. A length of stop rod, cut from flat or angle iron, completes the setup.

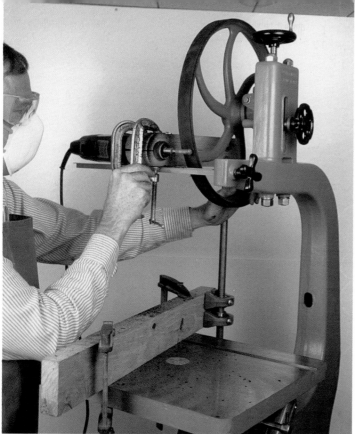

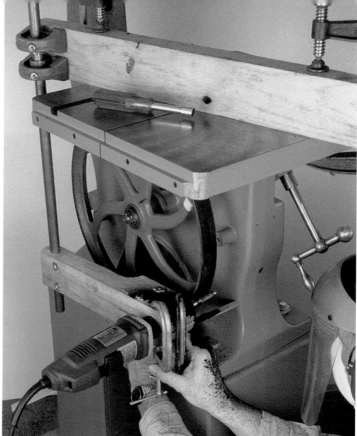

Vaughan's jig for trimming and crowning the tire holds an electric die grinder fitted with a flush-trimming router bit clamped in a pivoting bracket. He clamps the jig to the bandsaw with the pivot shaft extending up for working on the top wheel (left) or down for the bottom wheel (right). Each tire is trimmed twice at a slight angle from each outer edge to form a V-shaped crown.

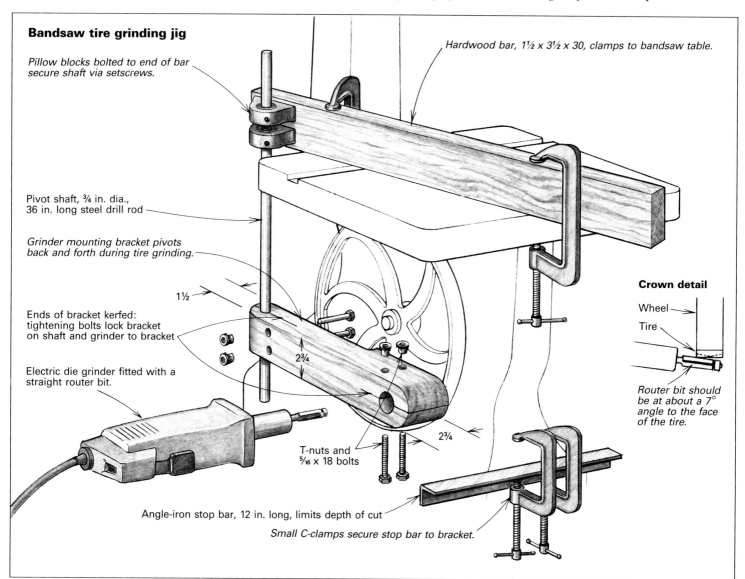

Bandsaw tire grinding jig

Pillow blocks bolted to end of bar secure shaft via setscrews.

Hardwood bar, 1½ x 3½ x 30, clamps to bandsaw table.

Pivot shaft, ¾ in. dia., 36 in. long steel drill rod

Grinder mounting bracket pivots back and forth during tire grinding.

1½

Ends of bracket kerfed: tightening bolts lock bracket on shaft and grinder to bracket

2¾

Electric die grinder fitted with a straight router bit.

2¾

T-nuts and ⁵⁄₁₆ x 18 bolts

Angle-iron stop bar, 12 in. long, limits depth of cut

Small C-clamps secure stop bar to bracket.

Crown detail

Wheel

Tire

Router bit should be at about a 7° angle to the face of the tire.

Photos: Robert Vaughan; drawings: Lee Hov

Before mounting the jig on the bandsaw, make darn sure that the power cord to both the die grinder and the saw are disconnected. Lightly clamp the hardwood bar to the saw table with the pivot shaft extending up for trimming the upper tire or down for the lower tire (see the photos on the facing page). Secure the die grinder in its bracket; then attach the bracket to the shaft with the T-nuts and bolts. Use a pair of small C-clamps to secure the stop rod to the bracket below the grinder. These C-clamps also make good operating handles for pivoting the bracket during trimming because they keep your hands away from the spinning bit.

Trimming each tire is done in stages: Three increasingly deeper passes cut one side of the V-shaped crown, and three cut the other. Trimming involves the somewhat tedious process of adjusting various parts of the jig to different positions, clamping and unclamping them to change the angle at which the bit contacts the tire and the depth of cut. It'll take time to get things right, especially on your first attempt, but the gratifying results outweigh the effort required.

You need to locate the axis of the jig's pivot shaft so that the axis of the bit relative to the surface of the tire is about 7° off. For a saw with 1¼-in.-wide wheels, this angle will allow the bit to trim about ¹⁄₁₆ in. more at the edge of the tire than at the center. Once you've set the correct angle, clamp the stop rod so that the first cut lightly trims the tire just at the edge. The stop rod is a crucial component of this rig. Without it, precision trimming is nearly impossible, not to mention dangerous.

Now, plug in the grinder (*not* the saw), and don a face shield and dust mask—this process sprays little black specks of rubber all over the place. Double check all clamps and setscrews (you need to be very sure that they are tight). Next, turn on the grinder, and then lock its switch on. Use one hand to turn the bandsaw wheel—very slowly—in the direction opposite the rotaton of the bit at a perimeter speed of about 1 in. per second. With your other hand, slowly pivot the cutter into the tire. If the wheel isn't turning when the bit enters the rubber, a jolting kickback will occur, and the tire might be gouged. Until you get used to this setup, start with a *very* light cut to prevent this accidental gouging, which can ruin the tire.

It takes about three full revolutions of the wheel to trim one side of the crown smoothly. The first pass will have little dips where the bit went in and out when the wheel-turning hand changed positions; the second pass cleans up most of these dips. The third pass should be very slow and smooth to take a light shaving and clean up more of the little dips (resist the temptation to turn the wheel fast). Don't let any tiny dips that remain disturb you. They don't affect blade-tracking performance, and I can't completely avoid them either. When one side of the crown is finished,

Rebalancing the wheel ensures vibration-free performance with the new tire. The wheel rides on pairs of ball bearings screwed to this simple jig. A heavy spot will consistently end up at the bottom, indicating where weight needs to be removed.

Keeping the wheel clean of sawdust and debris makes tires last longer. An old toothbrush bent and screwed into place serves that purpose.

shift the pivot shaft's axis point to set the angle to trim the other crown, and repeat the process. I overlap the cuts slightly at the center of the tire, taking care that the apex of the tire crown is centered after the second cut. In theory, this should leave a point, but because the rubber is so soft, the crown is actually slightly rounded. After trimming both sides of the tire, flip the hardwood bar and pivot shaft over. Remount the grinder bracket on the shaft, and then trim the other wheel.

Rebalancing the wheel

The new rubber tire can and usually does change the balance of the wheel. Therefore, you should remove each wheel from the saw after trimming to check the balance. My balancing rig shown in the top photo is crude compared to most static balancers, but the results are most satisfactory. I mounted pairs of ball bearings on the ends of some upright steel strips and then screwed these strips to a couple of bookend-style plywood platforms. Although it surely would be quicker to balance the wheels on the machine, usually there is too much natural resistance from the bearing seals and lubricant for sensitive results.

To use the jig, insert a very smooth shaft, like a drill rod, through the wheel's hub, and then set it between the bearings, as shown in the top photo. The principle is simple—the heaviest part of the wheel rolls to the bottom. Experimenting with different wheel orientations will soon tell you exactly where the heaviest spot is. If the same spot repeatedly ends up at the bottom, take the wheel to the drill press and bore one or more shallow holes at the heavy spot on the inside rim of the wheel with a ½-in. twist bit. Conservative drilling is in order here. If you're afraid to drill into your wheel, then wrap and tape pieces of electrical solder around the spokes or screw on weights directly opposite the heavy spot. Recheck and drill/weight each wheel until it can be spun on the balancing jig without the same spot settling to the bottom each time.

Brushing after every wheel

After all of this work, it's a good idea to install some sort of brush on the lower wheel of your saw to clean and protect your new tires. A brush that contacts the lower wheel sweeps away dust, pitch and other debris, which can build up and change the shape of the tire's crown and thus alter tracking. To make the brush, simply heat and bend a dogleg into the handle of an old toothbrush, as shown in the bottom photo, and screw it to the inside of the bottom wheel guard. □

Bob Vaughan is a contributing editor to Fine Woodworking *and a woodworking machinery rehabilitation specialist in Roanoke, Va.*

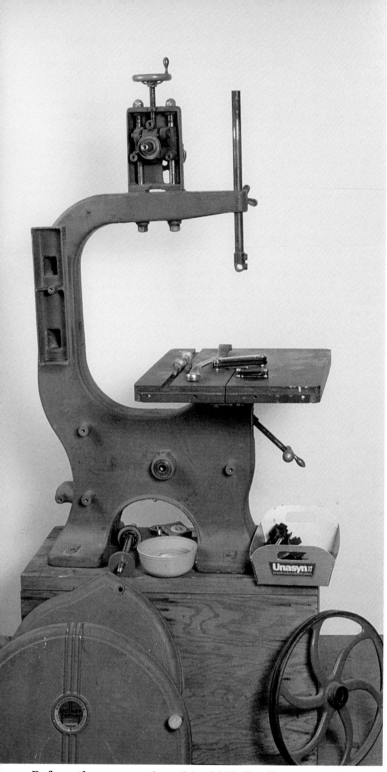

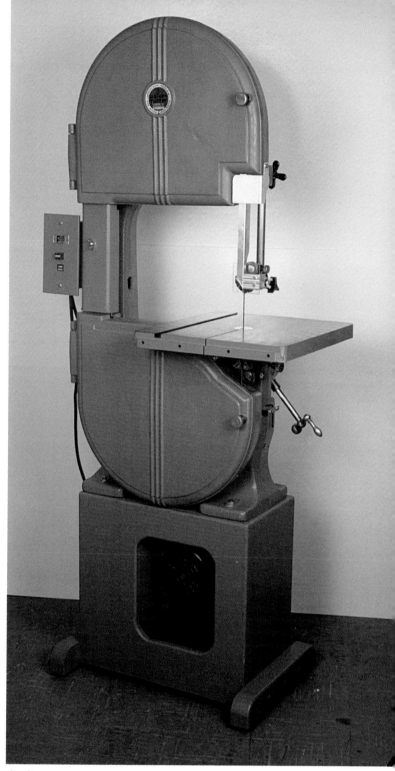

Before the restoration, *this old Walker-Turner wasn't much more than a pile of scrap iron. Sixty-five hours and four hundred dollars later, the author has a new (again), better-than-from-* *the-factory, vintage bandsaw. The saw's quality casting, 12-in. resaw capacity and 16-in. throat depth were all factors that made it worth restoring.*

Restoring Vintage Machinery
Bandsaw's lessons can be applied throughout the shop

by Robert M. Vaughan

From *Fine Woodworking* (January 1993) 98:74-79

What a bargain—a 16-in. Walker-Turner bandsaw for $80. All it needed was new tires, guides, motor, electricals, guards, stand, complete disassembly, cleaning and rust removal, one casting weld, repainting, reassembly and, of course, realignment of all the parts during reassembly. The good news was that all of the crucial components were there and in good condition; the other stuff I could fix. This wasn't an $80 bandsaw, but an $80 bandsaw kit. It was up to me to turn it back into a bandsaw.

I had to weigh the value of the restored bandsaw against commercially available machines. A resaw capacity of 12 in., 400 lbs. of quality American cast iron and a 16-in. throat depth are all factors that made this moderate-sized machine worth restoring. If this had been one of Walker-Turner's 14-in. models, I would have passed. The work required to restore it would have been the same, but the result would have been little better than a new Powermatic or Delta 14-in. model.

If you're thinking of restoring an old machine, it's important to realize that it's a very rare old machine that's ready to run. Almost all are like this machine was—a lot of cast iron with potential. Bearings, belts, pulleys, switches, wires and motor almost always need replacement. One reason that bandsaws are so popular to restore is that the parts that wear out can almost always be obtained from sources other than the original manufacturer. The important question to ask before diving into a restoration is whether the restored machine will be worth your trouble.

In this article, I'll discuss the general procedures common to restoring any old woodworking machine, as well as the more specific procedures that were necessary to get this bandsaw back into top form. And while the general procedures are applicable to just about any machine restoration, even the bandsaw-specific procedures illustrate ways of addressing problems common to all woodworking equipment—ways, for example, of dealing with dust, alignment problems and beat-up or missing guards. The principles of machinery restoration are the same regardless of the machine.

Moving the machine

Moving any heavy machine from one shop to another is always a chore. There are no rules on how to accomplish it other than to be prepared. I have help on hand for lifting. I generally bring resealable plastic bags for nuts and bolts and a note pad to record the disassembly sequence and to label parts bags. I also bring wrenches and WD-40 for disassembly of any heavy or protruding parts that might impede handling. I often remove the table, and any guards or pulleys, and I always try to remove the motor and cord. I make sure there are a couple of floor floats (four casters on a piece of plywood) ready in my shop, so I can move the machine around during the restoration process.

A fine-wire brush mounted on the author's wood lathe quickly and efficiently cleans away dirt, dried grease and even light rust. The wheel also imparts a slight polish, so Vaughan runs all fastener heads under the wheel for a few seconds.

Masking all parts ensures a clean, crisp, professional-looking paint job. A good way of masking holes is to wrap a piece of paper tightly around a dowel and then to release it inside the hole. The paper will expand to fit. To avoid a messy cleanup later, remove all the masking tape as soon as the paint is dry enough to touch.

First inspection

Once in the shop, I break out the air hose to blow out the years of accumulated dust and grease. *Always* wear a face mask or safety glasses when using an air nozzle. A 100-lb. blast of air into any of those little nooks and crannies can unleash hostile projectiles at bullet-like speed. If you don't have a compressor, a stiff bristle brush will remove most of the crud.

After I've cleaned off the bulk of the dust, dirt and grease, I begin disassembly, examining each component for further mechanical problems—things I may have missed when I bought the machine. Organization at this stage really pays off. As I take apart the various subassemblies of a machine, I use plastic trays, bins or boxes for the larger parts and resealable plastic bags to hold the little stuff. I note the sequence of washers, springs and other things that I'd otherwise forget. I bag individually any shims I find, along with a note showing where they came from. This not only makes reassembly infinitely easier but also allows me to move the multitude of parts and store them out of the way, without losing track of what's what and what goes where—no little consideration in a space-starved shop.

Next I buy or collect all of the big items I'll need. This includes the motor, wiring, switch, pulleys and belts—all the big-ticket items crucial to completion of the machine. Even when other unexpected expenses crop up, I know that the project will get finished.

Cleaning

Proper parts cleaning is the most time-consuming aspect of the restoration process, but it's also the most important. The purpose of a thorough cleaning is not only to please the eye but to make things work as they should. I've been hired to repair a lot of equipment that needed nothing more mechanically challenging than a good cleaning. Forty years of dust, dirt and resins have a way of adversely affecting the performance of the finest machine.

After covering my lathe bed (to protect it from flying dirt and debris), I mount a fine wire wheel on my wood lathe and use it to brush away any dirt or grit in threaded parts, to remove minor coatings of rust and to clean up any dried, caked-on grease (see the photo above). The wire wheel also polishes a bit, so I put the heads of all the old screws, nuts and bolts under the wheel.

I clean holes, with or without threads, with a brass brush (the kind used to clean rifle barrels) chucked into my electric drill.

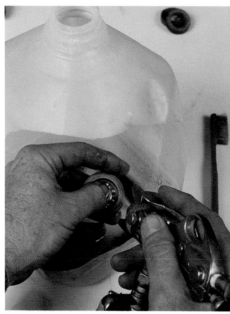

Forty years of dust, dirt and resin *had taken their toll on the back blade guides, but they weren't damaged—just frozen. Vaughan removed the bearing from the shaft with two screwdrivers (above), popped the cap off the bearing with a hammer and dowel (left) and sprayed the bearing clean with lacquer thinner (right). The cleaned guide works like new.*

If the hole isn't very deep, I'll follow this with a blast of air and then wipe with a clean or solvent-dampened rag.

Grease is best removed with a solvent; I prefer lacquer thinner because it's the quickest solvent I normally have around the shop. I spray-clean small parts, using a compressor-powered spray gun and spraying into a cut-out plastic milk jug. The milk jug catches most of the spray, which I use later to dampen rags for wiping down larger areas; I wipe with a dry rag after cleaning with a solvent-dampened rag. I've also found the refillable, rechargeable spray cans—which are available at most auto parts' stores—useful for cleaning larger areas. I just spray lacquer thinner on, then wipe clean with a dry rag. These cans are particularly handy in close quarters or when you don't want to drag the air hose around.

Think safety whenever working with solvents. Work in a well-ventilated area, wear a respirator and *always* set the dirty rags outdoors—away from anything flammable—to dry after use.

Cleaning an old machine is messy work. Chances are that your workbench (and many other areas of your workshop) will become spotted with grease and grime. Make sure you clean up thoroughly after working on the machine before you begin working wood again. It's incredibly annoying to find greasy dirt smeared all over a just-completed project. Rebuilding a woodworking machine may not be as bad as rebuilding your car's transmission in your shop, but it's close.

Dirt or grease from a machine you're restoring can mess up your shop, but shop dust and dirt can mess up a restoration as well. To avoid this, make sure any surfaces you'll be working on are clean before you begin. Also try to finish the restoration without interruption. If you have to put your restoration on hold in midstream to work on a woodworking project, both can suffer unless you're extremely careful about cleanup and protection.

Renewing the table

To clean up the rust on the tabletop, I started with 220-grit sandpaper wrapped around a block of wood, then moved up to 320-grit. After finishing with the 320-grit, I dampened the table with naphtha and rubbed with a hard Arkansas stone until the high spots shone like little mirrors. This makes any metal very slick and does wonders for planer and jointer beds—even new ones. It only has to be done once, and the results are well worth it.

General machinery repairs

Some repairs are specific to individual machines; others are general and apply to most machinery. I'll discuss general repairs below and the specifics of bandsaw repair in the story on pp. 94-95.

All four wheel bearings in this saw were contaminated with dust and dried-out grease and needed to be replaced. The top bearings were standard sized, and available locally (check the Yellow Pages for a bearing distributor near you), but the bottom bearings had an odd-sized inside dimension. My usual local sources of power-transmission products couldn't locate replacement bearings. I knew that Walker-Turner had some of its bearings custom-made for them, so I began to worry. I called Accurate Bearing Co. (1244 Capital Dr., Unit 1, Addison, Ill. 60101; 800-323-6548) and asked the sales manager about my bearings. He replied, "Sure. I have them right here. What else do you need?" I liked that.

To restore the outside threads of beat-up fasteners that can't easily be replaced, I used a thread-restoring file. These square files come in two sizes with eight different threads-per-inch sizes on each file. I set the file's teeth into the matching grooves of the fastener and filed. These files are particularly handy when the end of a threaded piece is smashed and when trying to start a threading die would risk cross-threading. You can find these files in most large industrial-supply catalogs.

The pulleys on the saw were cheap aluminum ones that no longer ran true. I replaced them with cast-iron pulleys from a local power-transmission distributor. The belt was equally worn, so I replaced it with a Browning cogged, high-strength industrial belt (from the same distributor) that's designed to transmit high torque smoothly. Any machine is only as good as its weakest component, so these simple substitutions of power train components really make a big difference in the overall performance of the restored machine.

Any time something is held in place by a setscrew, there's a good chance that the point of the setscrew will cause a crater. The raised sides of these craters will cause all kinds of difficulties in disassembly, often requiring gear pullers, presses, punches or a big soft-faced hammer. I usually file down the crater edges with a super-fine file or honing stone before removing the part from the machine. This avoids galling the inside of a hole or housing as the part is withdrawn.

The parts on this saw that need to be removed or adjusted to change the blade were fastened with nuts, bolts and slotted-head screws. Every time I wanted to change blades, I'd have to hunt down the proper tools, have the tools and all loose hardware laying around during the blade change, and then put them all back when I finished. To make the machine more user-friendly, I replaced common nuts with wing nuts, bolts with threaded studs and slotted screws with socket-head (Allen) screws. I then mounted a holder for the Allen wrench on the machine. Now

I can change the blade and adjust the guides without ever going on a tool hunt.

Painting

Repainting a restored machine may deter rust, but the real reason is that it looks nice and makes you feel better about your machine. Sawdust may come off *slightly* easier, but who are you kidding?

How far you want to take the paint job is up to you. I've stripped down to bare metal, done body work and built up the paint as though I was restoring an auto; other times, I've only needed to do touch-up work. Stripping may be necessary if the machine came from a school: often the color scheme will look as though it were designed by Stephen King and applied by King Kong. If you strip down old cast iron, you'll sometimes find that auto body filler was used to make a smooth surface.

On this particular machine, the existing paint had faded to olive-gray. I found original paint on an unexposed section of the machine and matched it with Krylon's #1608 Smoke Gray. It took five cans to do this bandsaw, including the stand. I didn't bother to strip because the paint film was in good condition. I simply cleaned the

surfaces with soap and water and then wiped them down with lacquer thinner. I had to spend a little more time and use a bit more solvent in some of the greasy corners and crevices, but there were no real trouble spots.

I mask all surfaces that take working parts, like shaft holes and ways. An easy way I have of masking the inside of a hole is to cut a small piece of paper and wrap it around a dowel. I then insert this into the hole and unwrap the dowel until the paper springs out to fill the hole.

I remove all masking tape and paper as soon as the part is dry enough to handle, so I won't have to deal with any sticky residue later. I paint the parts individually while they're disassembled. Bright, unpainted fasteners, new aluminum guards and crisply contrasting parts, such as handwheels, all add up to create a quality impression. A wash-over paint job says something else altogether.

Electrical

This machine, like many older machines, had a simple toggle switch inconveniently located on the front of the frame. I replaced it with a new heavy-duty, push-button

How to build a good machinery stand

Constructing a well-made wooden stand is the single most important thing you can do to eliminate bandsaw vibration. A good wooden stand is superior even to a steel stand because the wood absorbs much of the vibration rather than transmitting and amplifying it as steel will. Another advantage of a wooden base is it's easily modified to accept hanging accessories, such as fences and miter gauges.

I build my stand first because I'd rather not be bending over for the whole restoration. Placement of the motor and electricals, provision for sawdust evacuation, ventilation and machine maintenance are all factors I take into consideration when designing a stand.

The keys to a good stand are good materials and good construction methods. I use strong, dry hardwood and good-quality birch-veneer plywood. My construction methods are neither esoteric nor showy. Glued butt joints work fine as long as you use enough glue, and the joints fit tightly to begin with.

I push a joint together with the nose of my pneumatic staple gun, just until the glue begins to ooze out, and then I pull the trigger, squirting a 2-in.-long, wide-crown staple into the wood. The staple isn't for strength but rather to hold the joint tight

until the glue dries. Using staples or nails without glue results in joints that are guaranteed to vibrate loose. Bolts are forever having to be tightened because of machine vibration and seasonal wood movement. Glued joints are the only sure way I know of to make vibration-resistant wood joints. Biscuit joinery also works.

I glued the legs to the stand and then screwed large lag bolts through the leg, through the side of the plywood box and into a backing block (see the photo at right). The lag bolts compress the joint (providing clamping pressure) and add a comforting margin of safety against joint failure. I also glued in a panel to accept tracks for sliding motor mounts and drilled and installed T-nuts in the top of the stand to accept the bolts that would connect machine and stand.

Since no floor is really flat, I put in T-nuts and steel leveling feet. Distributing the machine's weight equally to each of the four feet is essential to reducing vibration. Why don't I put locking casters on the base? The bandsaw is tall, thin and has a high center of gravity, making it inherently subject to balance problems. Leaving a bandsaw permanently mounted on a wheeled base is trouble waiting to happen. —R.V.

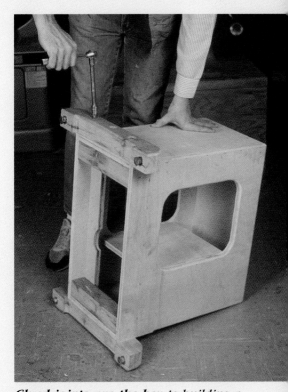

Glued joints are the key to building a good machinery stand, but lag bolts are good insurance against failed joints where the legs meet the carcase. Elaborate joinery isn't necessary for a strong and sturdy stand.

manual starter on the column (where it's easy to get to), but I had to cut a sheet-steel mounting plate for the switch first. After cutting and drilling the necessary holes in the mounting plate and mounting the starter, I drilled and tapped two holes in the bandsaw's cast-iron frame and attached the mounting plate assembly.

A rigidly mounted motor greatly reduces vibration. To mount the motor securely on this machine and still allow for tensioning of the belt, I cut a couple of short sections of folded steel U-channel (I used Unistrut from Grainger; 800-473-3473), drilled five holes in the bottom of each and screwed them to the base. Then I found a couple of pieces of steel that would slide in the channels and drilled and tapped them to accept the motor.

A good-quality new motor, switch, wire and plug will cost $200 to $300. It's money well spent. I've used a light switch, vinyl-covered cord and a cheap mail-order motor before. Performance was poor from the start. I ended up shelling out more money for the good stuff in no time.

Bottom line

Total material costs were just under $400, bandsaw included. Costs were so low because I used a reconditioned motor and a manual starter (both good quality but without any bells or whistles) and because I already had just about all the peripheral materials (sheet steel and aluminum, clear plastic, fasteners) on hand.

I also spent about 65 hours on the restoration. At $25 an hour, labor costs would be about four times my materials' cost—not out of line for this kind of project. I've explained how I overhaul a machine and, for the most part, the reasons why. I hope this both inspires and instructs others to restore old machinery because the result, when done well, is most gratifying. The adage "they don't make them like they used to" is true, but there's a reason for it. The sad and brutal truth is that most buyers of new woodworking machinery don't demand quality so much as they do low-priced look-alikes. The downward spiral in the quality of woodworking machinery is the result. "They don't make discriminating buyers and users of woodworking machinery like they used to" is probably a more apt phrase. But who can criticize the guy who's perfectly satisfied with a five-dollar socket set? □

Robert Vaughan is a contributing editor to Fine Woodworking *and a woodworking machinery rehabilitation specialist in Roanoke, Va.*

The particulars of the bandsaw

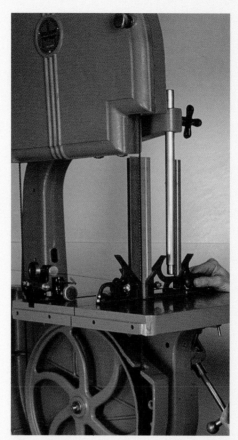

The saw table must be perpendicular to both blade and upper blade-guide post (which must be parallel to each other) for the bandsaw to work perfectly. The author adjusts the table for perpendicular, using combination squares to check for gap between the rule and the blade and between the rule and the blade-guide post.

Miter gauge, disc sander and a mitered push stick allowed Vaughan to grind the side blade guides with little effort. Other options, had the guides been irreparable, would have been to grind his own from steel bar stock, to replace them with new Delta guides or with guides made of graphite-impregnated phenolic resin (sold as Cool Blocks by Garrett Wade).

Many of the steps in the restoration of this bandsaw are just as applicable to a vintage jointer or planer as they are to the bandsaw. A good stand, new electrical and drive systems and clean, well-lubricated bearings are things that any old machine can profit by. But the procedures below are bandsaw-specific, and although it's a Walker-Turner I happened to be working on, the steps taken—and the conditions that necessitated these steps—are common to most bandsaws.

Table, blade-guide post, blade

For a bandsaw to work properly, the blade, blade-guide post and table must all be in proper relation to one another. If they're not, every time you move the upper guide up or down, you'll have to readjust the guides. You can either live with this long-term hassle or go through the one-time tedium of correcting these misalignments. This alignment has been adjustable on every bandsaw I've ever worked on, but I've never worked on inexpensive do-it-yourself-type bandsaws, so regretfully, I have no experience in that realm.

On C-frame bandsaws, such as this Walker-Turner, the upper blade-guide post's line of travel is dictated by the position of a hole in the casting. To make the blade travel in a line parallel to that of the post, the position of the wheels needs to be adjusted properly. On this machine, the upper wheel can be moved from side to side. I was also able to make slight adjustments to the position of the whole upper wheel carriage by loosening and retightening its mounting bolts. The bottom wheel can be moved in and out by adjusting the setscrew-held bearing stops. It took quite a few adjust-tighten-test sequences before the blade's line of travel was right (parallel to the upper blade-guide post), but now I won't ever have to worry about it again.

The next step was to set the table perpendicular to the blade's line of travel. I first put some good squares against the sides of the blade, loosened the tilt lock and tilted the table until both blades were parallel with the sides of the blade. Next, I put the squares' blades against the front and back of the blade and loosened the underneath bolts that hold the table to the trunnions. I slipped thin sheet-metal shims between the table and the trunnions, experimenting with different thickness shims until the table was perpendicular to the blade. If you can't get the table perpendicular, then all you can do is split the difference on either side of the blade. Once again, though, it's a one-time hassle with long-term benefits.

Restoring the old blade guides

Deep grooves were worn into the side guide blocks, and the back guide bearings were virtually frozen from sawdust contamination. Using a disc sander and miter gauge (see the bottom photo on the facing page), I reground the 45° angle on the steel side blade guides.

For both top and bottom back guides, I clamped the guide bearing's shaft in a vise and used two large opposing screwdrivers to pry off the bearing. I reversed the bearing and drove off the front dust cover with a wooden dowel, exposing the balls and cage. Then I flushed the bearings clean with lacquer thinner. Don't let the bearing spin freely under a blast of air because solvent will spew everywhere, and the bearing can be damaged at high speeds.

If either the side or back guides had been irreparable, I would have had to replace the defective part. For replacement side guides, I could have used graphite-impregnated phenolic resin guides (Cool Blocks), cut and ground new guides, or searched for compatible guides from another manufacturer. If the back ball-bearing guide for this particular machine had needed to be replaced, I could have had a new shaft machined to fit a standard 6203 size bearing—no big deal for someone with a metal lathe.

Before replacing a lot of individual guide components, though, I would first consider upgrading to a set of Carter guides. They make three good styles that fit this saw. Cost ranges from $140 to $185 for a complete set of guides, mounting brackets and studs. Carter Products can be reached at 437 Spring St., N.E., Grand Rapids, Mich. 49503; (616) 451-2928.

A new blade guard

Blade guards on old bandsaws, if they're there at all, are rarely in good working order, and this machine was no exception. After studying the old blade guard, with its worn-out sliding pieces, I decided that I could make one that would work better and be easier to maintain. The only hitch was that I had to have an aluminum block machined to accept the bent sheet-aluminum guard. Knowing a tall, single piece guard fastened to the upper blade guide could not fully extend up into the castings enclosing the upper wheel, I had to make two separate guards. One short guard was fastened to the upper wheel guard casting. It came down about even

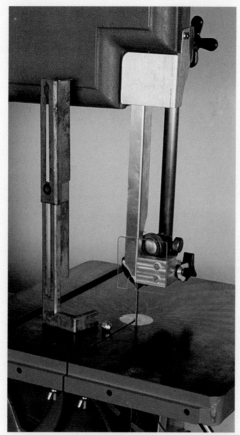

A new guard of bent sheet-aluminum seemed an easier and better solution than trying to get the rusted old steel guard (left) back into shape. Vaughan added the clear plastic to the front of the guard for more protection on the saw's infeed side.

Often the simplest solutions are the best. The author had noticed that the bottom back blade guides are almost always inundated with dust and tend to lock up much more quickly than the top ones. By placing an angled piece of clear plastic between the saw table and guide, he was able to deflect almost all of the dust away from the guide.

with the bottom of the upper wheel guard castings and was wide enough to let the whole upper blade guide slide up behind it. A tall, skinny guard was fastened to the upper blade-guide area. At the blade guide's lowest position, the top of this guard did not come below the guard I put on the upper wheel casting. This way, I could raise the blade guide all the way up and prevent the tall guard on the blade guide from hitting things in the upper wheel guard castings. As an afterthought, I put a clear plastic panel on the front of the blade-guide mounted guard to provide extra protection on the feed side of the saw (see the photo at left). I made this panel even with the actual bottom of the blade guard so that any stock that would fit under the plastic panel would fit under the upper blade guide.

Custom dust deflectors

Bandsaws normally flood the bottom blade-guide assembly with sawdust, causing these guide's bearings to fail long before the top guide bearings. Also, since the bottom guides are hidden from convenient inspection, they're rarely cleaned. I was able to eliminate more than half of the normal sawdust deluge with a clear plastic deflector, which I mounted above the guide. I experimented with cardboard and tape until I had a good pattern, and then I cut out what I needed from some scrap clear plastic. I bent, drilled and tapped a strip of aluminum to hold the plastic deflector. I then drilled and tapped one hole in the bottom wheel guard and threaded a bolt through from the inside. I fastened the deflector assembly with a wing nut for easy removal and for when I needed to change blades or set the saw table at a particularly steep angle (see the photo at left).

Even with the plastic deflector, I noticed dust being broadcast from the joints of the clamshell castings of the lower wheel guard. This dust would blow out on the table and pile up on the floor behind the machine. I found I could direct most of this dust toward the front of the saw with two simple baffles. After experimenting with cardboard again to get the best pattern, I cut baffles from aluminum flashing and then mounted them to the guard by drilling and tapping a single hole for each baffle (see the top photo).

The net result of all of this activity is that most of the sawdust created by the saw winds up right in front of it, where it can be easily swept away. If I used a vacuum system, I'd have cut and mounted a piece of 2-in. tubing in place of the plastic deflector to suck up the dust right as it comes off of the blade. —R. V.

Cutting Sheet Goods Down to Size

Alternative rigs for sawing and routing large panels

by Charley Robinson

The challenging job of cutting full sheets of plywood into manageable pieces is made easier by circular-saw accessories that guide a straight cut. Exac-T-Guide above uses a T-square (to which the saw is attached) guided in a U-channel to produce accurate results.

I hate plywood, but I've used a lot of it. And I've used plenty of medium-density fiberboard (MDF) in my time, too. The inherent stability of sheet goods makes them very convenient for cabinet carcases, built-in units and other remodeling projects. But trying to horse the heavy sheets through a tablesaw can be difficult, particularly if you work alone. And even with a helper, you still need almost 20 ft. of floor space to rip a full sheet.

Large commercial shops and lumberyards have used panel saws for years, but I couldn't justify $800 to $1,000 for such a specialized tool. My low-tech solution was to use a circular saw and the cutting guide shown in the sidebar on p. 98. The system works great for occasional use but can be cumbersome and time-consuming; the guide needs to be realigned and clamped for each cut.

At recent trade shows, three guide systems for cutting plywood with a circular saw caught my eye. Exac-T-Guide, Glide-Easy Saw and Blade Runner II (see the photo above and the photos on the facing page) all use a carriage to mount the saw and a fence or rail system to guide the carriage. Each manufacturer claims their guide system will rip and crosscut full 4x8 sheets, and two say they will replace the tablesaw for cutting sheet goods. The cost for these units, including the extras you will need to set them up for cutting plywood, ranges from $215 to $235. In addition, the systems all have router capabilities or will in the near future.

I wanted to try out these systems, so I designed and built some closet organizers and several sets of bookshelves to put the units through their paces. Typical of most sheet-good work, these projects required ripping panels to width, crosscutting them to length and routing dadoes and grooves. If you're used to working sheet goods on a tablesaw, it will take an open mind to see how versatile these tools can be. For example, when making a bookcase, shelf dadoes must align. With one of these units, I was able to rout dadoes across the panel before ripping it into individual bookshelf sides, thereby ensuring alignment. I'll describe how each system is set up and how they performed these basic functions.

Glide-Easy Saw

The Glide-Easy system suspends a circular saw above the workpiece on a pair of aluminum brackets. Nylon rollers ride along some 2-in.-dia., electrical conduit to guide the saw, as shown in the top left photo on the facing page. For $185, Intelligent Product Designs (see the sources of supply box on p. 99) includes the aluminum brackets that clamp to the saw's baseplate, a pair of plywood glide-rail supports and plywood height-adjustment blocks, as shown in the top right photo on the facing page. To this you need to add about $30 worth of materials: four 10-ft.-long 2x4s and two 10-ft.-long pieces of 2-in. inside diameter (ID) electrical conduit.

Once you have all the parts on hand, Glide-Easy can be put together in about a half hour. Fortunately, this system is simple because the instruction sheet that accompanies it is rather cryptic. The glide-rail supports clamp to the conduit, and the height-adjust-

From *Fine Woodworking* (July 1992) 95:82-85

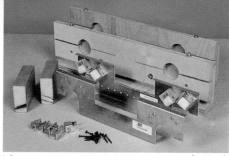

The contents of the Glide-Easy kit (above) are rather basic. A circular saw rides smoothly along 2-in.-dia. electrical-conduit guide rails (left) to make straight cuts. This unit can also crosscut and rip dimensional stock. Convenience and accuracy could be improved with such refinements as stops or a fence for making duplicate cuts.

Blade Runner II's strong suit is cross-cutting and mitering dimensional stock, but with the addition of 60-in.-long option-al rails (left), it can also rip and crosscut a 4x8 panel. An optional drop-in router mounting plate is available for quick changes from sawing to routing. The array of hardware and components (below) re-quired several hours to assemble.

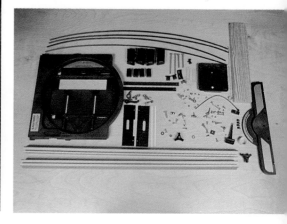

ment blocks, which are already attached to the glide-rail supports, are screwed to the four 2x4s. A 36-in.-long plywood crosscut gauge is screwed to the 2x4 base at one end of the unit perpendicular to the line of cut. Glide-Easy will rip and crosscut a full 4x8 sheet and will handle stock up to 2-in. thick.

Ripping and crosscutting—Glide-Easy is designed to be used on the ground with the workpiece supported by the 2x4 base and your body weight holding the workpiece in place. Before you can use the system, you must saw a kerf the length of the base 2x4 that is directly under the saw. This kerf serves as the reference for lin-ing up the workpiece. Then slide the panel in from the side, and align cut marks at each end with the sawkerf. Once the piece is positioned and held down with your body weight, push the saw carriage along the guide rails to make a straight cut. You can make crosscuts in the same manner but with the panel oriented perpen-dicular to the rails instead of parallel to them. Because of this con-figuration, Glide-Easy requires at least 10 ft. by 10 ft. of floor space.

Routing—The Glide-Easy system doesn't have a router carriage at this time, but the manufacturer plans to have one available soon.

Blade Runner II

When I unpacked Blade Runner II, I was reminded of the kid's toys labeled "some assembly required" that take several hours on Christmas eve to put together. There were seven different bags of hardware and 14 components, as shown in the bottom right photo, which took over three hours to assemble. Fortunately, the owner's manual gave detailed instructions.

Blade Runner II, as shown in the bottom left photo, is similar in function to Glide-Easy in that a tool carriage is guided above the work by a pair of rails that are screwed to a shopmade worktable. When properly set up, the plastic carriage glides smoothly on the extruded aluminum rails that include a rip gauge for the saw on one rail and a gauge for setting the router on the other rail.

In its standard form, Blade Runner II is designed for crosscut-ting, ripping, mitering and routing standard lumber up to 2 in. thick and 27 in. wide and sells for $135. I added the optional 60-in.-long rails ($80) to extend the length of cut to a full 48 in., so I could crosscut and rip full sheets of plywood. Including the plywood base, out-of-pocket costs will run about $235 to get this unit ready.

Ripping and crosscutting—The manufacturer suggests making a wider worktable for better support if you are going to be doing a lot of ripping. To rip on Blade Runner, rotate the saw plate in the carriage so that the blade is parallel to the adjustable fence. The saw is positioned using the rip scale on the guide rail and clamped in place with the carriage locking knob. The hairline pointer on the carriage makes accurate setups easy. The workpiece is then fed through the saw as if you were using a tablesaw, so you'll need

To rout dadoes across panels with Exac-T-Guide, clamp the T-square in place at both ends, and slide the router on the mounting plate along its long arm, as shown. Exac-T-Guide is the only unit that has a stock mounting plate that accepts a wide variety of tools.

Exac-T-Guide

Exac-T-Guide shown in the photo on p. 96 takes a different approach to guiding the cutting tool. The saw (router, biscuit joiner, jigsaw or laminate trimmer) mounts on an easily detached glass-filled plastic mounting plate. The mounting plate slides on the extruded-aluminum long arm of a large T-square. The stamped-steel short arm of the T-square, in turn, rides in a U-channel screwed to the edge of a 4x8 plywood work surface. (The $224 it took to set up Exact-T-Guide includes $199 for the tool and $25 for the plywood.) In addition to the U-channel, I screwed a perpendicular end stop to the work surface and completed the setup by assembling and truing the T-square.

When I was setting up Exac-T-Guide, I thought I could skip the cut-and-adjust procedure described in the instruction sheet by instead using the factory edge of another panel to align the U-channel. But I found that factory edges may not be as perfect as I had thought. My first cut bowed ³⁄₃₂ in. from the ends to the middle of a 7-ft.-long piece. By readjusting the fence as prescribed, I eliminated all of the bow. The entire setup is a simple procedure that shouldn't take more than about an hour, including setting the U-channel.

Ripping and crosscutting—Sheet goods up to ⅞ in. thick are ripped on the work platform with the T-square guided by the U-channel, as shown in the photo on p. 96. The panel is placed on the work platform and butted against the U-channel. Any width rip-cut up to 4 ft. can be accommodated by sliding the saw mounting plate along the long arm of the T-square and then tightening a knob to lock it in place. The scale on the T-square's long arm and the hairline indicator on the mounting plate make accurate adjustments a snap. The short arm of the T-square rides in the channel and guides the saw parallel to it.

Other materials, such as doors, that are too thick for the U-channel can be ripped or crosscut by guiding the short arm of the T-square along an edge parallel to the cut while pushing the saw forward.

Although panels can be crosscut as described above for doors, I found it easier just to swing the panel 90° and, like a ripcut, use the

about 20 ft. of floor space to push the panel through the saw.

Blade Runner II's carriage has a removable plate that holds the circular saw. The plate can be rotated in the carriage to position the saw perpendicular to the rails for rip cuts or parallel to the rails for crosscuts. For crosscutting, slide the workpiece under the rails and against the adjustable fence. A kerf in the lead board attached to the fence serves as a reference for aligning the cut. If the fence is accurately set, pushing the saw through the piece will result in a square crosscut. Sliding a large piece of plywood into position, however, can exert sufficient leverage to affect the accuracy of the fence. I found it best to mark the workpiece on both edges and then align one cutting mark with the kerf in the lead board and the other edge with the sawblade.

Routing—An optional drop-in router mounting plate ($36) is available for fairly easy tool changes. To rout dadoes, position the stock under the rails and against the fence, and then push the carriage-mounted router along the rails (the same as crosscutting). To rout grooves the length of the panel, follow the ripcutting-setup procedure, and then push the panel past the bit.

Double-edged cutting guide and sturdy worktable

Before I had a shop that could handle full sheets of plywood, I used a couple of simple cutting guides that relied on the factory edges of a sheet of medium-density fiberboard (MDF) to make accurate cuts. At first, I had an 8-ft.-long and a 4-ft.-long guide for both my router and my circular saw. But for easier handling and to cut down on shop clutter, I modified the design so that one guide would work for both the router and saw, as shown in the drawing on the facing page.

I used to cut sheet goods with a couple of 2x4s stretched between some wobbly, old sawhorses and invariably had to try to catch one side or the other as I was finishing my cut. I've found that the knockdown worktable shown in the drawing allows me to concentrate on cutting, instead of catching, by fully supporting the entire sheet of plywood. And the folding sawhorses (Pack Horses by Davalco Products, see the

sources of supply box), are stable and strong. I found their height to be just right, and they fold into self-storing packages that can be latched together and lugged around by their carrying straps with just one hand. Also, Pack Horses' sawhorses fit easily into a trunk.

Making the cutting guide: The dual-purpose cutting guide is made by cutting two strips from the edge of a sheet of ½-in.-thick MDF. The first strip is the 5-in. or 6-in.-wide center guide, and the second strip, about 14 in. wide, serves as the cutting-guide base. The actual width of the base will depend on the circular saw and router that you will be using with the guide (see the drawing detail at right). If you are making a dual-purpose guide, the center-guide strip will need to be run through a tablesaw, with the factory edge against the fence, to true up the edge that's

cut and make it parallel to the factory edge.

Measure the baseplates on your saw and router to determine the position of the center guide on the cutting-guide base, and then glue and screw the center guide to the base. Now a pass with the circular saw on one side and with the router on the other side will trim the edges of the guide so that they coincide with the sawblade and the router bit. Be sure to trim the guide with the same router bit that you will be using with the guide. I used a special 18mm-dia. (²³⁄₃₂-in.), down-shear straight bit (available from Woodhaven, see the sources of supply box), so I can rout dadoes that fit tightly to the metric plywood I use. The appropriate edge of the cutting guide is now easily lined up with the layout marks on the plywood. Don't forget to mark each side of the guide, so you'll know which side is for the saw and which is for the router. *C.R.*

U-channel to guide the T-square. However, swinging the panel will require at least 10 sq. ft. of floor space. The manufacturer indicates an accessory mount is being developed that allows the mounting plate to be rotated 90° yet still slide along the long arm of the T-square. With this mounting, you could cut perpendicular to the U-channel for crosscuts without having to turn the panel.

Routing—Exac-T-Guide provides very controlled router movement, both across the panel and along its length. Grooves are easily routed in the same fashion as ripcuts: Clamp the mounting plate at the desired position along the long arm of the T-square, and push the T-square, guided by the U-channel, the length of the panel. Rout dadoes by clamping both ends of the T-square in place and then sliding the router on the mounting plate along the long arm of the T-square (see the photo on the facing page). By using a set of four accessory stops ($40) to control router movement, it's easy to rout stopped grooves, dadoes or even a square opening anywhere in the panel.

The bottom line

Although all these tools can cut a straight line, there is a considerable difference in their ease of use. Lining up cuts on the Blade Runner II is a little fussy, and repetitive cuts are a real irritation because there is no provision for setting a stop. Ripping sheet goods on Blade Runner II has the same problems as ripping on a tablesaw: It needs 20 ft. of floor space to push the heavy, awkward panels through the saw. And the overhead rails make it difficult to use a push stick to feed panels through the saw. I also found it difficult to rout a straight groove the length of an 8-ft. piece by pushing the stock past the bit. In addition, the router mounting plate flexes enough to create uneven depths when trying to plunge cut for a stopped dado.

Glide-Easy can cut sheet goods or dimensional lumber as well, but it's a pain to line up the workpiece with the sawkerf in the 2x4. I'd get one mark lined up only to have it move while aligning the other end. Also, Glide-Easy has no fence or stops for making repetitive cuts. Glide-Easy's ground-level working arrangement means you don't have to lift heavy panels to a raised table, but bending over the work and crawling along a panel can be hard on your back and knees. And, finding a flat place to set up could be a challenge on a job site.

My favorite tool for working with plywood is Exac-T-Guide. It produces ripcuts and crosscuts that are more accurate than possible with my tablesaw and with a lot less stress and strain. The built-in carriage locks and accessory stops make it easy to set the saw for repeat cuts that yield exactly the same size panels. This tool would also be useful for straightening the bowed edge of a board up to 8-ft. long, which is something that can't be easily done on a tablesaw.

Exac-T-Guide is equally adept at controlling a router. But I discovered that both ends of the T-square must be clamped when routing dadoes; otherwise, there's enough play in the free end of the T-square to allow the dado to drift off course by ⅛ in.

Exac-T-Guide can also be used for taper cuts and routing or cutting circles. Although Exac-T-Guide's mounting plate is the only one that will accept a variety of tools, I would opt for an extra mounting plate (about $50). Then, with just the twist of a knob, I could switch from the saw to a router in a matter of seconds to conveniently and easily handle most of the work I need to do on sheet goods. □

Charley Robinson is an assistant editor for FWW.

Sources of supply

Exac-T-Guide, BradPark Industries, Inc., 91 Niagara St., Toronto, Ont. Canada M5V 1C3; (416) 594-9455, (416) 461-1601.

Glide-Easy Saw, Intelligent Product Designs, 1556 Halford Ave. #363, Santa Clara, CA 95051; (408) 296-4066.

Blade Runner II, Professional Tools, Inc., PO Box 672525, Houston, TX 77267-2525; (713) 872-1885.

Pack Horse sawhorses, Davalco Products, 301 West 53rd St., Suite 3D, New York, NY 10019; (800) 945-9545.

Carbide-tipped, shear-dado router bits (metric and standard diameter), Woodhaven, 5323 W. Kimberly Road, Davenport, IA 52806; (800) 344-6657.

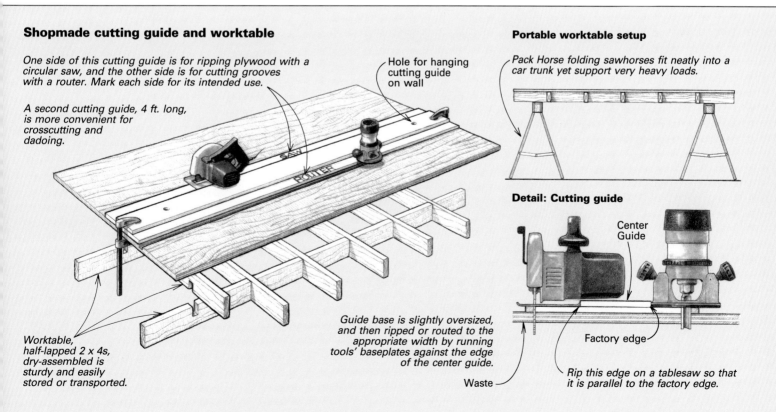

Shopmade cutting guide and worktable

One side of this cutting guide is for ripping plywood with a circular saw, and the other side is for cutting grooves with a router. Mark each side for its intended use.

A second cutting guide, 4 ft. long, is more convenient for crosscutting and dadoing.

Hole for hanging cutting guide on wall

SAW

ROUTER

Worktable, half-lapped 2 x 4s, dry-assembled is sturdy and easily stored or transported.

Guide base is slightly oversized, and then ripped or routed to the appropriate width by running tools' baseplates against the edge of the center guide.

Portable worktable setup

Pack Horse folding sawhorses fit neatly into a car trunk yet support very heavy loads.

Detail: Cutting guide

Center Guide

Factory edge

Waste

Rip this edge on a tablesaw so that it is parallel to the factory edge.

Mehler uses his shopmade crosscut box to square the end of a heavy maple board on the table-saw. He also made the Lexan guard, which rides on the workpiece.

A Tablesaw Crosscut Box

Safe and precise cutting with a shopmade jig

by Kelly Mehler

From *Fine Woodworking* (July 1991) 89:72-75

Plywood tablesaw crosscut box

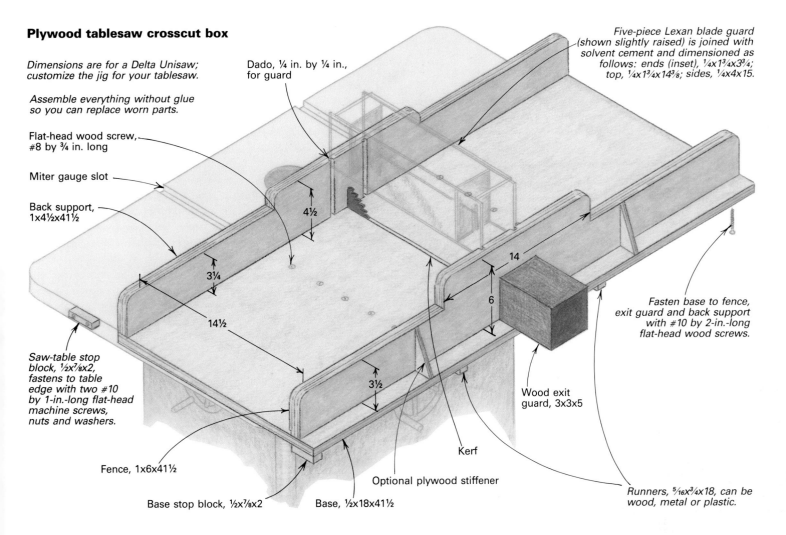

Dimensions are for a Delta Unisaw; customize the jig for your tablesaw.

Assemble everything without glue so you can replace worn parts.

Dado, ¼ in. by ¼ in., for guard

Five-piece Lexan blade guard (shown slightly raised) is joined with solvent cement and dimensioned as follows: ends (inset), ¼x1¾x3¾; top, ¼x1¾x14⅜; sides, ¼x4x15.

Flat-head wood screw, #8 by ¾ in. long

Miter gauge slot

Back support, 1x4½x41½

4½

3¼

14½

14

6

3½

Saw-table stop block, ½x⅞x2, fastens to table edge with two #10 by 1-in.-long flat-head machine screws, nuts and washers.

Fasten base to fence, exit guard and back support with #10 by 2-in.-long flat-head wood screws.

Wood exit guard, 3x3x5

Kerf

Fence, 1x6x41½

Base stop block, ½x⅞x2

Base, ½x18x41½

Optional plywood stiffener

Runners, ⁵⁄₁₆x¾x18, can be wood, metal or plastic.

Crosscutting boards on the tablesaw with a miter gauge isn't easy. Even with a long auxiliary fence, the board drags on the table and skews off at an angle, which causes an inaccurate cut. This is one reason why I don't crosscut with a gauge anymore; instead I use a shopmade crosscut box that carries the workpiece past the sawblade for consistently accurate cuts—even on wide doors. And by clamping auxiliary fences to the box, I can quickly and safely cut perfect open mortises, tenons and finger joints.

The plywood base of my crosscut box, shown in the drawing, is screwed to two hardwood runners that slide in the miter-gauge slots milled into the saw table. Since the base is cut in half the first time the box is used, a fence and a back support are screwed to the base to hold the halves together. To make the box an accurate cutoff tool, I took special care to square the fence to the kerf. When crosscutting with the box, I align the cutoff mark on the workpiece with the kerf in the box, hold the piece against the fence and push the box past the sawblade until the piece is cut. For safety, I made a clear Lexan guard, which fits between the support and the fence; I also added a wood exit guard, which covers the blade where it comes through the fence, and a stop on the saw table, to keep the box from going so far that the blade cuts through the exit guard. Besides the midsize box shown in the photo on the facing page, which has a 14½-in.-wide capacity, I also have a box for 12-in. workpieces and a box for 30-in. panels; and I made a similar box for my router table.

I use the mid-size box the most, and so I'll tell you how to make it, as well as its Lexan guard. Although it's sized for my Delta Unisaw, you can easily adapt it to your machine. Your box's accuracy will depend on three factors: Your sawblade must be parallel to the miter-gauge slots (see "Tuning Up Your Tablesaw," *FWW* #78);

the box's fence must be perpendicular to the blade's line of cut; and you must build the box with stable material.

Cutting the parts—The main parts for the crosscut box are from high-quality, 9-ply, ½-in.-thick birch plywood. I made the 1-in.-thick fence and back support by laminating two pieces of plywood. The base should extend 1 in. wider than your saw table to attach the stop and to clamp workpieces on the end. The fence and support should be the same length as the base. After laminating the fence and back support, I jointed their bottom edges square, and rabbeted the fence's inside bottom edge ⅛ in., so sawdust wouldn't prevent the workpiece from laying tightly against it. I also cut ¼-in.-wide by ¼-in.-deep dadoes across the inner face of the fence and support to receive the ends of my Lexan blade guards: a standard guard (see the drawing) and an auxiliary guard for cutting tenons and other joints (see the center photo on the next page). Then I bandsawed the fence and support to the dimensions in the drawing (proportion yours to your saw table). The fence is higher in the center to hold a workpiece vertically (to cut finger joints, mortises and tenons) and lower on the ends, to clamp narrow pieces to the box.

Rip the runners to fit snugly side to side in the miter-gauge slots, but leave them thinner than the depth of the slots to allow for dust. (Most saws have ¾-in.-wide by ⅜-in.-deep slots.) After screwing the base to the runners, as described below, you can scrape them until they slide easily. I used osage orange runners on this crosscut box, but any vertical-grained hardwood (to minimize shrinkage), aluminum or plastic would work as well.

Attaching the base to the runners—Before you begin assembling your box, let me caution you: don't use glue. Instead, fasten all parts together with countersunk flat-head wood screws (as shown in the drawing). To fasten the base to the runners, put them in the miter-gauge slots and place the base on top of them with its front edge aligned with the front edge of the saw table and its left edge extending 1 in. beyond the saw table. Mark the base over the runners' centerline and extend these lines across the base with a straightedge. Drill pilot holes and countersink for #8 by ¾-in.-long wood screws every 4 in., alternating the screws ¹/₁₆ in. on either side of the line, to prevent drilling and screwing into the same grain line and splitting the wood runner. Don't put screws under the fence or support, or you'll have to remove these components before you can replace the runners.

The runners should fit tightly in the table's miter-gauge slots, and so you'll probably have to pry the base from the table. Now, cut off the runner's excess length and scrape their edges until they slide easily in the slots. Scrape the high spots only, as indicated by dark marks left on the runners after sliding the box back and forth. If the slots are clean and don't leave a distinctive mark, coat them with a graphite marking crayon or pencil lead. When the runners slide easily in the slots, without sideways play, rub them with paraffin to seal and lubricate them.

Attaching the fence and back support—The base is fastened to the back support with screws spaced 3 in. apart. Be careful not to drive any into the dadoes for the Lexan guard or where the tablesaw blade will cut through the base. The back support doesn't need to be square to the blade, but for your box to be accurate, the fence must be absolutely straight, flat and square to the sawblade.

I used a square to check that the face of my fence was perpendicular to the base. Joint the edge if it's not, and recut the rabbet if necessary. Then fasten the base to one end of the fence with one screw from underneath, and clamp the opposite end to the base so it's aligned with the front edge. Make sure the inside face of the fence is flat. When I made this box, the plywood fence was warped, and so I temporarily clamped a stiff straightedge to the outside of the fence until I completed alignment. Next, to square the fence to the blade, raise the blade until it just barely cuts through the base. Then, slide the fixture in the slots and cut through the base, but stop before you saw into the fence. Now, turn off the saw, pull its plug and raise the blade to its maximum height. Squaring the fence is easy, but it takes some patience. Slack off on the clamp that binds the fence and base, and use a square to align the fence 90° to the sawkerf in the base. Check for square-

More than a crosscut jig

If you have been using a miter gauge to cut wide, heavy pieces, you'll appreciate how easily a crosscut box handles large pieces. And accuracy is so great that I even use the box to cut small pieces. I keep large pieces flat against the base by clamping a hold-down block to the fence above the workpiece. You can hold light, narrow pieces with your hand, as you would on a miter gauge. But I hold small pieces down with an L-shaped block, as shown in the left photo below.

It's easy to accurately align the cutoff mark on the workpiece with the box's saw-kerf. If you need to cut many pieces to the same length, clamp a stop block to the right side of the fence, so it is the required distance from the kerf. Then, crosscut one

end of each piece by holding it against the fence on the left of the kerf and cut it to length by sliding it to the right against the stop. If the end of the piece extends beyond the end of the box, clamp a long L-shaped stop to the fence. Be sure you cut the correct end by stacking workpieces so that you pick them up and put them in the box without flipping or rotating them.

Joinery on the crosscut box: I use my crosscut box to cut open mortises and tenons by clamping a vertical support to the fence so that it is square to the base, as shown in the center photo below. I made an auxiliary Lexan guard (see the center photo below) for this type of joinery. You can secure three corners of the guard

in the dadoes in the back support and fence, but make the guard's top and one side shorter to accommodate the auxiliary vertical support.

The box is also great for cutting finger joints using the auxiliary jig shown below in the photo at right. This jig is shaped like the box's fence and it has an index pin (a headless #6 screw) ⅛ in. from the box's ⅛-in.-wide kerf, to cut equal-width fingers and spaces. For the finger-joint jig, I made a Lexan guard that is the same width as the one I use for crosscutting, but it is shorter to accommodate the jig and workpiece. Instead of fitting the jig in the slots, I clamp its ¾x4x3¾ plywood end, which is screwed flush to the end of the three-sided Lexan guard, to the support. —*K.M.*

To cut a small workpiece, Mehler puts the guard on top of it, holds the workpiece down with an L-shaped block, and pushes the crosscut box with his other hand.

The crosscut box becomes a tenoning jig when a vertical support is clamped to its fence. Open mortises, like the one above, can also be cut with this setup.

Mehler clamps his finger-joint jig to the box's fence with the jig's index pin ⅛ in. away from the ⅛-in.-wide blade to produce equal-width spaces and fingers.

ness on both sides of the blade; when you're satisfied, retighten the clamp. Remove the box from the tablesaw, and secure the base to the fence with one screw through an extra-large hole in the base near the clamp. Now remove the clamp.

Before drilling for the rest of the screws, replace the box on the saw and cut through a wide scrap piece. Test the cut with a square; if you need to adjust the fence further, loosen the screw in the enlarged hole, tap the fence into alignment, retighten the screw, and again cut and check the test piece. Continue this process until you're satisfied, and then drill for and drive the rest of the screws at 3-in. intervals.

If you repeatedly cut heavy pieces, you can help maintain the squareness of the fence with plywood stiffeners (shown in the drawing). They not only help strengthen the fence, but also make replacing the fence easier because you need only align a new one on the stiffeners and guard. Keep the stiffeners about 8 in. from the ends of the fence so you can still clamp a stop to the fence when repetitively cutting stock to the same length.

Making blade guards — A blade guard is a necessity. The clear Lexan guard I made shields my fingers from the blade and helps protect me from offcuts and sawdust that may fly off the blade. I don't find the guard restrictive as some woodworkers might claim. Since the ends of the guard's extra-long sides slide in dadoes in the fence and back support, the guard can be lifted to accommodate up to a 3½-in.-thick workpiece. You could make the guard with clear acrylic plastic, such as Plexiglas, but the polycarbonate Lexan can resist a stronger impact. I cut the parts on the tablesaw and then glued the guard together with Weldon 3 solvent cement, although Weldon 35 is recommended for polycarbonate (both are available from IPS, PO Box 379, Gardena, Cal. 90248; 213-321-6515). I clamped the assembly with the top centered between the sides and with the ends inset about 1 in. Then, following the directions on the cement, I ran a thin stream of it into the joints, as shown in the top photo at right. Put only enough in the joint to fill it; too much and it will run down the sides. To run a stream of solvent into the end joints, stand the assembly up vertically. The ends strengthen the guard, even though the blade will cut through them.

Since the sawblade comes through the fence when it's raised to maximum height, I made an exit guard for crosscutting a thick workpiece. The guard in the drawing fits my 10-in. tablesaw, but you can adjust the dimensions if your saw is larger. The guard should be 2 in. to 3 in. wide, at least ¼ in. above the blade at its maximum height, and extend at least 1 in. in front of the blade when the blade is centered on the face of the front fence. Fasten the guard to the box by driving two screws through the fence and into the guard. I countersunk them into the bottom of the Lexan guard dadoes. Finally, screw the base to the bottom of the guard, and finish all the wood with Watco oil. Then I fastened stop blocks to the box and saw table to keep from sawing through the exit guard. I screwed a ½x⅞x2 stop block to the base where it overhangs the saw table (near its left, front corner), and I screwed another one to the edge of the table. The block on the base should be about 1/16 in. from the table edge (so it won't bind), and the block on the table should stop the box when the center of the fully raised blade reaches the face of the fence. I fastened the block to my table by countersinking two #10 by 1-in.-long flat-head machine screws, washers and nuts into 3/16-in.-dia. holes through both. Before you do this, make sure there aren't any obstructions under the table where you intend to drill the holes. Then slightly round over the corners of the block screwed to the table, so you don't take flesh off if you bump it.

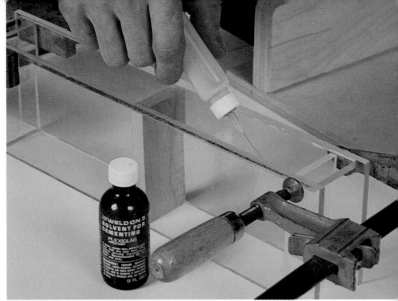

With the Lexan guard parts clamped together, Mehler squeezes one-minute cement into the joints. The ends of the guard's sides slide into dadoes in the box's fence and back support.

To demonstrate the capacity of his wide cutoff box, Mehler trims the end of a 30-in. paneled door. A wedge between the door and support presses the workpiece against the fence.

Making other crosscut boxes — To cut wider panels, such as the 30-in. door in the bottom photo above, I made another crosscut box with a base as wide as my saw table from front to back. Since more than half of its width extends over the back of the saw at the end of a cut, it should be supported on an outfeed table. If you make a box much wider than this, I think you will also need a support in front of your saw. I recently attached an outfeed table to my saw and now wonder how I lived without it for so long. Instead of an outfeed table, you could use outfeed rollers (which are best when attached to the saw), a separate table, saw horses or even an adjustable ironing board.

Finally, since crosscut boxes help make such accurate cuts, I also made a 14-in.-wide by 26-in.-long box, which is more convenient for narrow workpieces. This box doesn't overhang the left side of the table, and so I stop the box's travel short with a dowel in the outfeed table. With a little imagination, I'm sure you'll come up with variations, such as a mitering box, a crosscut box with an adjustable angle or a beveling box. □

Kelly Mehler operates Treefinery Woodshop and Gallery in Berea, Ky.

Working with Portable Planers

Low-cost surfacers rise to new levels

by William D. Lego

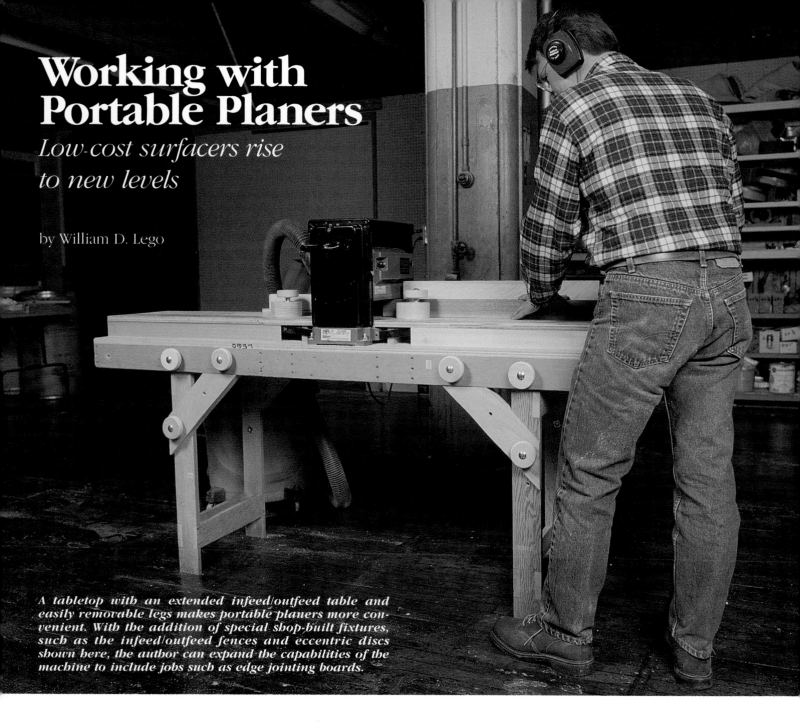

A tabletop with an extended infeed/outfeed table and easily removable legs makes portable planers more convenient. With the addition of special shop-built fixtures, such as the infeed/outfeed fences and eccentric discs shown here, the author can expand the capabilities of the machine to include jobs such as edge jointing boards.

Several years ago, United Parcel Service brought a Ryobi AP-10 surface planer to my door, and my shop hasn't been the same since. This compact, portable machine can produce a nearly scraper-fine finish at a very affordable price. Since then, several other companies have begun marketing similar planers. They lack the stability and power of the large, stationary machines, but they can do a lot of high-quality work, especially if you build a few simple jigs. In this article, I'll describe planer setups I've developed for edge jointing boards, beveling stock and tapering table legs. These jigs evolved from one-time affairs cobbled from scraps into carefully constructed setups that can be quickly and easily installed, removed and conveniently stored.

Most of these small planers don't come with a base. After kneeling on the floor running test pieces through my new machine, I soon realized my first project would be to build a planer stand. Also, since the 19 in. of total support provided by the standard infeed and outfeed rollers was insufficient to eliminate the bounce at the end of long boards, which created a washboard surface on the stock, I decided to expand the stand into a 6-ft.-long box-beam table with support on both ends of the machine.

My first table sat atop two sawhorses and could be leaned against the wall for easy storage. Later, I added legs to the table (see the photo above). Because I did not want to eliminate the planer's portability features, I designed a table with light, yet strong legs that can be removed and stored within the framework of the tabletop, shown in the photo on p. 106. The whole stand can be made for $50 to $75.

Building the table—The basic box frame for the table is assembled with straight, clear Douglas fir 1x4 dimensional lumber and drywall screws. Even though this unit is durable enough to withstand the rigors of daily commercial use (I've been using mine for more than three years), I recommend using fir 2x4s, as shown in figure 1 on the facing page, for a table that will frequently be dragged in and out of a truck. The framework is made by fitting crossmembers into ¾-in.-deep dadoes and rabbets in the front and rear rails. The box frame is then covered with a ¾-in. birch-veneer plywood tabletop. Make sure the frame is flat and well supported on the floor or a bench before screwing on the plywood, otherwise you may build a permanent bow into the table. Next, I centered and bolted the planer to the plywood top. Poplar strips, screwed to the tabletop, support the ¾-in. birch-veneer plywood infeed/outfeed table at the exact height of the planer bed, as shown

From *Fine Woodworking* (May 1990) 82:66-69

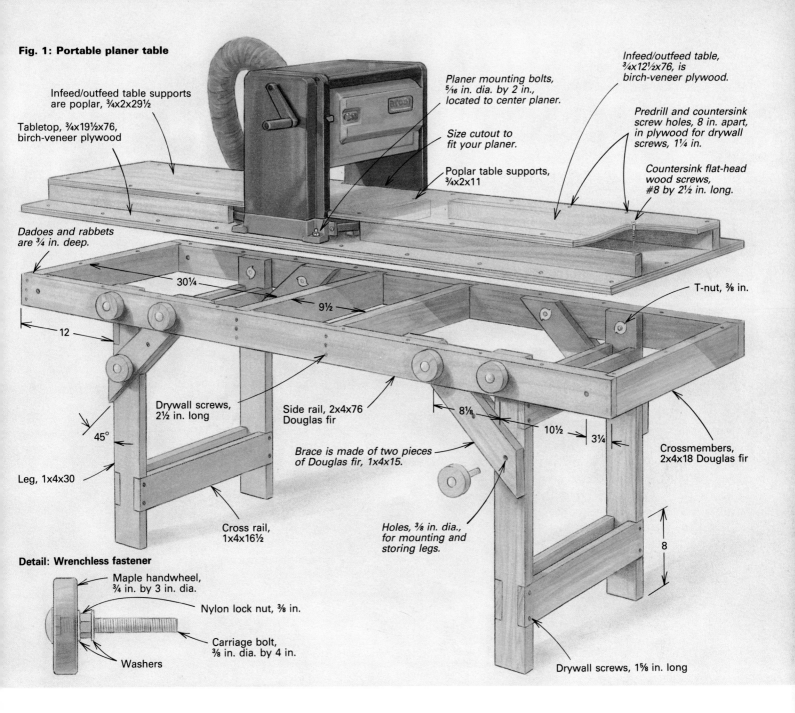

Fig. 1: Portable planer table

Infeed/outfeed table supports are poplar, ¾x2x29½

Tabletop, ¾x19½x76, birch-veneer plywood

Dadoes and rabbets are ¾ in. deep.

30¼

12

45°

Leg, 1x4x30

9½

Drywall screws, 2½ in. long

Cross rail, 1x4x16½

Side rail, 2x4x76 Douglas fir

Brace is made of two pieces of Douglas fir, 1x4x15.

Planer mounting bolts, ⁵⁄₁₆ in. dia. by 2 in., located to center planer.

Size cutout to fit your planer.

Poplar table supports, ¾x2x11

8⅛

10½   3¼

Holes, ⅜ in. dia., for mounting and storing legs.

Infeed/outfeed table, ¾x12½x76, is birch-veneer plywood.

Predrill and countersink screw holes, 8 in. apart, in plywood for drywall screws, 1¼ in.

Countersink flat-head wood screws, #8 by 2½ in. long.

T-nut, ⅜ in.

Crossmembers, 2x4x18 Douglas fir

8

Drywall screws, 1⅝ in. long

Detail: Wrenchless fastener

Maple handwheel, ¾ in. by 3 in. dia.

Nylon lock nut, ⅜ in.

Carriage bolt, ⅜ in. dia. by 4 in.

Washers

in figure 1. To install the infeed/outfeed table, set the planer to its maximum thickness of cut, and then feed the table diagonally through the planer until it can be laid flat on the bed of the planer and screwed to the support strips fastened to the main table. Although the infeed/outfeed table reduces the planer's depth of cut by ¾ in., it provides a long, smooth, sturdy support for stock being run through the machine.

The leg assemblies of 1x4 fir, shown in figure 1, are also box-beam-type construction for strength and lightness. These legs are bolted to the table frame and braced at each end by a pair of leg supports, positioned at 45° angles to virtually eliminate any wobble. When the table needs to be moved, the legs unbolt and store inside the table frame.

To make changing the legs and attaching the jigs even easier, I developed wrenchless fasteners, shown in the detail in figure 1. These fasteners are simply ¾-in. maple handwheels secured to the end of a carriage bolt. The handwheels can be turned on a lathe or cut out with a 3-in. hole saw. To sand each handwheel after cutting, mount it on its ⅜-in.-dia. carriage bolt, chuck it in the drill press and run it against a belt sander. Once the table is assembled, you're ready to go to work.

Edge jointing on the planer—Since I don't have a jointer in my shop, I tried to true the edges of the stock by running the boards on edge through the Ryobi. This resulted in strips that were less than perfectly square: they looked like little parallelograms in cross section. I first tried screwing squared blocks to the infeed/outfeed table to hold the stock vertically, but this left my table looking like a pincushion. I eventually developed the setup shown in the photo on the facing page. The jig uses round eccentric discs that adjust to hold stock between ¼ in. and 1¼ in. thick (up to 4⅜ in. wide) on edge as it is fed through the planer. These discs hold the stock against fixed fences secured to the planer's infeed/outfeed table with wrenchless fasteners. As you can see in figure 2 on the following page, the infeed fence consists of a faceplate screwed at 90° to a baseplate and reinforced with five braces. A wear plate, attached to the front of the faceplate provides a renewable working surface. I used ¾-in. lumbercore, birch-veneer plywood, although straight maple or other hardwood will do. Begin making the infeed fence by fastening the faceplate to the baseplate with 1¼-in. drywall screws. Predrilling all the holes will help prevent splitting and ensure that the screws are fully countersunk. The 90° braces are held in place with two screws through the baseplate and one

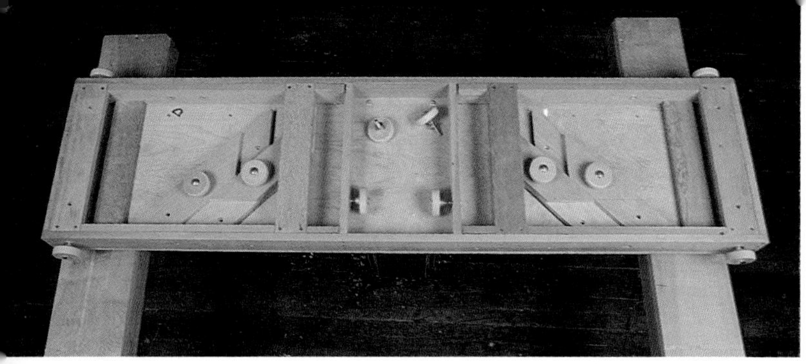

A view of the underside of the planer stand shows how the detached legs fit within the framework of the table and are held in place by shopmade wrenchless fasteners and leg braces.

screw through the faceplate. Finish up the fence by attaching the wear plate with $1\frac{1}{4}$-in. drywall screws through the back of the faceplate. The outfeed fence is easily made by screwing a block of maple to a piece of $\frac{3}{4}$-in. lumbercore plywood and rounding the infeed corner to prevent the stock from hanging up. The eccentric discs, which must be carefully made to hold stock perpendicular to the planer bed, can be turned on the lathe or made with a drill press and belt sander. Drill a $\frac{3}{8}$-in. hole in each disc, $\frac{1}{2}$ in. off center, to create the eccentricity. I used wrenchless fasteners, built as previously described, and $\frac{1}{4}$-in. carriage bolts to hold the fences in place. For tighter clamping with the eccentric discs, I used $\frac{3}{8}$-in. bolts in the fasteners.

To install and operate the edge-jointing jig, mount the infeed and outfeed fences and the eccentric discs as shown in figure 2 below. Use a straightedge to align the front edges of the fences before tightening them in place on the table. To use the jig, place a piece of stock to be edge jointed against the infeed and outfeed fences. Now, rotate the eccentric discs until they just touch the stock and then back them off a few thousands of an inch until the stock just slides between the fences and the discs. If the discs are adjusted correctly and the stock has been planed to the same thickness, this setup will create a straight, square edge on your stock. Although my edge-jointing jig will only work on stock up to $4\frac{3}{8}$ in. wide, I find it invaluable for dressing edges on face frames, door frames and drawer sides.

When not in use, the eccentric discs store on the back of the infeed fence, secured with wrenchless fasteners. I usually leave the fences in place on the infeed/outfeed table when thickness-planing stock up to 5 in. wide. However, to plane stock from 5 in. up to the full 10-in. capacity of the planer, I remove the fences.

Planing beveled edges–About the time I got my Ryobi AP-10, I was commissioned to make a walnut frame-and-panel bar with a 45° angle in the middle. To get clean, accurately cut edges, I decided to use the planer to bevel the stiles where they met at the 45° angle. This required making a jig similar to the one shown in figure 3 below, only I made this one as a temporary device with a $22\frac{1}{2}$° angle. The jig consists of $\frac{3}{4}$-in. by $2\frac{1}{2}$-in. hardwood cut at the desired angle to form inclined blocks that are screwed to a plywood baseplate. Another piece of plywood screwed to the blocks forms the inclined table for feeding the stock through the planer. A hardwood cleat, screwed to the inclined table, supports the bottom edge of the board being planed. The jig is held in position by fastening the baseplate to the infeed/outfeed table.

Additional jigs with inclined tables of 30°, 45° and $67\frac{1}{2}$° were developed for different jobs, the only difference in each being the angle of the inclined blocks. Like the initial edge-jointing jig, the beveling jigs were screwed to the infeed/outfeed table, but they were so handy I made permanent fixtures. In addition to being sturdier, the new jigs have baseplates dimensioned the same so a uniform mounting system incorporating T-nuts and wrenchless fasteners can be used. In use, the jigs are centered, front to back, under the planer on the infeed/outfeed table and held in place with wrenchless fasteners made with $\frac{1}{4}$-in.-dia. by $2\frac{1}{2}$-in.-long carriage bolts. By varying the side-to-side position of the baseplates on the table, the wear on the planer blades is more evenly distributed; but make sure the wrenchless fasteners don't interfere with stock being fed through the jig.

The degree of accuracy used in cutting the inclined blocks will determine how precise the jigs will be. A power miter box or accurately adjusted radial-arm saw will yield good results, but test

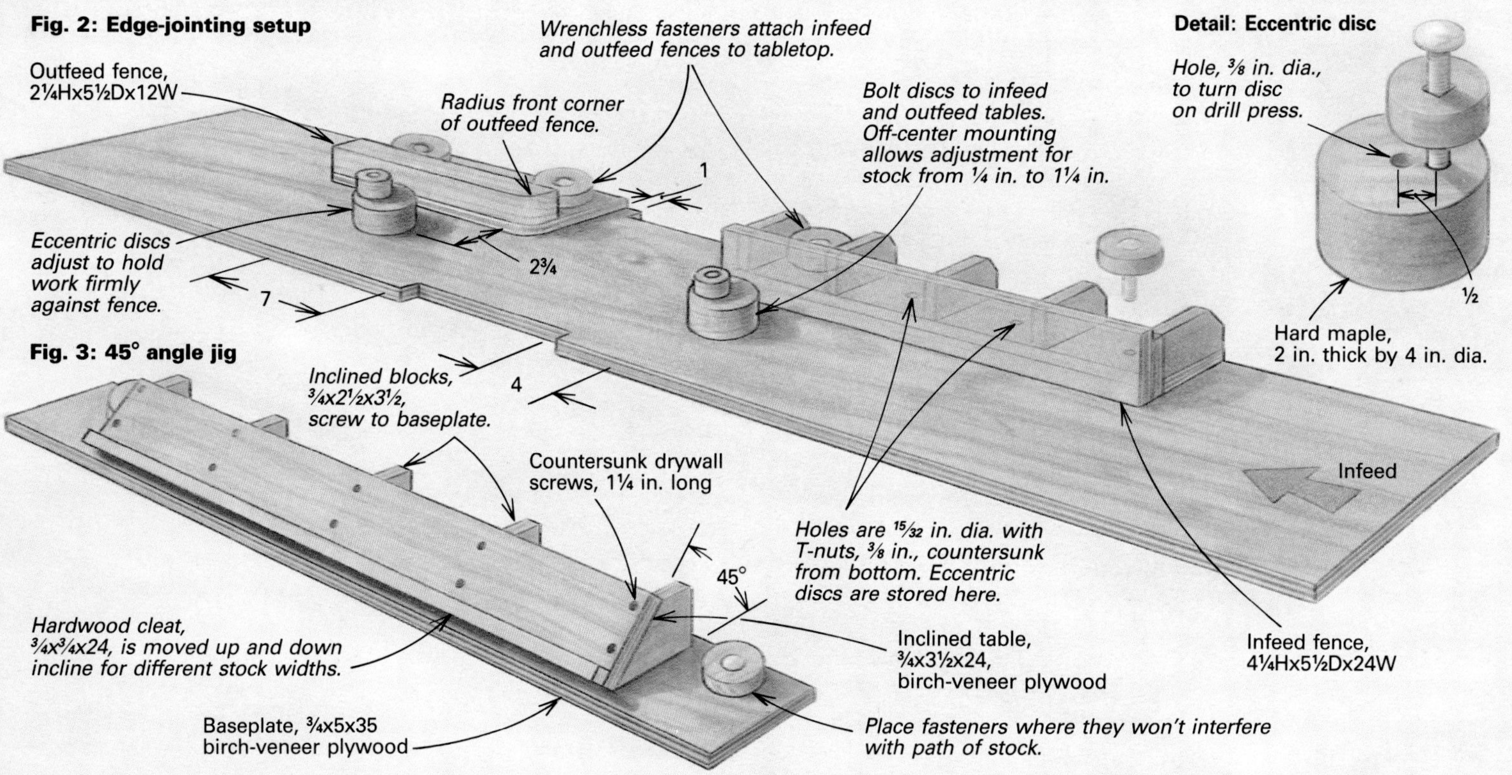

Fig. 2: Edge-jointing setup
Outfeed fence, 2¼Hx5½Dx12W
Wrenchless fasteners attach infeed and outfeed fences to tabletop.
Radius front corner of outfeed fence.
Bolt discs to infeed and outfeed tables. Off-center mounting allows adjustment for stock from ¼ in. to 1¼ in.
1
2¾
Eccentric discs adjust to hold work firmly against fence.
7
4
Detail: Eccentric disc
Hole, ⅜ in. dia., to turn disc on drill press.
½
Hard maple, 2 in. thick by 4 in. dia.
Fig. 3: 45° angle jig
Inclined blocks, ¾x2½x3½, screw to baseplate.
Countersunk drywall screws, 1¼ in. long
45°
Holes are 15/32 in. dia. with T-nuts, ⅜ in., countersunk from bottom. Eccentric discs are stored here.
Infeed
Hardwood cleat, ¾x¾x24, is moved up and down incline for different stock widths.
Inclined table, ¾x3½x24, birch-veneer plywood
Infeed fence, 4¼Hx5½Dx24W
Baseplate, ¾x5x35 birch-veneer plywood
Place fasteners where they won't interfere with path of stock.

the jigs before using them on a project. To test the 45° beveling jig, for example, cut four little pieces from scrapwood run through the jig, and fit them together like pieces of a pie. If they do indeed make half a pie, then the jig is right on. If not, adjust the jig by running a strip of iron-on plywood edgebanding tape along the bottom of the baseplate. The angle of cut can be either decreased or increased by adding the tape to the front or back edge of the baseplate. When fine-tuning your jigs, it is better to err on the side of a smaller angle because this ensures the visible outside of the assembly will show a tight joint.

Shortly after completing my new set of beveling jigs, I had the opportunity to put them to use. This time the project was a three-sided frame-and-panel desk with the sides coming together at a 135° angle, as described in the sidebar on the following page.

Another angle on planing—Tapering table legs usually calls for cutting the taper on a tablesaw or bandsaw and then handplaning and sanding to the final dimension. If I were an antique restorer, replacing a damaged leg or even making legs for a table or two, I would probably make them in the traditional manner. But for limited production runs, I saw the initial taper and run the legs through the planer with the jig shown in the photo at right. This method produces uniform surfaces that are ready for finish-sanding much quicker than hand methods.

The jig is made of two leaves of ¾-in. birch-veneer plywood hinged together at one end as shown in figure 4 below. The top leaf, reinforced by two hardwood strips, is held at the desired angle by sliding supports. I made up six of these supports to accommodate a variety of angles, but normally only use three of them at a time. They are held in place by ¼-20 hex bolts that run through slots in the bottom leaf into T-nuts in the support base. My jig handles legs up to 34 in. long by 2⅝ in. square, but can be easily modified for specific applications. Cut the blank a couple of inches long so any surfacer snipes at the ends can be cut away when the leg is trimmed to its finished length. The leg blank is held in place by ¼-in.- to ¾-in.-thick cleats screwed into the top leaf on both sides and top and bottom of the blank. Be sure these cleats hold the leg firmly, and place a shim under the untapered portion of the leg to prevent any movement that would alter the taper.

Cleaning up the sawn tapers is easy. Begin by using a square to draw a reference line around the top of the leg where the taper will end; I usually leave 5 in. of untapered stock at the top of my legs. After rough-sawing the taper to shape, position the leg blank on the top leaf and secure it with cleats and the wedge, as shown in figure 4. Set the jig to the desired angle and run it and the leg through the planer until the taper reaches the reference line. Turn the blank 90° and repeat this procedure for each side you want to taper.

In developing jigs, whether for the planer or other tools, I try to expand the utility of the particular tool; but I also focus on the design and safe use of these jigs. As a general guideline when developing your own jigs, protect your hands by keeping adjustments away from moving blades and bits; be sure metal parts don't interfere with cutting edges; mark blade paths if the jig will cover the obvious path of the blade; make guards and dust pickups an integral part of the device whenever possible; and use nuts with nylon anti-loosening inserts in the threads to prevent the nuts from vibrating loose. When first using a jig, try to anticipate any problems and be extra vigilant, ready to shut the tool down at the first sign of any problem. Check for loose bolts, nuts or screws during the shake-down period and then enjoy the convenience and accuracy that jigs can add to your shop. □

William Lego builds custom cabinets and furniture in Rockford, Ill.

Sources of supply

Grizzly Imports Inc., 1821 Valencia St., Bellingham, WA 98226; (800) 541-5537, (800) 523-4777.

Jet Equipment and Tools, Box 1477, Tacoma, WA 98401; (800) 243-8538.

Makita USA, 1450 Feehanville Drive, Mt. Prospect, IL 60056; (708) 297-3100.

Penn State Industries, 2850 Comly Road, Philadelphia, PA 19154; (800) 288-7297, (215) 676-7609.

Ryobi America Corp., 1424 Pearman Dairy Road, Anderson, SC 29625; (800) 323-4615.

Sears Power Tools, 9390 Bunson Parkway, Louisville, KY 40220; (800) 366-3000.

Shopsmith, Inc., 3931 Image Drive, Dayton, OH 45414; (800) 543-7586.

Sunhill, 1000 Andover Park E., Seattle, WA 98188; (800) 544-1361.

Williams & Hussey, Box 1149, Wilton, NH 03086; (800) 258-1380, (603) 654-6828.

This birch-veneer plywood planer jig cleans up sawn tapers on legs more quickly and uniformly than handplaning, leaving a surface ready for final-sanding and finishing.

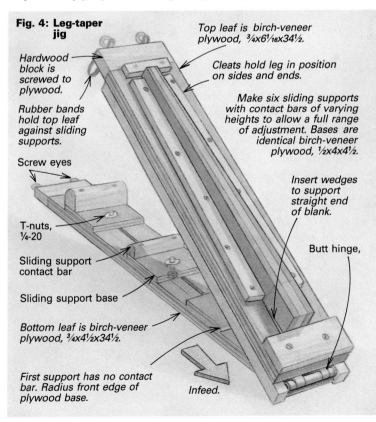

Fig. 4: Leg-taper jig

Top leaf is birch-veneer plywood, ¾x6¹⁄₁₆x34½.

Hardwood block is screwed to plywood.

Cleats hold leg in position on sides and ends.

Rubber bands hold top leaf against sliding supports.

Make six sliding supports with contact bars of varying heights to allow a full range of adjustment. Bases are identical birch-veneer plywood, ½x4x4½.

Screw eyes

Insert wedges to support straight end of blank.

T-nuts, ¼-20

Butt hinge,

Sliding support contact bar

Sliding support base

Bottom leaf is birch-veneer plywood, ¾x4½x34½.

First support has no contact bar. Radius front edge of plywood base.

Infeed.

The Spindle Shaper
Basic techniques for a shop workhorse

by David DeCristoforo

A cope-and-pattern cutter shapes the end of a cabinet rail, held in the sliding-table jig shown in figure 2. Table inserts normally under the cutter head and guards have been removed for clarity in this article, but guards must always be used for actual cuts.

In years gone by, a woodworker's tool chest contained a large selection of wooden handplanes. With skill and enormous labor, the craftsman could cut rabbets, grooves and moldings. Contemporary craftsmen still must perform the same operations, but they're more likely to switch on a spindle shaper than reach for a handplane for raised panel work or large moldings. Again, skill is essential for a good job, but the shaper drastically reduces the labor and time involved.

The shaper is a simple machine—a large horizontal worktable with a vertical spindle projecting through a circular opening. The spindle height is generally controlled by a handwheel on the front of the machine. Cutters are mounted on the spindle, which is driven by a powerful motor, either direct drive or belt driven. At first glance, the shaper may look like a glorified router table, but even the largest router can't match its power or continuous cutting ability.

In times past, you'd grind a steel knife to the shape you wanted and bolt it into a cutter head. In recent years, a broad range of sophisticated cutter systems have become readily available, making the shaper even more versatile than ever. These cutters, which have knives permanently brazed to a heavy steel body, can be arranged in various ways on the shaper's spindle to cut a wide variety of molding profiles, do basic mortise-and-tenon joinery, cope-and-stick moldings for doors and windows, and numerous other tasks. Once you've learned to use collars, templates and hold-downs, the shaper is ideal for rapidly producing odd-shaped parts in large numbers.

Shaper sizes—Shapers are most often classified by spindle size, which, to a large extent, determines the horsepower of the motor; as spindle size increases, so does motor size. I don't think any serious craftsman should consider a machine with a spindle

smaller than ¾ in. and with less than a 2-HP or 3-HP motor. A ½-in. spindle with a 1-HP motor may be sufficient initially for lightweight molding work for furniture, but most workers quickly outgrow these machines. Also, small shapers can handle only small cutters, which generally aren't available in as many patterns as larger cutters. Heavy-duty machines—those with at least ¾-in. spindles—often have interchangeable spindles, which offer greater flexibility in mounting cutters and router bits. My heavy-duty Delta shaper (Model 43-822), for example, has ½-in., ¾-in. and 1-in. spindles, an extra-long ¾-in. spindle and a router collet, all driven by a 3-HP reversible motor with a two-speed (7,000 RPM and 10,000 RPM) pulley setup. The smaller spindle accepts cutters with smaller bores, which usually have smaller outside diameters and can shape tighter curves than large cutters.

Most shapers come from the factory equipped with a split fence. Both halves can be adjusted independently so the fences can be offset, as shown on the next page, in much the same way that jointer tables are offset. If the outfeed fence (fence halves are designated infeed or outfeed according to feed direction) is offset about ⅟₃₂ in., it can support the stock if the entire edge is removed, as when shaping a half round. If only part of the edge is removed, the fences are set flush or replaced with a one-piece fence that spans the opening in the cutter shroud, as shown in figure 1. Factory fences are very limiting; in fact, you may feel they're provided as a token gesture. This is especially apparent with large cutters that won't fit inside the cutter shroud. Also, large cutters often produce enough waste to clog factory-made shrouds and any dust collector attachments. (You'll really need a dust collector if you use many large cutters.)

Shaper safety—Consider safety before using a shaper. It is an extremely dangerous machine and over the years I've developed

From *Fine Woodworking* (March 1988) 69:48-53

Fence halves can be adjusted independently, just as you would set jointer tables so that a wide straight cutter can be used to true edges of stock. The offset shown above is about $\frac{1}{32}$ in.

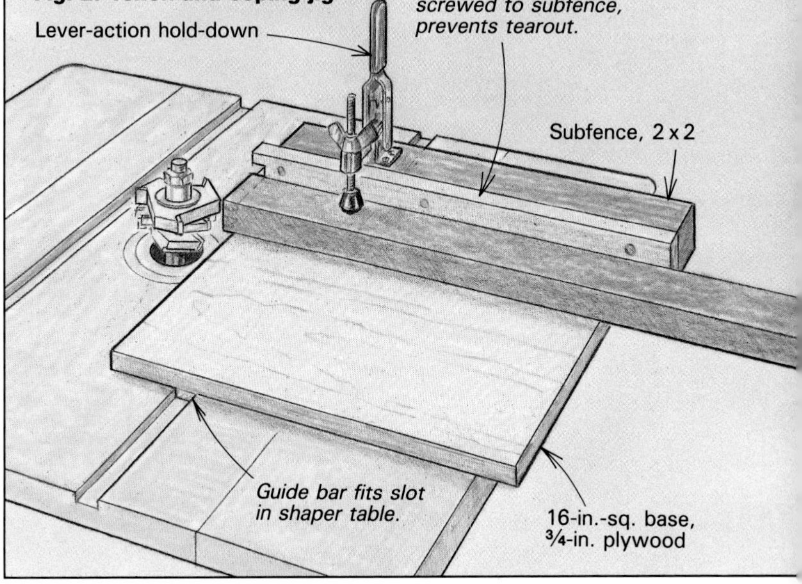

a very healthy respect for it. Read the owner's manual carefully. Some of the safety rules are cut and dry, others enter gray zones where common sense is crucial. Unplug the machine before mounting cutters. Check the speed rating marked on each cutter and don't exceed the recommendation. Never shape narrow stock that would bring your hands within 3 in. to 4 in. of the cutter. Rather, shape the edge of a wider piece and then rip it to size. Push sticks aren't recommended, as they might be with a tablesaw, because of the danger of the stick contacting the cutter. A 2-lb. chunk of steel spinning at 7,000 RPM under 2 HP or 3 HP can tear a push stick out of your hand with ease, exposing you to serious injury. The push blocks with non-slip rubber faces often used to move stock facedown over a jointer are useful for some cuts. If you must shape narrow stock, use featherboards or hold-downs, or better yet, a power feed, which can mechanically guide the stock past the cutter and let you keep your hands well out of the way. Be equally careful with short pieces or when shaping the endgrain of boards. Never attempt to shape a piece that's less than five times as long as the width of the fence opening. For endgrain work, such as tenoning, where the danger of the cutter suddenly grabbing the piece is high, I use a sliding table to hold the stock.

Never stand directly behind the stock or allow anyone to stand in its path in case it's kicked back and ejected. Don't leave the machine with a cutter loose on the spindle—it's too easy to start the motor, forgetting that the nut is not tightened. If you've never been seriously frightened, this will do it. Last but not least, always lock the spindle elevation mechanism and make sure the cutter clears all fences and guards before starting the machine.

Spindle size versus horsepower—It's unwise to mount a cutter more than $2\frac{1}{2}$ in. in diameter and 1 in. in height on a $\frac{1}{2}$-in. spindle, and even using those sizes on spindles this small can be risky. I have seen a $\frac{1}{2}$-in. spindle with a 5-in.-dia. panel cutter bend enough to jam the cutter into the table. On a 3-HP machine, a $\frac{1}{2}$-in. spindle is seriously overpowered, even with a smaller cutter. For this reason, I rarely use the $\frac{1}{2}$-in. spindle, relying instead on the more substantial $\frac{3}{4}$-in. or 1-in. spindles.

Shaper work can be divided into two broad categories: straight-line work and curved work. With either category, the workpiece must be securely supported at all times—before it reaches the cutter, continually during the cut and until the piece is safely away from the cutting edge. Straight-line work usually involves a fence and a combination of hold-downs, featherboards or factory-supplied tensioning devices to snug the workpiece against the fence and table without endangering fingers.

Fences and associated jigs also can do double duty as guards. I have several panel-raising cutters, for example, which don't clear

Fig. 1: Customized fence
Clamp one end of fence to table so assembly can be rotated into spinning cutter until desired projection is reached.

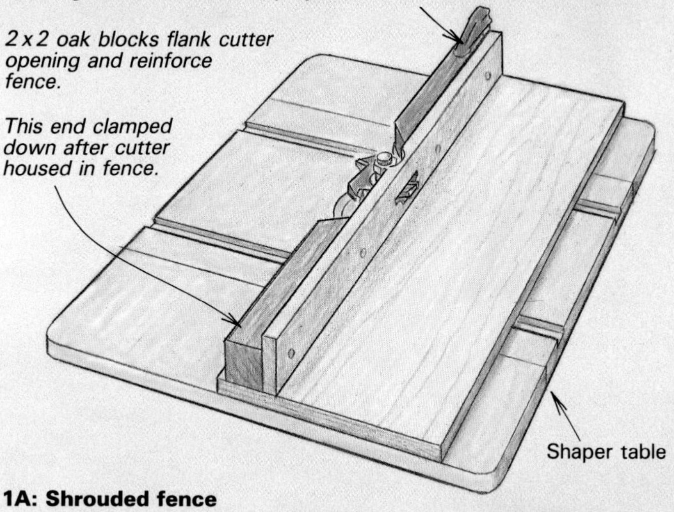

2 x 2 oak blocks flank cutter opening and reinforce fence.

This end clamped down after cutter housed in fence.

Shaper table

1A: Shrouded fence

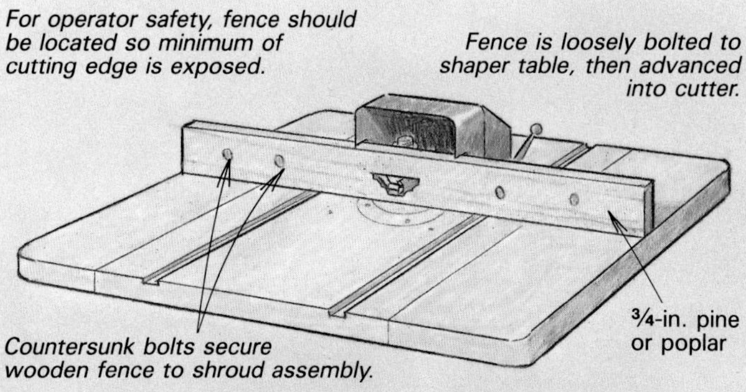

For operator safety, fence should be located so minimum of cutting edge is exposed.

Fence is loosely bolted to shaper table, then advanced into cutter.

Countersunk bolts secure wooden fence to shroud assembly.

$\frac{3}{4}$-in. pine or poplar

Fig. 2: Tenon and coping jig
Lever-action hold-down

Removable 2 x $\frac{3}{4}$ fence screwed to subfence, prevents tearout.

Subfence, 2 x 2

Guide bar fits slot in shaper table.

16-in.-sq. base, $\frac{3}{4}$-in. plywood

the shroud on my Delta shaper, so I built the panel-raising jig shown on the next page for each cutter. One approach to designing these setups is to draw out the cross section and the stock as it will have to pass the cutter to produce the shape you want. Then, simply construct an appropriate stock-support system that can be mounted on the machine—fences don't necessarily have to be mounted square or parallel to the table. To achieve the desired shape, the stock may have to pass the cutter at an angle or vertically, so some of your jigs may be complex and involve considerable time and effort. The time needed to come up with a safe and reliable system is well spent; the consequences of a jig

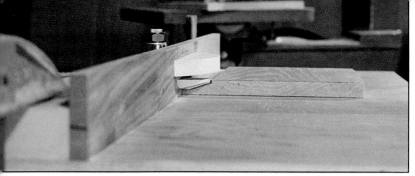

Shopmade fence and guard assembly shields large-diameter panel-raising cutter. Even though these large cutters won't fit within factory-made shrouds and fences, they should never be used without guards. Make a separate guard for each cutter.

Fig. 3: Auxiliary table for panels

Customize guard for individual cutter.

Screws through fence secure ¾-in. softwood guard over panel cutter.

Screw base and fence to support blocks.

¾-in. plywood base, 12 in. wide and as long as the shaper table.

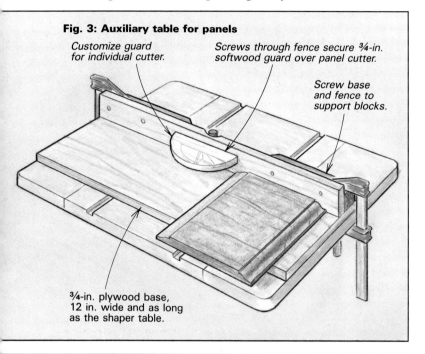

A typical shaper cutter setup includes, from top to bottom—lock nut, lock washer, collar, thin spacer, cutter guard, thin spacer, bushing, cutter, bushing and collar. When the cutter is mounted above the stock, the concentric inserts, shown below, should be installed in the table to provide maximum stock support.

failing could be horrible. These jigs are important, so store them carefully. It's helpful to make notes on the jig itself explaining how it is used and tape on samples of the shaped stock.

Mounting cutters—The exact sequence for mounting cutters and accessories on the spindle depends on the requirements of the cut. A typical setup is shown in the second photo at left. You must always consider the limitations of the machine when determining setups—the major adjustments involve changing the cutter height, either with shims or by raising or lowering the spindle, and changing the distance between the cutter and the fence and/or any template being used to guide the workpiece. Some workers also build tilting fences to support the stock at various angles for specialty cuts; some manufacturers offer tilting arbors for the same purpose.

As an example of the setup adjustments, here's how to shape a cove and bead on a table edge. My cutter has been designed for stock facedown (submerged), counterclockwise rotation, as discussed in the accompanying article on cutter selection. We must first remove enough table-insert rings to provide cutter clearance; the remaining concentric rings help support the stock from below. I usually place a thin ¼-in. collar on the spindle first so the cutter body is not stressed against the spindle-bearing housing. Then the cutter is placed on the spindle with the profile facing up. If the spindle cannot be raised enough for the cutter to project sufficiently, a thicker collar must be placed under the cutter. Several more collars are placed on top of the cutter. I leave at least 1½ times the nut thickness of thread above the last collar so I can get a good grip with the spindle wrench when I tighten the locking washer and nut. Now set the spindle at the approximate elevation needed for the cut. Mount the fence on the machine and set it for the approximate cutter projection. After the fence is locked down and any necessary guards and hold-downs attached, a test cut can be made. Then the elevation and projection can be fine-tuned as needed by adjusting the spindle height and fence location.

I generally feed the stock manually past the cutter, against the direction of cutter rotation. A smooth, steady feed is best. If you feed too fast or the spindle speed is too slow, the cutter will take off bigger chunks of wood, making tearout likely. Shapers are powerful enough to make most cuts in a single pass, but on tough woods or with large cutters, you might get a smoother finish by making a couple of passes. If the grain is really contrary, I'll sometimes feed the wood in the same direction as the cutter rotation, an operation called climb cutting. This is dangerous without a power-stock feed, so don't attempt it freehand. If you get hooked on shaper work, you'll eventually want a power feed anyway, because it gives much more uniform results with less effort and greater safety than hand-feeding allows.

Shaping curves—I generally support curved workpieces with templates, used in conjunction with fences, guide pins inserted in the shaper table itself and guide collars over the cutters. The starting pin supports a curved piece until it can bear on guide collars on the spindle, as shown on the next page. Most shapers have several holes bored into the table for optimal positioning of these tapered pins. Never move a curved piece into the cutter without using the pin. The safest method is to maintain contact with both the pin and the collar, however, it's sometimes necessary to move the work away from the pin to turn a tight curve. Keep in mind that you cannot shape an inside radius or an inside angle smaller than the radius of the cutter. Finish these areas by hand.

Spindle-mounted guide collars can be either fixed or ball bearing and can be mounted either under or over the cutter. A ball-bearing collar functions just like a ball-bearing pilot on a router bit and works more smoothly than a fixed collar. If only a portion of the stock is to be shaped and the uncut edge is at least ⅛ in. thick, that edge can ride directly on the bearing. Otherwise, a template must be used. I usually make my templates out of ¼-in. tempered hardboard and fasten them to the workpiece with small brads. If I'm shaping many duplicates, say legs for a run of chairs, I make a heavier template, commonly called a carrier, out of ¾-in. plywood. The carrier can be fitted with handholds for extra security and several hold-downs to secure the stock as the carrier runs against the guide collar to move the stock past the cutter. Regular straight fences can sometimes also be used for curved work, as when shaping the face of a curved piece like the one shown at right. Templates can also increase the versatility of the guide collars, which are generally sized to a specific cutter. Rather than spending $35 to $45 for a separate collar for each cutter, you can customize templates so one collar can be used with different-size cutters. It is helpful to visualize a line tangent to the ball bearing. If this tangent were the face of a fence, the distance from this face to the outer edge of the cutter would equal the cutter projection. The size of the template can now be adjusted to move the stock closer to or further from the cutter.

I always tell beginners that the best way to understand cutters is to actually make some test cuts. After just a short time, most people begin to understand the toolmakers' logic and have little difficulty setting up cutters to produce the patterns they need. □

David DeCristoforo is a designer/craftsman and writer. He lives in Davis, Calif.

A starting pin and a ball-bearing rub collar are needed to shape a radiused edge. The pin supports the template until it securely bears against the collar.

A shopmade high fence supports the workpiece while it is rotated past the cutter, shaping a relief into the radiused face.

Shaper cutters: infinite varieties, endless possibilities

In the past, every woodworker had to make his own shaper cutters by grinding down steel knives and mounting them in specially designed heads, which had a bad reputation for launching knives from time to time. Now, good-quality shaper cutters are available in a great variety of shapes and styles, and most workers opt for the convenience and greater safety offered by commercial cutters. I don't recommend shopmade knives, especially for inexperienced workers, because of difficulties in shaping, balancing and aligning the knives. Some companies do, however, manufacture cutter heads with improved locks for securing the knives and a variety of useful interchangeable knives.

The other types of commercial cutters range from single-profile cutters to elaborate combination systems that offer a relatively low-cost way to acquire the cutting capability of scores of individual cutters. All the major manufacturers also give the buyer the option of specifying how the cutter will run—clockwise or counterclockwise with the stock facedown (submerged) or counterclockwise with the stock faceup (cutter over). Submerging the cutter is advisable when shaping long or large workpieces unassisted. Should the stock lift off the table during the cut, it won't be forced into the cutter. If you need to observe the progress of

Cutter components: top—ball-bearing rub collars; center, left to right—bushings, spacers, collars and shims; and bottom—Delta's spindle-mounted cutter guard.

the cut, the cutter must be over the stock. Actually, any cutter can be run either facedown or faceup by flipping it over and reversing the spindle rotation, assuming your shaper motor is reversible. This won't cause problems as long as you securely tighten the nut when running the spindle clockwise.

In addition to the basic cutter shape, you'll need a variety of spacers, collars, shims and guide collars, as shown above, for mounting cutters. Spacers are sometimes needed between cutters when more than

one cutter is mounted on the spindle at one time to cut multiple patterns. Shims come in sets of varying thicknesses, generally from 0.003 in. to 0.03 in., and are useful for fine-tuning cutter spacing. Collars take up empty space on the spindle, so you don't have to run the nut all the way down the spindle to secure a single cutter. Guide collars are used for shaping curved edges.

Here is a rundown on common cutters:

Straight cutters: Straight cutters are available in thicknesses from ¼ in. to 3 in. for grooving, rabbeting, dadoing and slotting, and can be stacked with spacers to form tongues. Several narrow cutters can be stacked to make wider cuts, too. For the smoothest and quietest cut, always stagger cutters when stacking them. I've also found that a 2-in. straight cutter gives the shaper several advantages over a jointer. Jointing the edges of wide stock is easier because the wood lies flat on the broad shaper table. Also, using a power feed and climb cutting against the grain, I can joint difficult grain without chipping. On the minus side, stock thickness is limited by the cutter height, and face planing is not practical. Since the face-grinding operation used in sharpening carbide cutters reduces their diameter slightly, it is a good idea to have all your straight cutters sharpened at the same time. This will ensure that all the cutters maintain the same diameter so they can be stacked for tongue cutting. Also, remember that as sharpening changes the cutter diameter, it also changes the relationship between the cutting edge and any ball-bearing collar that might be used with it. You may eventually need to adjust your templates or get smaller collars.

Detail cutters: Detail cutters, available in a multitude of profiles, are used for general molding work. These profiles include ogees, ¼ and ½ rounds, fluting, various cove-and-bead combinations and numerous others. While it is nice to have a good selection of cutters, it is difficult to say which could be considered as "basic." My approach has been to buy cutters as I need them, including their cost in my job estimate. As my inventory of profiles builds, I offer clients designs that incorporate molding profiles already paid for by previous jobs, returning the savings to them in the form of a reduced bid.

Reversible cutters: These cutter profiles interlock when reversed and joined. They can be molding profiles or special cutters like the glue-joint cutter shown below. The rule of thumb with all reversible cutters is that their centerline must line up with the stock's centerline. Some trial and error is necessary to get the cutter elevation just right, so it is a good idea to save a correct stock sample for future setups. The lock-miter cutter is the most difficult reversible cutter to set up because cutter elevation and fence depth both affect its fit. Adjusting this cutter for the first time is a lot like the old rub-your-tummy-and-pat-your-head bit. I like to leave a slight flat at the long point of

A narrow straight cutter cuts a ¼-in. groove in the edge of a board. Both halves of the split fence are aligned with each other to support the stock before, during and after the cut.

The glue-joint cutter will produce the joint shown by simply flipping the stock over for every other pass. This joint has about 2½ times more glue surface than a simple butt joint.

Staff

Shaper cutters range from straight cutters to elaborate molding patterns. Shown above, clockwise from top left, are a Delta ¾-in. straight cutter, a Freeborn straight-top groover, a 3-knife jointing cutter from F.S. Tool Corp., a door lip cutter from LRH Enterprises and a Freud Perfecta combination cutter, which can cut 39 molding shapes.

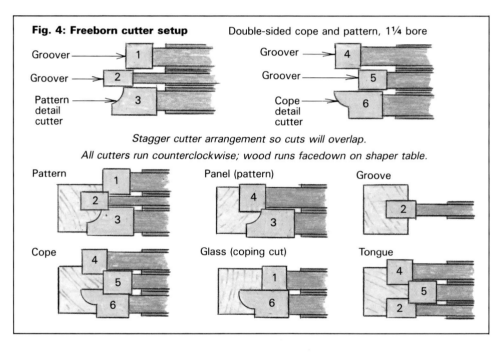

the miter rather than cut right down to a sharp point. I plane away the flat after the pieces are joined.

Combination cutters: Many inexperienced workers find combination cutters too intimidating to use, especially since they often don't come with clear-cut directions. Freud's line of combination cutters, for example, come only with diagrams showing the cut and the numbers of the cutters in the set needed to produce it. A Freud spokesman said these are purchased by experienced woodworkers who don't need detailed instructions. Freud cutter kits aimed at furnituremakers and small shops come with detailed instruction booklets. The Freeborn Tool Co. also provides instruction sheets with its cutters. The guide for the company's double-sided cope-and-pattern cutters (1¼-in.

bore) is shown in figure 4. These patterns can be stacked though, and it's fairly clear how the individual shapes are formed and where the spacers and shims must be used.

For more-complex patterns, cutters sometimes can be stacked together to produce the pattern shown, but often multiple passes must be made, as shown in figure 5. Begin with accurately milled stock and unless you retain a square surface to run against the fence and the table, you will have to build a special support system to hold the piece as it passes by the cutter. If you must remove a great deal of material, you might remove much of the waste with a tablesaw cut before starting the shaper. I usually start with the deepest pattern cut first, reasoning that the setup required would call for the cutter to extend the most, and that the guard devised for it would offer protection for the remain-

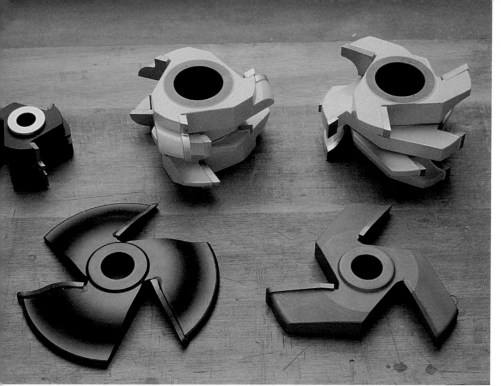

Specialty cuts range from interlocking patterns to wide beveled fields. Above, clockwise from top left: a carbide-tipped glue-joint cutter from Delta; a set of Tantung-tipped cope-and-pattern cutters from Freeborn; and two styles of panel raisers—one from DML that cuts a flat field and a second from F.S. Tool that creates a gently curved field.

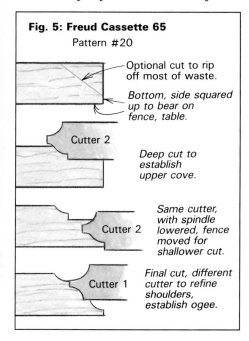

Fig. 5: Freud Cassette 65

Pattern #20

Optional cut to rip off most of waste.

Bottom, side squared up to bear on fence, table.

Cutter 2 — Deep cut to establish upper cove.

Cutter 2 — Same cutter, with spindle lowered, fence moved for shallower cut.

Cutter 1 — Final cut, different cutter to refine shoulders, establish ogee.

ing cuts. Also the deeper cuts would be made while the stock is thickest and most resistant to flexing. The shallower cuts are made last.

Cope-and-pattern cutters: The cope-and-pattern cutters are sold in sets for the construction of doors and other frame-and-panel work. They go by a number of aliases, among which are cope-and-stick, stile-and-rail and male-and-female cabinet door sets. These cutters can be confusing to the novice, but a few practice cuts will clear everything up. The sets consist of two stacks of three cutters each. One stack is used to shape the inside edges of stiles and rails, forming a molded edge and a groove for a panel insert. The second stack is used to cope the ends of the rails, forming an exact mating joint. These sets are available in different thicknesses from ¾ in. to 1¾ in. I usually make the cope

cuts first, using the tenon-and-coping jig shown in figure 2. Endgrain is likely to tear out, but the long-grain pattern cuts usually remove most of the damage. Once all the stock ends are coped, use one of the pieces as a gauge to set the correct height for the pattern cutter. These cutters are factory ground for a correct fit, but sharpening will loosen the fit. Usually, a thin shim under the molding cutter in the cope stack will tighten the joint sufficiently. In any event, cutters in these sets should all be sharpened at the same time. One other hint: Always make more than you need when making interlocking parts—it's easier than setting everything up again to make another matching piece.

Custom cutters: If you or your client want something unique, most manufacturers will custom-make carbide or composite-alloy cutters. You must send an accurate, full-size drawing of the desired profile and your configuration requirements to the manufacturer for bid. These cutters will be expensive. I once paid more than $700 for two cutters to shape a large edge banding. However, I ended up with a one-of-a-kind molding profile I could use over and over.

Panel-raising cutters: Panel raisers can be hair-raisers. They are generally quite large in diameter, often making you feel that you're using a helicopter rather than a woodworking tool. Panel raisers are sized for a specific stock thickness, usually ⅝ in. or ¾ in. They are designed to cut a full profile in the specified thickness, leaving a ¼-in.-thick tongue. A ¾-in. panel raiser cannot be used on material of less than ¾-in. thickness without sacrificing part of the molding profile or part of the tongue thickness. If this same cutter is used to shape ⅞-in.-thick material, you will end up with a ⅜-in.-thick tongue. However, you could rabbet the back of the panel to reduce the tongue thickness. Many manufacturers of-

Sources of supply

Additional information on shapers is available from the following companies:

Andreou Industries Inc., 22-69 23rd St., Astoria, NY 11105.

Cascade Precision Tool Co., P.O. Box 848, Mercer Island, WA 98040.

Chang Iron, U.S. distributor, Woodworker's Supply of New Mexico, 5604 Alameda N.E., Albuquerque, NM 87113.

Delta International, 246 Alpha Drive, Pittsburg, PA 15238.

Farris Machinery (Kitty tools), 2315 Keystone Drive, Blue Springs, MO 64015.

Grizzly Imports, Inc., P.O. Box 2069, Bellingham, WA 98227.

J. Philip Humphrey International Inc., 210 Eighth St. S., Lewiston, NY 14092.

Jet Equipment and Tools, P.O. Box 1477, Tacoma, WA 98401.

Kölle, U.S. distributor, Woodworking Specialties, Quality Lane, P.O. Box 70, Rutland, VT 05701.

Mini Max, 5933 Peachtree Industrial Blvd., Norcross, GA 30092.

Northwood Industrial Machinery, 11400 Decimal Drive, Louisville, KY 40299.

Parks Woodworking Machine Co., 1501 Knowlton St., P.O. Box 23057, Cincinnati, OH 45223.

Powermatic, Morrison Road, McMinnville, TN 37110.

Scheppach America, P.O. Box 135, North Miami Beach, FL 33163.

Sunhill, 1000 Andover Park E., Seattle, WA 98188.

Total Shop, P.O. Box 25429, Greenville, SC 29616.

Transpower, 11000 E. Rush St., #18, S. El Monte, CA 91733.

TWS Machinery, P.O. Box 55545, Seattle, WA 98155.

Wilke Machinery Co., 120 Derry Court, York, PA 17402.

Shaper cutters are available from these manufacturers and their distributors:

Cascade Precision Tool Co., (see above).

Delta International, (see above).

DML, a division of Vermont American Corp., 1350 S. 15th St., Louisville, KY 40201.

Freeborn Tool Co. Inc., 3355 E. Trent Ave., Spokane, WA 99202-4459.

Freud Inc., 218 Feld Ave., High Point, NC 27264.

F.S. Tool Corp., P.O. Box 530, 210 Eighth St., Lewiston, NY 14092.

LRH Enterprises, 6961 Valjean Ave., Van Nuys, CA 91406.

Reliable Grinding, 145 W. Hillcrest Ave., San Bernardino, CA 92408.

TWS Machinery, (see above).

fer a panel-back cutter that can be mounted on the spindle with the panel raiser to simultaneously shape the back of a thicker panel.

Due to their extreme size and cutter projection, panel raisers require extreme caution and should never be mounted on a spindle of less than ¾ in. dia. Never mount them any higher on the spindle than necessary, and guards should always be used.   —D.D.

Workshop Solvents

Selecting the right chemicals and using them safely

by George Mustoe

The alchemists of the Middle Ages alternated their attempts to transmute lead into gold with the search for a universal solvent—a liquid capable of dissolving all materials (had they succeeded, I wonder how they'd have packaged their discovery). Six hundred years later, I'm still following in the alchemists' footsteps. As a chemist, I'm frequently asked to dilute a dish of gooey stuff or to dissolve some residue without damaging the underlying material. Woodworkers often face similar problems. Luckily, if you know a little chemistry, you can select a solvent that not only does the job, but also poses the least health and safety hazards.

Reactive and inert solvents

Despite the rising popularity of water-base finishes (see *FWW* #89, pp. 52-55; *FWW* #69, p. 80 and *FWW* #47, pp. 65-66), sooner or later you will need to use another solvent besides water. Solvents work in one of two ways. Inert solvents, like mineral spirits and lacquer thinner, reduce the viscosity of finishes and allow deeper penetration, more even application and faster drying. They don't alter the composition of the oils or resins used in the finish. In contrast, reactive solvents attack the chemical structure of the materials they dissolve; for example, when methylene chloride is applied to paint, it becomes a paint stripper.

Reactive solvents can dissolve stains or glues and strip finishes because they break apart the molecular bonds. These solvents change substances permanently, so they can't be used to thin paint. Reactive solvents must be chosen carefully, because you don't want them to dissolve

more than you had intended. Some compounds in finish removers, for example, will also attack plastics.

Not all reactive solvents require you to don rubber gloves and eye protection, however. Water is a reactive solvent when it is used with soap (a surfactant), because it alters the structure of grease and dirt molecules, making them water soluble. In addition, solvents may act very selectively. Sugar dissolves readily in water but not in lacquer thinner, even though the latter instantly attacks the varnish on your table. The reactions are not the same because the molecular geometry of the two substances causes great differences in solubility.

Inert solvents make good thinners (diluents), degreasers and cleaners because they can freely intermix with a substance without disturbing its molecular structure. This ability is related to a phenomenon chemists call polarity. Depending on their structure, chemicals have a wide range of polarities. For example, two atoms of hydrogen bond to one oxygen atom to give a water

molecule (H_2O) a wishbone shape (shown on the bottom of the facing page). This arrangement is polar because the hydrogen end has a slight positive charge compared to the end with the oxygen atom. In contrast, methane (CH_4), is non-polar. Its symmetrical structure causes the internal charges to be evenly distributed. The methyl alcohol molecule (CH_3OH) is weakly polar. Its central carbon atom is surrounded on three sides by hydrogen atoms. But on one side, the oxygen atom disturbs the symmetry of electric charge.

A useful rule based on this polarity lesson is "Like dissolves like." Oil, grease and wax have non-polar molecules, so they dissolve easily in non-polar solvents such as paint thinner, not as easily in weakly polar solvents like acetone, and not at all in water, which is strongly polar. When a substance (such as sugar) dissolves readily in water, it's proof that the material's atoms have a polar arrangement. When choosing a solvent for a particular task, you can eliminate a lot of guesswork by referring to the chart on the facing page. For instance, suppose sticky residue from a label has marred your new tool.

If a dab of mineral spirits (non-polar) won't dissolve the gum, don't waste your time by trying turpentine or naphtha. Instead, try alcohol (slightly polar) or water (strongly polar).

Solvent precautions and safer alternatives

You should use less dangerous chemicals in place of highly toxic solvents whenever possible. For example, save your lacquer thinner for its intended purpose, and use mineral spirits, instead, for cleaning brushes. And when diluting shellac, ethanol (denatured, ethyl or grain alcohol) can be substituted for the much more toxic methanol (wood or methyl alcohol).

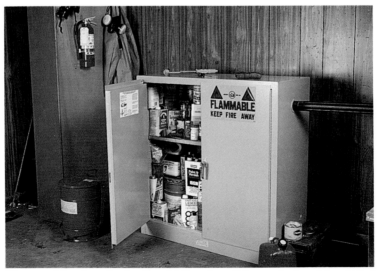

Flammable chemicals should be stored in a steel cabinet that is vented to the outside. A lidded, metal bucket (at left above) provides temporary safe storage for solvent-laden rags.

Photo this page: Alec Waters

Common Shop Solvents

Solvent	Applications	Chemical Type	Toxicity[1] TLV (Threshold Limit Value) in PPM	Flammability[2] * FP (Flash Point) in Degrees F	Usual Route of Absorption L = Lung, S = Skin
Mineral spirits	General-purpose thinner, degreaser, brush cleaner, wood filler	Non-polar	200	86-105	L, S
Turpentine	General-purpose thinner, degreaser, brush cleaner, wood filler	Non-polar	100	95	L, S
VM&P naphtha (benzine)**	Quick-dry thinner, degreaser cleaner	Non-polar	300	20-55	L, S
Xylene, toluene	Some paints and glues	Non-polar	100	40-81	L, S
Hexane	Rubber and contact cements	Non-polar	50	−7	L, S
Lacquer thinner	Quick-dry thinner	Non-polar	100	−50	L, S
Halogenated solvents: methylene chloride†‡, perchloroethylene, trichloroethylene, methyl chloroform	Paint and varnish removers, refinishers, contact cement, aerosols, adhesives, some paints, degreasers	Non-polar	25-350	0-90	L, S
Ethanol (denatured or ethyl alcohol)	Shellac, spirit stain thinner	Weakly polar	1,000	55	L
Isopropanol (isopropyl or rubbing alcohol)	Surface cleaner	Weakly polar	400	53	L, S
Methanol (methyl alcohol)†	Shellac, spirit stain thinner, finish stripper, blush	Weakly polar	200	52	L, S
Acetone	Cleaner, thinner for epoxy and plastic cement	Weakly polar	750	1.4	L
Methyl ethyl ketone	Aerosols, plastic cement	Weakly polar	200	21	L
Methyl isobutyl ketone	Aerosols, plastic cement	Weakly polar	50	73	L
Ethyl acetate	Aerosols, plastic cement	Weakly polar	400	24	L, S
Water	Latex finishes, grime remover	Strongly polar	None	None	NA

Notes

1. Toxicity—highly toxic: less than 101 PPM; moderately toxic: 101-500 PPM; slightly toxic: more than 500 PPM
2. Flammability—extremely flammable: less than 21°F; flammable: 21°F-99°F; combustible: 100°F-150°F
*   Even moderately flammable solvent vapors will ignite readily if exposed to heat sources, sparks or open flames, provided the solvent's temperature exceeds the FP. Vapors may be explosive if they are allowed to accumulate.
** Benzine is not to be confused with benzene (a known carcinogen).
†   This solvent's vapors pass freely through filters of most respirators.
‡   No FP, but flammable when vapors reach 14%-22% by volume at 77°F.

Halogenated hydrocarbons are the only petroleum-base solvents that are not combustible, but this safety feature is often counterbalanced by serious health risks. Carbon tetrachloride is a halogenated hydrocarbon that some older books recommend as a degreaser, but a single exposure to its strong vapors can be fatal. Instead, use mineral spirits or naphtha to remove oil or wax residues. Another familiar halogenated solvent is methylene chloride, a major ingredient in most paint removers and non-flammable brands of contact cement. This liquid is very effective as a stripper because it attacks the adhesion layer of a finish right at the wood, allowing the old coats of finish to be conveniently removed as a gelatinous layer. The acute toxicity of methylene chloride is relatively low, but the vapors have strong narcotic effects and may disrupt your heartbeat. Methylene chloride is also one of two solvents that pass freely through the filter cartridges of organic-vapor respirators (the other is methyl alcohol). Goggles are important since splashed droplets can cause serious eye damage.

The diluents used in both compressor-powered sprayers and spray-can finishes also are highly toxic. And since sprayers require liquids with exactly the right viscosity and drying rate, it's best to follow the manufacturer's recommendations for thinners. Most of these solvents are identified only by a trade name; they are typically a mixture of petroleum distillates and can produce health problems ranging from eye and throat irritation to neurological damage, liver and kidney injury, and blood diseases, so it's best to limit your use of them. One way of minimizing exposure to these solvents is to use brushes or rollers whenever possible, rather than spray guns or aerosol cans. With direct applicators, like brushes, you won't need to dilute the finishing mate-

Chemical polarity in solvents

Strongly polar

Non-polar

Weakly polar

Water (H₂O)

Methane (CH₄)

Methyl alcohol (CH₃OH)

rials as much, which greatly reduces the amount of toxic vapors that are emitted.

Many petroleum-base liquids can be used as thinners for brush-on varnishes and paints, and even though most of these organic solvents perform similarly, their toxicities vary widely. The least-hazardous choice for brush-on varnish and paint thinner is mineral spirits. Turpentine also has low toxicity, but it's more likely to cause allergic skin reactions. In fact, prolonged or repeated skin exposure to most solvents (except water) can cause skin irritation. This occurs because many solvents, like acetone, ethanol and ketones, extract natural oils from skin layers, which results in severe chapping. If you need a thinner that dries quickly, naphtha is safer than most other fast-evaporating solvents, but be aware that quick-dry solvents all pose substantial fire hazards. Woodworkers are usually surprised to learn that the most flammable shop solvent is acetone—a liquid that's often handled with very little caution.

Most finish removers contain solvents that are toxic to some degree when inhaled or absorbed through the skin. Some non-chemical refinishing alternatives are safe, but they require a bit more time and effort. Sanding and cabinet scraping are two methods that don't rely on chemicals. And the new, so-called safe strippers, such as Wood Finisher's Pride, Easy-Off, Bix Hydro Stripp and 3M's Safest Stripper, are other possible alternatives. These products utilize relatively safe compounds like methyl pyrrolidone (NMP), dibasic ester (DBE), d-limonene or citrus extracts. However it's still a good idea to conduct a test before using any of them to refinish one of your favorite antiques.

If you do have to use a highly toxic solvent, you can guard yourself against absorption and inhalation by avoiding spills, wearing goggles and butyl gloves, and using a chemical-cartridge respirator with an organic-vapor canister. And, of course, the warnings to "use with adequate ventilation" should be heeded. For more information on

Will new VOC regulations affect you?   by Michael Dresdner

Twenty-three years ago, Americans launched Earth Day to emphasize the environmental damage caused by humans. Since then, more attention has been paid to the hazardous wastes we've been putting into our air. Among these are hydrocarbon solvents called volatile organic compounds (VOCs) that evaporate into the air and are widely used by wood finishers.

The media has chronicled the problems associated with ozone depletion caused by the release of chloroflourocarbons (CFCs) into the upper atmosphere. Although CFC pollutants continue to thin our protective ozone layer, the VOC/ozone problem acts in reverse and occurs in our lower atmosphere. Since VOCs are photoreactive, sunlight causes them to create, rather than destroy, ozone. But excess ozone in our surface air makes breathing difficult and combines with particles to form smog. Unfortunately, the surplus ozone in our troposphere (surface atmosphere) doesn't travel high enough to benefit our stratosphere (upper atmosphere).

Since most of the solvents that make up finishing materials are ozone-producing VOCs, it's actually easier to name the three groups of VOC exceptions. First, there are additives, like ammonium hydroxide used in latex paint, which are not organic compounds. The second group contains VOCs that produce little or no ozone. Alcohol (a shellac solvent) and methylene chloride (a solvent in paint remover) fall into this category. The third group contains VOCs that evaporate so slowly they aren't counted in a paint's formula. Virtually everything else used to thin paint and varnish is an ozone-producing VOC.

As a way to reduce tropospheric ozone, the 1990 Clean Air Act restricted the amount of VOCs finishers (and everyone else) are allowed to release.

Presently, there are two actions being taken to reduce VOCs, and together they can create even more significant reductions. The first is for solvent users to increase their transfer efficiency (TE), which is a percentage of the amount of finish that actually contacts the wood. The TE rates the application method used on the wood and not the finish's solvent content.

Brushes, paint pads and rollers boast TE's of almost 100%. By contrast, a typical compressed-air spray gun operates at only a 35% TE; two-thirds of the finish leaves via the spray-booth fan without ever touching the work. Between these application methods are high-volume, low-pressure (HVLP) turbine sprayers and airless systems with TEs from 60% to 85%.

The second VOC action deals with the finishes. Finish and paint formulators are redesigning coatings with lower solvent levels and, in some cases, replacing a portion of their product's VOCs with alternative diluents such as water. Most current water-base finishes still contain VOCs, but less of them.

Each state is responsible for meeting the national ambient air-quality standards. Regulations vary from state to state. The toughest come from the south coast air-quality management district (SCAQMD), the southern California area that includes Los Angeles. SCAQMD regulates both VOC content in finishes and the minimum TE of application methods.

Many states will eventually pass similar legislation, but in the interim, the Environmental Protection Agency (EPA) has suggested that all states use the Chicago, Ill., standards (see chart below) as a minimum guideline if stricter laws aren't already in place. Companies that want to find out a state's regulations can contact their local air-quality department. For information, call the EPA at (703) 308-8721.

Hobbyists and shop owners will, in most cases, be exempt from regulations because they represent a small part of the problem. In comparison, big furniture manufacturers put out more VOCs in one day than a dozen small shops produce in a year. But that doesn't mean small users shouldn't be concerned with the VOC issue. Voluntary compliance with these regulations sets a good example for other finish producers and sends a message to lawmakers. Considering the current state of our environment, we simply can't afford to look the other way. ☐

Finishing Material Limits		
Item	(grams/liter)	(lb./gal.)
Clear topcoat	670	5.6
Opaque stain	560	4.7
Pigmented coat	600	5.0
Repair coat	670	5.6
Sealer	670	5.6
Transparent stain	790	6.6
Wash coat	730	6.1

Grams of VOC per liter of coating less water and any exempt compounds for the eight-county Chicago, Ill., area. Limits are given as guidelines by EPA for other states.

Michael Dresdner is a finish consultant, woodworker and author in Perkasie, Pa.

Chart courtesy of *Custom Woodworking Business*, summer, 1991, p. 68

safely using hazardous chemicals, see *FWW* #80, pp. 58-63.

Proper ventilation and fire safety

Adequate ventilation consists of a steady flow of fresh air across a work area in a direction that carries fumes away from the worker. Indoors, this means opening all the doors and windows for good cross-ventilation. If a strong odor is present or you develop dizziness, headache or nausea, leave the area immediately. But don't trust your sense of smell to protect you from all vapors. For example, the legal maximum limit considered safe for workplace exposure to methyl alcohol is only 200 parts per million (PPM), but most people can't smell it until the vapor level reaches 2,000 to 6,000 PPM. Also, most solvent vapors are two to four times heavier than air, so fumes accumulate near the floor. Because of this, ventilation is especially important for basement shops and storage areas. An air-to-air exchanger and a spark-free exhaust fan are ideal for basements.

The proper handling and storage of solvents are important for fire and ventilation safety. It's risky to stockpile large amounts of solvents; a few gallons will satisfy the needs of most shops. Woodworkers should not be using gasoline or kerosene except for its intended use as a fuel. Besides its high flammability, gasoline may also contain toxic tetraethyl lead or benzene. Kerosene is less

hazardous and may work for degreasing machine parts, but like gasoline, it is a poorly refined petroleum product that has relatively inferior handling properties when used as a shop solvent. Frequently used solutions are best stored in a flame-proof safety can (shown at right). Keep solvent-contaminated rags in lidded, metal disposal cans (see the photo on p. 114) that are located away from potential fuels. Flammable vapors must be protected from heat in case of a shop fire, to delay ignition so that occupants can escape. Rather than putting solvents in glass jars or using open containers to park used paint brushes, keep them in sealed cans. To store cans, buy a double-walled steel, flammable-liquid storage cabinet, like the one shown in the photo on p. 114, or build a fire-resistant locker. Most state require that the lockers be vented to the outside and limit the total amount of solvents that you can legally keep on hand. And some states have now imposed restrictions on the use of solvents that are volatile organic compounds (VOCs). See the sidebar on the facing page for more information on VOCs.

Records compiled by the National Fire Protection Association reveal that spontaneous combustion is a leading cause of woodshop fires. Turpentine and oil finishes are particularly hazardous because of their tendency to oxidize in air. A heap of oil- or turpentine-soaked rags can reach ig-

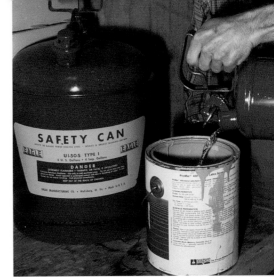

Safety cans are ideal solvent containers. *The cans have flash arrestors and caps that release pressure, dissipate heat and retard vapor ignition. Here, Mustoe adds mineral spirits via a can's triggered spout.*

nition temperature in a few hours. Soaking rags in water can delay combustion, but it's best to dispose of solvent-laden wastes each day. Fortunately, there are many environmentally sound options for removing waste solvents (see the sidebar below). Finally, make sure your shop's fire extinguisher is suited for flammable liquids, and keep it handy. ☐

George Mustoe is a geochemist in Bellingham, Wash. His part-time woodworking projects include skis, snowshoes and Irish harps.

Disposing of solvents responsibly
by Jeff Jackson

As woodworkers, we use solvents and other finishing products that may end up as hazardous wastes, so it's important to keep abreast of environmentally responsible waste-disposal methods. The *Code of Federal Regulations* (Title 40—Protection of the Environment) defines hazardous waste and establishes reportable quantities for releases of certain chemicals. However, these laws don't apply to most woodworkers because they use such small amounts of organic compounds, such as solvents.

Nevertheless, even small quantities of hazardous wastes can contaminate the environment. A quart of stripper carelessly discarded in a stream can contaminate millions of gallons of water. But there are some safe ways to dispose of small amounts of waste finishing products, as follows:

● Air-dry brushes, rags and waste liquids left in containers outdoors or in well-ventilated areas, away from pets, children and ignition sources. Even though this pollutes the air with hydrocarbons, sunlight and air will break down common volatile chemicals in hours or days. Dry wastes discarded in landfills are less likely to become part of the leachate (liquid) that may ooze into groundwater under a landfill or into nearby surface water. Also, solidified waste is more easily handled by municipal waste-disposal firms.

● Mix waste finishes and solvents with non-reactive absorbents, like cat litter, and dry the material or seal it in a container. Don't use sawdust because it could lead to spontaneous combustion.
● Never pour flammable solvents or hazardous-waste compounds down the drain. This could create a fire hazard, upset your septic system or allow the solvents to enter your groundwater. If you're on a municipal sewer system, the compounds may not be removed during waste-water treatment.
● Never pour hazardous liquids in surface water or ditches. When poured into the soil, chemicals may eventually enter the groundwater via rainwater or melted snow.
● Recycle waste finishes and solvents by brushing them on an old shed or other outbuilding. Also, take advantage of community recycling efforts and exchange programs for paints and varnishes. Check to see if your town's health department has a program to handle small volumes of hazardous wastes.
● Rethink your finishing processes to reduce or eliminate hazardous materials. If you need a quart of stripper, but the gallon container is on sale, buy the quart anyway. It's a small price to pay for reducing waste volume. ☐

Jeff Jackson is an environmental engineer and part-time woodworker living in Taylors, S.C.

Toggle Clamps

Get a grip on workshop problems with these handy devices

by Ed Hoffman

Toggle clamps come in a wide variety of styles, shapes and sizes. *Here, pull-action toggle clamps firmly, yet temporarily, attach an outfeed table mounted on wheels to a tablesaw. By just flipping a couple of handles, the table can be rolled away for other uses.*

We've all done it—hand-held that small piece of wood to drill, shape or cut it on a power tool while thinking there must be a safer way to do the job. Those of us who were lucky can still count 10 fingers. The others will wish they had heard of toggle clamps before they made that cut. It's been more than 50 years since the Detroit Stamping Co., now De-Sta-Co, introduced the toggle clamp. Although there are more manufacturers today and toggle clamps are available from most woodworking mail-order sources, the clamps are just now appearing with regularity in woodworking shops. Toggle clamps exert exceptional holding force, have a positive locking action and are fast and easy to use with just one hand. These features combined with reasonable cost ($5 to $20 for most clamps) make toggle clamps ideal for holding workpieces to jigs, fixtures and workshop tools.

Toggle clamps operate through a system of pivots and levers joined together so force applied to the knee lever (or handle) straightens the arrangement of pivot points and creates endways pressure on the mechanism (see the drawing). When fully extended to its locked position, the middle pivot point is moved slightly beyond the centerline of the outer pivot points. The clamping force now creates endways pressure to push the middle pivot point down against a stop, locking the toggle clamp in position.

Mechanical toggle clamps

Toggle clamps come in a dizzying variety of styles. In fact, toggle clamps offer more mechanical, pneumatic and hydraulic varia-

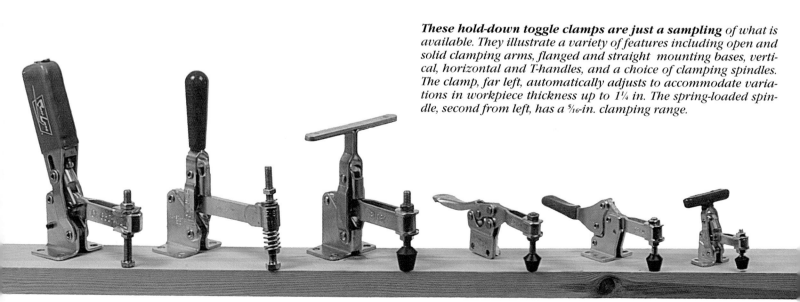

These hold-down toggle clamps are just a sampling *of what is available. They illustrate a variety of features including open and solid clamping arms, flanged and straight mounting bases, vertical, horizontal and T-handles, and a choice of clamping spindles. The clamp, far left, automatically adjusts to accommodate variations in workpiece thickness up to 1¼ in. The spring-loaded spindle, second from left, has a ⁵⁄₁₆-in. clamping range.*

tions than any other type of clamp. Some of the major differences in the mechanical clamps are the handle design (arrangement and placement), mounting styles and holding capacity. Holding capacity, which ranges from 60 lbs. to 16,000 lbs., is defined as the maximum amount of force that can be applied to the clamping bar in the closed position without permanently deforming the clamp.

The basic mechanical toggle clamp is available in four different types: hold-down, straight-line, pull-action and squeeze-action clamps, as shown in the photos below. The hold-down and straight-line types have proven to be the most useful in the woodworking shop. The straight-line clamps have a push or pull action, and some of these clamps can apply pressure at either end of the clamp stroke. Pull-action clamps draw parts together much like the lock on an extension table. And squeeze-action toggle clamps, also called toggle pliers, hold parts with a pinching action, operating like a parallel clamp or C-clamp.

***Hold-down clamps*—**Hold-down toggle clamps offer the most design options, including a T-handle or a straight handle in a horizontal or vertical format; solid or open clamping arms with a high, low or angled profile; and flanged or straight mounting bases. The open-arm style has the greatest clamping flexibility because it allows the adjustable spindle assembly to be moved along the clamping arm and positioned to suit the task. The threaded spindle can be adjusted up and down to accommodate workpieces of varying thicknesses. To get the maximum holding force, the spindle assembly should be positioned close to the handle. For maximum reach, the spindle is moved to the other end of the clamp arm. The solid-arm clamps generally use a welded-on bolt retainer to mount the adjustable spindle. Or a customized workholder could be welded or bolted onto the arm. Although a flanged base is the most frequently used mounting system, hold-down clamps are available with a straight base for special applications. (The photo below shows a variety of handles, arm styles and mounting bases.)

Hold-down toggle clamps can increase the quality of work when used, for example, to eliminate stock creep while crosscutting miters on the tablesaw, as shown in the top right photo on p. 120. These toggle clamps can also increase safety by keeping the fingers away from the cutters when template routing small pieces, as shown in the top left photo on p. 120.

***Straight-line clamps*—**Straight-line toggle clamps provide a pushing or pulling action; most straight-line clamps will lock in the

Straight-line clamps (two at left below) *can push or pull and work well for jig and fixture applications.* ***Pull-action clamps (two at right below)*** *are great for making band clamps or for securing machinery and guards.*

Squeeze-action clamps (at right) *are available as hand-held toggle pliers or in a larger form that can be machine mounted .*

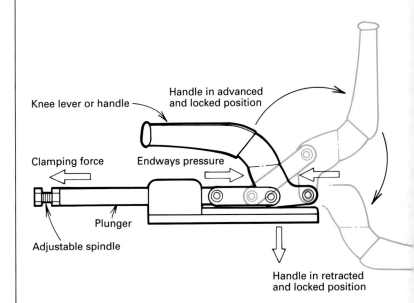

Toggle clamp basics

Knee lever or handle

Handle in advanced and locked position

Clamping force

Endways pressure

Plunger

Adjustable spindle

Handle in retracted and locked position

In the fully extended position, endways pressure on the lever from the clamping force pushes down on the middle pivot point, which is slightly below the centerline of the outer pivot points, to lock the clamp.

Photos below: Susan Kahn

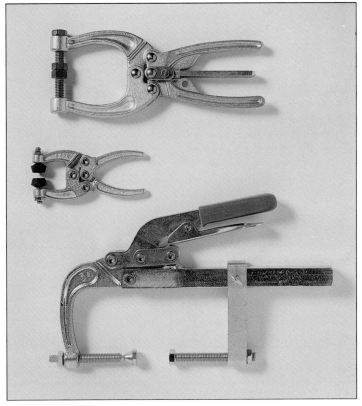

A hold-down clamp quickly secures the workpiece for safer and more accurate work. The toggle clamp (above), unusual because it can automatically accommodate variations in workpiece thickness up to 1¼ in., prevents stock movement when cutting miters on a sliding table.

Jigs and fixtures should include a stop or fence (left) to resist the force of the tool and should support the workpiece opposite the clamping force to prevent distortion.

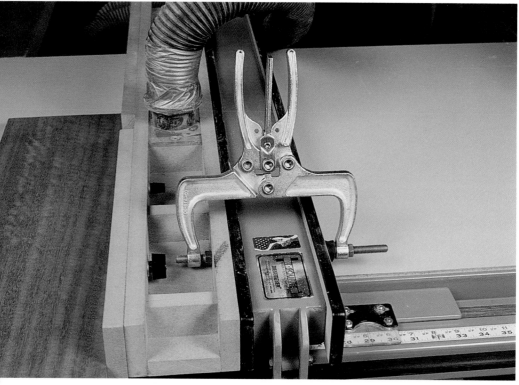

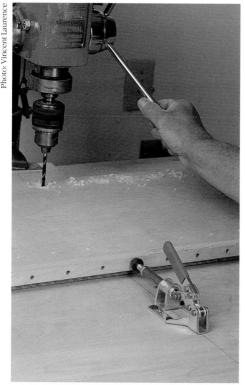

Photo: Vincent Laurence

A cone-shaped tip on this straight-line clamp (above) automatically registers the workpiece for shelf-bracket holes while holding the workpiece in place.

Squeeze-action clamps, or toggle pliers, (left) make easy work of clamping an auxiliary fence in place. These clamps are particularly useful when the clamped object is frequently adjusted or when it's removed and replaced.

Sources of supply

Due to their increased popularity in woodworking applications, toggle clamps are available from many hardware and tool stores, home centers and most mail-order catalogs. However, if you can't find the clamps locally or if you want a complete catalog, you can contact the following manufacturers directly.

Carr Lane Manufacturing Co., 4200 Carr Lane Court, PO Box 191970, St. Louis, MO 63119-2196; (314) 647-6200.

De-Sta-Co, PO Box 2800, 250 Park St., Troy, MI 48007-2800; (313) 589-2008.

Te-Co, 109 Quinter Farm Road, Union, OH 45322-9796; (513) 836-0961.

fully extended or retracted position. The plunger is generally internally threaded to accept a standard hex head bolt. The bolt serves as an adjustable spindle for fine-tuning clamping position and force. Some styles of this clamp have an externally threaded plunger to mount custom workpiece holders. Straight-line clamps are available with either a flange mount or a threaded body for mounting the clamp directly through a panel, plate or angle bracket.

For woodworking applications, straight-line clamps are handy for gluing jigs where items of the same size, like the frame parts for cabinet doors, are regularly assembled. Used with a special cone-tipped spindle, these clamps are also great for positioning and holding work (see the bottom right photo on the facing page).

Pull-action clamps—Pull-action clamps, or latch clamps, are designed to draw two parts together. A familiar application is the common toolbox latch. With this clamp, the handle is raised to advance the clamping element, usually a hook or U-bolt. Once the clamping element is engaged, the handle is moved to a horizontal position to pull the pieces together and lock the clamp. Threaded ends on the hook or U-bolt allow the clamps to be precisely adjusted. These clamps also are available in a right-angle configuration that pulls perpendicularly to the base. Pull-action clamps can make quick work of applying a band clamp, securing machinery guards or, as shown in the top photo on p. 118, for holding equipment in place.

Squeeze-action clamps—Squeeze-action clamps combine the normal grip of a pair of pliers with a toggle action. The hand-held type, often called toggle pliers, is designed for applications where C-clamps might ordinarily be used. These clamps use either one threaded spindle with a fixed jaw or two threaded spindles to set the clamping thickness. Most toggle pliers include a lever between the handles that will quickly release the clamp when squeezed. Toggle pliers are especially helpful when the clamped object needs to be repositioned frequently, such as the auxiliary fence shown in the bottom left photo on the facing page.

Automatic toggle clamps

For all their many benefits, one drawback to standard toggle clamps is their limited ability to compensate for different workpiece sizes. Once set to a clamping height, most toggle clamps can only accept slight variations in stock thickness. Although an optional, spring-loaded spindle is available, it only increases the clamping range to 5/16 in. Larger variations often require readjusting the clamp spindle.

A new toggle clamp shown in the top right photo by Carr Lane Manufacturing Co. (see the sources of supply) has resolved this problem. A standard toggle clamp is made of fixed-sized components connected by pivot pins to provide the clamping action. With this new toggle clamp, however, one of the fixed components (the handle) has a variable length; the clamp correctly adjusts itself to fit the workpiece by automatically altering the pivot length within the handle with a self-adjusting and self-locking wedge arrangement.

In use, the adjustable spindle of the automatic toggle clamp is set at the average workpiece height. Once set, the clamp automatically adjusts to suit workpieces that are up to 3/8 in. thicker or thinner than this setting. The clamping force of the automatic toggle clamp can be adjusted, up to a maximum of 500 lbs., by turning the screw located in the end of the handle.
☐

Ed Hoffman is a writer and consulting engineer in Colorado Springs, Colo.

Putting toggle clamps to work

by Douglas W. Ruffley, P.E.

Because of the wide variety of toggle clamps available, you should select the appropriate clamps for the job before designing any jigs or fixtures on which the clamps will be used. Clamps should be selected on the basis of holding force, action, configuration and mounting, as discussed in the main article. Once the right clamp is at hand, you also need to consider the clamp setup and proper jig design.

Clamp setup: The adjustable spindle can affect the clamp's exerting force (the force with which the clamp holds a workpiece). The exerting force can be adjusted from very light pressure up to the maximum-designed holding force (the point at which the clamp deforms) of the clamp. The force should be snug, but it should not be adjusted so tightly that the clamp becomes difficult to operate. Sixty lbs. is about the maximum amount of force an operator can exert repetitively; however, for safer and more comfortable operation, the spindle should be adjusted to require handle forces from 30 lbs. to 40 lbs. If the clamp is too hard to operate, the operator's hand may slip into the machinery. When applying force to a clamp handle, it is best to keep the wrist straight because the operator can generate more force with less stress on the arm's muscles and tendons.

Optional spindles: In addition to the standard adjustable hex head spindle, there are a variety of other spindles that are better suited to woodworking applications. Spindles tipped with a flat-bottom, molded-neoprene cushion, as shown in the top left photo on the facing page, help protect the wood from being damaged by the clamping force and help compensate for slight variations in stock thickness. The cone-shaped, neoprene tip, as shown in the bottom right photo, is excellent for clamping into holes, slots and corners. Also available is a swivel-foot spindle in a variety of materials with a steel, stainless steel or delrin clamping pad for holding sloped or irregular surfaces. A spring-loaded spindle that can compensate for up to 5/16-in. variation in stock thickness is handy, but this unit requires welding the spindle retainer to a solid-arm clamp.

Jig considerations: Clamped parts should be positioned against a fence or a fixed stop so that tool forces are resisted by the stop, not the clamp. Be certain that the clamp bar, including the spindle, clears the area for easy loading and unloading of the part. Clamped pieces should be supported opposite the clamping force by the jig, fixture or work surface. Otherwise, parts could distort, and the part could vibrate and move out of position. If vibration or an overhead mounting position might cause a clamp to open accidentally, use a clamp with an added locking-release lever. And, finally, for the safety of tool and operator, be sure that all parts of the clamp clear the tool path. ☐

Doug Ruffley is the chief engineer for De-Sta-Co Industrial Products Group in Troy, Mich.

How to Buy Used Hand Tools

You can find high-quality tools at flea markets and auctions

by Robert Hubert Jr.

***Behold the language** of auctioneer Richard Crane. Most auctioneers initially start the bidding low; later, they'll open items high.*

I was excited. I had finally saved up a little extra cash to put toward new hand tools for my shop. I gathered up all my dog-eared woodworking catalogs to pick out planes, chisels and other tools. The shock came when I hit "total" on my calculator; my modest savings would buy only a fraction of the tools I wanted. But thanks to a neighbor who told me about an old plane he had seen at a local flea market, my tool-buying strategy changed.

The next Sunday I bought that plane, a usable Stanley #5, for just $15. Three years later, my collection of vintage hand tools has cost me less than half the price of new tools. And here's the best part: By carefully purchasing and reselling a few extra tools for a profit, my tool buying has begun to pay for the rest of my shop.

Preparing for a tool hunt

Whether you call them antique tools, vintage tools or just plain old tools, hunting for used tools requires preparation. The better equipped you are, the better your chances of acquiring high-quality tools at reasonable prices. Here's the systematic approach I use.

Make a tool "want list" for the woodworking you do. Use catalogs to jog your memory of your shop needs. Be specific. Don't just list "bench plane," put down "Stanley #3," and list whether you want a wood plane or an all-metal one. Being specific will keep you focused and help you avoid buying tools you don't need.

Study the tools you'll be buying. Start by becoming familiar with tool classes and makers. Certain tools, like drawknives, have changed little over the years. Others, like planes, have changed dramatically. One place to learn about hand tools is in original or reprinted owner's manuals and catalogs. Product literature can help you identify a tool as well. In addition, there are books and associations (see the sources of supply on the facing page) that offer a tour of secondhand tools and sellers, as well as supply information about repairing and using old tools. As a beginner, you can go a long way by studying up on Stanley tools alone.

Learn about fair prices and value of used tools. Although you shouldn't completely rely on price guides, current guides can give you ball-park figures for tools. If you're buying for speculation, the guides can tell you how valuable a tool is. Collectors typically look for limited-production tools or tools from unusual makers. Stay away from these tools if you want a bargain tool for woodworking. Always jot down a fair price range for each of the tools on your want list. An entry in my notebook looks something like this: "Jack Plane—prefer Stanley #5 w/corrugated sole—$15-$25."

Four basic rules for buying vintage tools

As I head into an uncharted used-tool market with my want list in hand and my head full of knowledge, I follow four basic rules.

Rule #1: Thoroughly inspect the tools you're buying. If a tool has many parts, take it apart and examine the pieces. I carry a simple tool-disassembly kit that consists of two screwdrivers, an Allen wrench set and a pair of pliers. A hidden crack (see the photo on p. 125) can make an old tool useless. Therefore, after you take a tool apart, wipe away grime with a rag. Then, check the tool's stress points. On a plane, the blade area and mouth are susceptible to stress and so is the rear tote (for more on this, see the story

Wise tool prospectors, *armed with want lists and notes, scope out a table of handplanes and box lots of tool parts during the auction preview. A few of the bidders will snatch up bargains at the end of the auction just by outlasting their competitors.*

on p. 124). On chisels, check for mallet-caused damage and for splits where the tang meets the handle.

Check for missing or substitute parts. Here again, a manual makes it easy to compare a parts list against the actual tool. At the least, a catalog will show a drawing or photo of what the tool should look like. In addition, the tools themselves can reveal where parts are absent. A threaded hole with nothing attached may indicate a missing fence, for example.

Rule #2: Look at what tool collectors don't. One of my best bargains came about because a collector shunned a tool. The owner of a panel-raising plane had restored his tool by refinishing it. The tool looked beautiful to me, but not to a collector. Without its original finish, the plane sold for one-tenth of its value.

Rule #3: Buy parts and pieces. Occasionally, it's a good idea to buy a box lot or two of tool parts because you'll often find a tool with something missing. The tool may be offered cheaply and be in good shape otherwise. To complete the tool, you can simply connect the right part from your stock. My best hand tools have come this way (see the bottom photo at right).

Rule #4: Take it easy. There will always be another tool like the one you want. Don't feel forced into buying a marginal tool or one that costs more than it's worth. It took me nearly three years to put together my assortment of hand tools, and I'm still refining it.

Where to acquire old hand tools
Vintage tool hunters basically have three avenues where they can buy tools: flea markets, auctions and dealers. Depending on where you live, the used-tool scene can be quite disorganized and the prices arbitrary. Always remember, it's "buyer beware."

Flea markets offer the best bargains, but they'll cost you energy and time (pleasant work for me). At many flea markets, you may only find one tool. But, it's likely you'll be able to buy it cheap. My favorite buy was a mint-condition Millers Falls bit brace—just $3. You can cover a flea market quickly once you learn to spot tool tables from a distance. When you find a tool, don't be afraid to barter. Rarely have I had to pay the marked or asking price.

Auctions provide the best selection of tools, but be wary of auction fever. There'll be lots of tools for sale, so wait for a good

There are other places to look for secondhand tools besides auctions and flea markets. Here, Hubert asks about a pair of calipers being offered by a tailgate dealer, who temporarily has set up shop in the parking lot outside the Cabin Fever Auction. This old-tool auction is held every February in Nashua, N.H.

Put together for less than one-fourth the price of a complete plane, this Stanley combination plane is the author's pride and joy. Assembled from parts acquired from flea markets, auctions and tool dealers, this non-original plane makes a perfectly good woodworking tool, even though it's unacceptable to a collector.

Sources of supply

For a more complete list of tool groups, dealers, auctions and publications, send $1 to Bob Vogel, New England Tool Collectors Assoc., 164 Chestnut St., N. Easton, MA 02356-2611.

Associations, auction houses and workshops:

Early American Industries Association, PO Box 2128, ESP Albany, NY 12220-0128

Society of Workers in Early Arts and Trades, 606 Lake Lena Blvd., Auburndale, FL 33823

Tool Group of Canada, 112 Holmcrest Trail, Scarborough, Ont., Canada NT M1C 1V5

The Tool and Trades Historical Society, 60 Swanley Lane, Swanley, Kent, U.K. BR8 7JG

Your Country Auctioneer Inc., 63 Poor Farm Road, Hillsboro, NH 03244

National Antique Tool Auction, 4729 Kutztown Road, Temple, PA 19560

David Stanley Auctions, Stordon Grange, Osgathorpe, Leicester, U.K. LE12 9SR

Warwick Country Workshops (plane clinics), 1 E. Ridge Road, Warwick, NY 10990

Antique and used-tool dealers:

Tom Witte's Antiques, PO Box 399, Mattawan, MI 49071

Bob Kaune Antique and Used Tools, 511 W. 11th St., Port Angeles, WA 98362

Two Chislers, 1864 Glen Moor Drive, Lakewood, CO 80215

Iron Horse Antiques, PO Box 4001, Pittsford, VT 05763

Roger K. Smith, PO Box 177, Athol, MA 01331

Martin Donnelly Antique Tools, 31 Rumsey St., PO Box 281, Bath, NY 14810

Books and publishers:

Dictionary of Woodworking Tools, R.A. Salaman, revised by Phillip Walker, 1990, The Taunton Press Inc., PO Box 5506, Newtown, CT 06470

The Antique Tool Collector's Guide to Value, Ronald S. Barlow, 1985, Windmill Publishing Co., 2147 Windmill View Road, El Cajon, CA 92020

Restoring, Tuning and Using Classic Woodworking Tools, Michael Dunbar, 1989, Sterling Publishing Co., 387 Park Ave. S., New York, NY 10016

Astragal Press, PO Box 338, Mendham, NJ 07945

tool at the right price. To minimize overbidding, first get the auction preview list, even if you have to buy it, and then use preview time wisely (see the bottom photo on p. 122). Some auctions have previewing the day before; and some require an admittance fee. After I check off items from my want list, I allow five minutes for inspecting each tool. This gives me enough time, even when there's a crowd. If there's no preview list, try to arrive when previewing begins. Do a once over to spot-check all the tools. Then go back and fully inspect items that interest you.

Second, mark down the maximum price you're willing to pay for a tool. I often write the figure on the back of my bidding card along with the lot number (this prevents me from bidding on a tool that looks identical to the one I want). Once you've arrived at a figure, don't exceed that limit. You'll be strongly tempted to bid another five dollars in hopes of winning a tool, but this rarely works. One exception is when you're bidding against a dealer—they're usually conservative, disciplined bidders. Once they reach their cutoff, you can often buy an item at just a slightly higher bid. On the other end of the spectrum are the collectors. Avoid getting in a bidding war with a collector—they often bid quite aggressively when pursuing a tool for their collection.

Third, to save yourself grief, don't bid on something you haven't inspected. I've wound up with lemon tools because I didn't inspect them first. If you can't attend an auction, you may still be able to place a sight-unseen absentee bid, but it is risky. If you're determined to take a risk at an auction, buy a cheap box lot.

Fourth, check out the tailgate tool market, where dealers peddle their wares in event parking lots (see the top photo on p. 123).

Dealers have hard-to-find tools, but their prices are frequently higher than those at flea markets and auctions. Many tool dealers sell via mail order and issue some kind of catalog. The catalogs usually list prices and describe tools and their condition. Before you order from a dealer, verify that he has a flexible return policy. Most dealers also have a listing service in which they'll locate something from your want list. Finally, keep an eye open for antique dealers who double as tool dealers. □

Bob Hubert Jr. works for an architectural firm. He likes to build period and modern furniture for his Harvard, Mass., home.

Stalking the secondhand plane

by Maurice Fraser

Acquiring a new handplane can mean spending good time tuning it or else spending dearly for a ready-to-use deluxe model (see the photo below). Another option is to hunt for a usable old classic. So you won't have to hunt in the dark, I'll describe what to watch for when pursuing a used plane, and I'll explore their inner workings.

Basic plane anatomy
A plane is, essentially, a chisel locked in a guiding body. Standard bench planes are of three types—each for a special job. The jack plane (14 in. to 15 in. long) zaps wood to dimension, the jointer plane (18 in. to 24 in.) straightens curves, and the smooth plane (8 in. to 9½ in.) polishes surfaces. Except for size, the three types are built alike.

British and American traditions
The best metal planes are either the wooden-core British models, exemplified by the classic Norris, or the open-shell cast-iron planes, perfected by the Stanley plane-makers of Connecticut.

Norris and Stanley-type metal planes boast parallel-thicknessed irons, which ensure that the mouth-to-blade fit is constant. In addition, both Norris and Stanley blades have a cap iron bolted to them called, collectively, the "double iron." Both planes lock the double iron to the throat opening with a pivoting lever cap.

Norris-type lever caps are on an axle and tighten to the blade by the turn of a bolt. Stanley-type lever caps are captured under a bolt head and snap tight with a clever cam action: The lever cap consistently forces the blade onto the back of the throat (cutter seat). However, the ideal, integral seat isn't feasible in a cast body, so Stanley-types have a screw-on cutter seat or frog, which allows adjustment. But, often more a liability than an asset, the frog permits chatter on heavy cuts, and its blade-positioning range can be narrow. Furthermore, Stanley-type frogs wander during adjustment, and realignment is by tedious trial and error. By contrast, the Norris-type cutter seat is simple. It is cut into the solid wood interior and needs no adjustment.

Adjusters: Stanley vs. Norris
Both Stanley and later Norris metal planes rely on mechanisms to control both depth of cut and side-to-side evenness. Stanley planes separate the two modes of adjustment. For depth, a brass wheel's rotation pushes a forked lever downward, carrying the blade with it. Sideways movement is via a pivoting upright lever, whose end is captive in a blade slot. Norris planes combine the two motions in a single ingenious, but awkward, mechanism (see the inset photo on p. 125).

Stanley's two-part adjustment system is re-

**Inspiring smoothers:** The mint-condition used planes in the background (an A-6 Norris, left, and a Stanley #4½, right) are hard to find. But, a few new planes borrow features from these originals, as shown in the foreground: Bristol Design's P-40 (left center), J. Warshafsky's 04 Reed (left front) and Record's Calvert-Stevens CS-88 (right front).

Checking used plane parts

A Stanley "Bailey" #4 smooth plane assembled

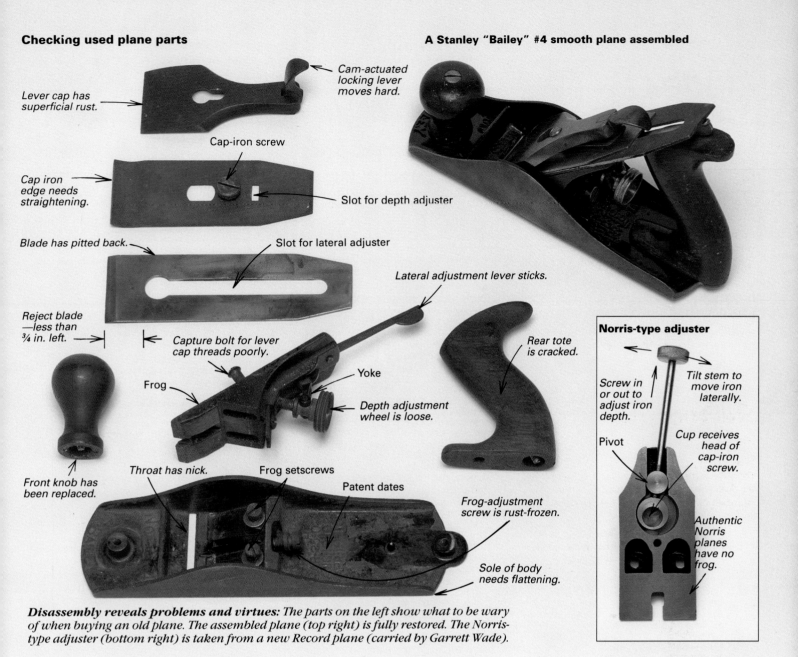

Lever cap has superficial rust.

Cam-actuated locking lever moves hard.

Cap-iron screw

Cap iron edge needs straightening.

Slot for depth adjuster

Blade has pitted back.

Slot for lateral adjuster

Lateral adjustment lever sticks.

Reject blade —less than ¾ in. left.

Capture bolt for lever cap threads poorly.

Frog

Yoke

Rear tote is cracked.

Depth adjustment wheel is loose.

Front knob has been replaced.

Throat has nick.

Frog setscrews

Patent dates

Frog-adjustment screw is rust-frozen.

Sole of body needs flattening.

Norris-type adjuster

Screw in or out to adjust iron depth.

Tilt stem to move iron laterally.

Pivot

Cup receives head of cap-iron screw.

Authentic Norris planes have no frog.

Disassembly reveals problems and virtues: The parts on the left show what to be wary of when buying an old plane. The assembled plane (top right) is fully restored. The Norris-type adjuster (bottom right) is taken from a new Record plane (carried by Garrett Wade).

liable and responsive. Even over-used Stanleys adjust with finesse. But a well-preserved Norris adjusts less finely, and it's easy to over-tighten the lever cap.

What to look for

Since Norrises are rare and ultra expensive, start by looking for the upper-end Stanley models: Bailey, Bed Rock and Gage. Liberty Bell and Defiance are Stanley's lesser models and may not tune up as well. Most generic "Stanleys" (unsigned) are cheapies and no bargain. Leave exotic brands to the collectors, and as a rule, avoid (or haggle for) planes with mixed parts.

If you're patient and observant, you can avoid buying a plane that will need major work. The photo above shows a few features that can make or break a deal.

Body: Normal rust and pitting won't affect a plane's function, but cracks (common around the mouth) are risky and can worsen. Check the sole against a straightedge or a sole of known flatness. If light shows

through, the sole will need flattening.

Handles: Avoid planes without totes. In addition, broken or badly mended totes are like ill-fitting running shoes—no bargain is worth the misery. Note that the totes of long and short planes are not interchangeable. Broken or missing front knobs are replaceable. You can remedy a loose knob or tote by screwing in the retaining bolt or shortening it.

Blades: Original blades are best, but replacements are acceptable. A blade ground down to ¾ in. or less from its long slot has little life left (and may have only unhardened steel left in it). Rust pitting on a blade's bevel face is acceptable, but *not* on the cutting face. The blade's back should be unscored—and flat—or proper cap-iron fit will be impossible. Avoid bent blades.

Cap iron and lever cap: When screwed tight, no light should show at the cap iron's junction with the blade's edge (chips will

clog here). If the cap iron is a substitute, its adjuster slot may not align with the depth lever. This limits blade extension, so check out the blade-depth range. A chipped lever cap corner won't affect planing, but the leading contact edge should be straight.

Adjuster and threaded parts: If the brass wheel is rust-frozen, applying WD-40 or oil may or may not free the motion. The yoke should be astride the wheel and freely move with it without rattling. Reject a broken yoke. The lateral adjustment lever can be bent and still function perfectly. Screws should all turn and have reasonably crisp slots and rust-free threads. The lever-cap capture bolt *must* turn to allow tension adjustment, but rusted frog bolts may never require further use if the frog is set right ...it's one of the risks of the hunt.

□

Maurice Fraser teaches woodworking at the YWCA's Craft Students' League in New York City.

Index